Latin American Studies Series

Series Editors Michael C. Meyer John D. Martz Miguel León-Portilla

After a decade of dictatorship, the resurrection of democratic forces in Chile began with the debt crisis and recession of the early 1980s. Mass demonstrations erupted and political parties revived with unexpected vigor despite the repression of General Augusto Pinochet's regime. The United States pressed for democratization. In 1988, to the astonishment of the world, Pinochet allowed his opponents to win an honest plebiscite and accepted the resulting transition to democracy. *The Struggle for Democracy in Chile, 1982–1990* is the first book to discuss in comprehensive detail that unusual transition. Showing the evolution and erosion of the military dictatorship over two decades, it concludes with the installation of Patricio Aylwin as the democratically elected president in 1990. Here, eleven leading experts examine how the most significant social and political sectors reacted to liberalization in the 1980s, and how the opposition took advantage of the dictatorship's own legality to bring about an end to authoritarian rule.

The Struggle for Democracy in Chile, 1982–1990

Edited by Paul W. Drake and Iván Jaksić

University of Nebraska Press
Lincoln and London

The paper in this book meets the
minimum requirements of
American National Standard for
Information Sciences—
Permanence of Paper for Printed
Library Materials,
ANSI Z39.48–1984.

Library of Congress Cataloging-in-
Publication Data

The Struggle for democracy in
Chile, 1982–1990 / edited by Paul
W. Drake and Iván Jaksić.
p.   cm. — (Latin American studies
series)
Papers presented at a conference
held in March 1989 which was
sponsored by the Center for Iberian
and Latin American Studies at the
University of California-San Diego,
the Center for Latin American
Studies at the University of
California-Berkeley, and the
Institute of the Americas in La Jolla.
Includes bibliographical references
(p.   ) and index.
ISBN 0-8032-1691-2 (cloth). — ISBN
0-8032-6588-3 (pbk.)
1. Chile—Politics and
government—1973- —Congresses.
2. Authoritarianism—Chile—
History—20th century—
Congresses. 3. Government,
Resistance to—Chile—History—
20th century—Congresses. 4. Civil-
military relations—Chile—
History—20th century—
Congresses. 5. Representative
government and representation—
Chile—History—20th century—
Congresses. I. Drake, Paul W., 1944– .
II. Jaksić, Iván, 1954– . III.
University of California, San Diego.
Center for Iberian and Latin
American Studies. IV. University of
California, Berkeley. Center for
Latin American Studies. V. Institute
of the Americas. VI. Series.
F3100.S86   1991
983.06'5—dc20
91-7216
CIP

This book is dedicated to our
children: Joshua, Elizabeth, and
Katherine Drake, and Ilse Jaksić

Contents

Preface

This book catches Chile at a crossroads in its history. The 1988 plebiscite closed an authoritarian episode and opened the door to a new experiment in democracy. To the astonishment of the world, a dictator allowed his opponents to win an honest referendum and accepted the resulting transition to democracy. Those results heartened struggling democratic forces throughout the hemisphere. The plebiscite was followed by a competitive election for president in 1989, again won by the opposition to the authoritarian regime. The victors took power in 1990, dedicated to the task of redemocratization.

Whatever the degree of democracy achieved by the new Chilean regime, this is a prime moment to analyze the transition from authoritarianism in a long-term and comparative perspective. This book places the 1988 watershed in the context of Chile's structural and political transformations since the economic crisis of 1982. It also locates that country's experience within the framework of the process of democratization that engulfed Latin America in the 1980s. Chile provides an exceptionally rich and poignant case study because of its unusually open and reformist democracy from 1932 to 1973 and its extraordinarily closed and reactionary dictatorship from 1973 to 1990.

The purpose of this volume is to explain the gradual breakdown of the authoritarian regime from its peak at the start of the 1980s to its demise at the end of the decade. The main emphasis is on the evolution from military rule toward democracy, from the collapse of the economic model in the crash of 1982 to the defeat of the political model in the plebiscite of 1988. Virtually all of the chapters concentrate on the 1980s, though to give the reader a full picture they include brief summaries of developments that took place during the first decade of military rule and an assessment of the legacy for its democratic successor. The only exceptions are Arturo Valenzuela's background essay on the consolidation of the dictatorship and Felipe Larraín's discussion of the economic challenges facing the opposition as they take power. Most of the papers were commissioned in 1987 and completed between the 1988 plebiscite and the 1989 elections, and some material was added thereafter to incorporate the 1989 electoral results and the final steps to civilian rule in 1990.

Space limitations forced us to include only chapters on the most crucial actors in the struggle between the military regime and its opponents in the 1980s. Other worthy topics—such as the roles of the Roman Catholic Church, human rights groups, shantytown dwellers, and students—had to be subsumed within the existing chapters. For example, although the Church is discussed at several junctures, it was not allotted a separate chapter; that institution declined in importance as the main shelter for the opposition in the late 1970s to its role as an ally behind the more significant players—especially political parties—in the mid-1980s. After the introduction, the chapters are organized from the regime and its supporters (Valenzuela, Varas, Silva, Campero) to the regime's opponents (Valenzuela, Angell, Garretón, Portales, Larraín).

The editors of this anthology believed that the climactic 1988 plebiscite would unleash redemocratization, whether rapidly under a victory for the opposition or much more slowly under a win by the government. Therefore, in 1986 we began organizing a research conference on "Transformation and Transition in Chile" to convene in the aftermath. That workshop, held in March 1989, and this volume were co-sponsored by the Center for Iberian and Latin American Studies at the University of California-San Diego, the Center for Latin American Studies at the University of California-Berkeley, and the Institute of the Americas in La Jolla. Further support came from the Center for Latin American Studies at San Diego State University, the Programa de Estudios Conjuntos Sobre las Relaciones Internacionales de América Latina and the Facultad Latinoamericana de Ciencias Sociales in Santiago, and the Social Sciences, the Chancellor's Associates, and the Department of Political Science at the University of California-San Diego. In addition to the contributors to this volume, participants included Harry G. Barnes, Jr., Sergio Bitar, Paul Boeker, David Collier, Ann Craig, Peter DeShazo, Sebastián Edwards, Mark Falcoff, Albert Fishlow, Angel Flisfisch, Joseph Grunwald, Carlos Huneeus, Arend Lijphart, Brian Loveman, David Mares, Timothy McDaniel, Michael Monteón, Frederick Nunn, Philippe Schmitter, Cathy Schneider, Peter H. Smith, Barbara Stallings, Alfred Stepan, Luciano Tomassini, J. Samuel Valenzuela, Carlos Waisman, and Peter Winn.

Suzanne Wagner handled all the arrangements for the conference with consummate skill and good cheer. The first drafts of translations of the papers in Spanish were done by Elizabeth Hutchison, Sulamita Sragovicz, Carol Gallo, and Carolina Arroyo. We are grateful to them as well as to Julie Kline and Sandi Naylor for their assistance during the preparation of the manuscript.

Abbreviations

ACUSO	Acuerdo Social por el No
ANPT	Asociación Nacional de Productores de Trigo
ASEP	Asesoría Política
ASEXMA	Asociación de Exportadores de Manufacturas no Tradicionales
ASIMET	Asociación de Industriales Metalúrgicos
ASUSENA	Academia Superior de Seguridad Nacional
AN	Avanzada Nacional
BID	Banco Interamericano de Desarollo
CCHC	Cámara Chilena de la Construcción
CDL	Centro Democrático Libre
CDT	Central Democrática de Trabajadores
CEL	Comité por Elecciones Libres
CEP	Centro de Estudios Públicos
CEPCH	Confederación de Empleodos Particulares de Chile
CIEPLAN	Corporación de Investigaciones Económicas para América Latina
CMD	Concertación de Mujeres por la Democracia
CMT	Confederación Multigremial del Trabajo
CNC	Comisión Nacional Campesina
CNI	Central Nacional de Informaciones
CNS	Coordinadora Nacional Sindical
CNT	Comando Nacional de Trabajadores
COAJ	Comité Asesor de la Junta
CODELCO	Corporación del Cobre
CODEM	Comité de Defensa de los Derechos del Pueblo
CONARA	Comisión Nacional de Reformas Administrativas
CPA	Confederación de Productores Agricultores
CPD	Concertación de Partidos por la Democracia

CPME	Consejo de la Pequeña y Mediana Empresa
CPC	Confederación de la Producción y el Comercio
CTC	Confederación de Trabajadores del Cobre
CUT	Central Unica de Trabajadores
CUT	Central Unitaria de Trabajadores
CUT	Confederación Unica del Trabajo
DINA	Dirección Nacional de Inteligencia
ENAER	Empresa Nacional de Aeronáutica
FACH	Fuerza Aérea de Chile
FEES	Fondo de Educación y Extensión Sindical
FMS	Federación de Mujeres Socialistas
FPMR	Frente Patriótico Manuel Rodríguez
IC	Izquierda Cristiana
IDLPM	Instituto Internacional para el Desarollo del Liderazgo Político de la Mujer
MAPU	Movimiento de Acción Popular Unitaria
MDP	Movimiento Democrático Popular
MEMCH-83	Movimiento Pro Emancipación de la Mujer 1983
MIR	Movimiento de Izquierda Revolucionaria
MOMUPO	Movimiento de Mujeres Pobladoras
MSU	Movimiento Sindical Unitario
MUDECHI	Mujeres de Chile
ODEPLAN	Oficina de Planificación Nacional
PAIS	Partido Amplio de Izquierda Socialista
PC	Partido Comunista
PDC	Partido Demócrata Cristiano
PEM	Programa de Empleo Mínimo
PET	Programa de Empleo y Trabajo
PPD	Partido por la Democracia
PH	Partido Humanista
PN	Partido Nacional
POJH	Programa Ocupacional para Jefes de Hogar
PS	Partido Socialista
RN	Renovación Nacional
SIM	Servicio de Inteligencia Militar
SNA	Sociedad Nacional de Agricultura
SOFOFA	Sociedad de Fomento Fabríl
SONAMI	Sociedad Nacional de Minería
UDI	Unión Democrática Independiente
UDT	Unión Democrática de Trabajadores
UP	Unidad Popular

Paul W. Drake and Iván Jaksić

Introduction: Transformation and Transition in Chile, 1982–1990

From 1982 to 1990, Chile underwent a protracted transition toward redemocratization. The plebiscite of October 5, 1988, marked the climax of that process. In the balloting, the victory of the opposition forces over General Augusto Pinochet Ugarte opened the way for competitive presidential and congressional elections in December 1989 to select a civilian government to take office in March 1990. That transition captured world attention because, prior to 1973, Chile had sustained one of Latin America's most durable and progressive democracies and, since 1973, it had endured one of the most prolonged and reactionary dictatorships. Moreover, policy-makers acclaimed the adroit role the United States played in the transition as an exemplary case of subtle foreign intervention to encourage democratization. Whether Chile could return fully to the democratic camp was seen as a litmus test of the trend that swept the hemisphere in the 1980s.[1]

Chile evolved toward democracy amid profound transformations in the nation's economy, society, and politics. The government of Christian Democrat Patricio Aylwin, elected in 1989, inherited a country far different from the one that had existed in the recent past. Redemocratization will not mean a reversion to the status quo that prevailed before the 1973 coup d'etat. Nor will it take place within the narrow confines of the project launched in the 1970s by the military regime, whose economic, social, and political models reached the height of their power in 1980–81. The situation at the beginning of the 1980s was analyzed in the most important previous international scholarly collection on Pinochet's Chile.[2] Since the early 1980s, however, when the papers for that anthology were written, profound changes have occurred in all dimensions of the Chilean situation. Those transformations made the transition to democracy both possible and different from what it would have been a decade ago.

This volume emphasizes the changes that have taken place in Chile since 1982 in five crucial and connected domains:

First, in the economic realm, the international recession in 1982 created the worst depression in Chile since 1930. That calamity provoked changes in the neo-liberal model, but not its abandonment.

Second, although General Pinochet rode out the storm in the early 1980s by retaining the loyalty of most leaders of the armed forces and the business community, dissent broke out in the previously solid ranks of regime supporters.

Third, after a decade of enforced quiescence, civil society—especially the lower classes—reawoke through the protests that erupted in 1983. Those demonstrations spread from organized labor through the middle sectors and were finally concentrated in the urban shantytowns.

Fourth, the previously repressed and dormant political parties experienced a renaissance after 1982. Despite an initial reluctance to accept the new electoral rules as part of the institutionalization of Pinochet's system, political parties took command of the showdown in the plebiscite and of the competitive elections thereafter.

Fifth, the international environment also experienced a sea change, as democratization redrew the political map. Once surrounded by like-minded governments and a largely indifferent United States administration during Ronald Reagan's first years as president, the Pinochet regime by the mid-1980s found itself isolated from its democratic neighbors and pressured by industrialized powers to join the liberal fold.

Chilean Democracy before 1973

Looking ahead to post-authoritarian politics, commentators at the end of the 1980s wondered to what extent the future held a fundamental realignment of issues and actors or a virtual restoration of pre-Pinochet patterns. From 1932 to 1973, Chilean democracy had been distinctive in Latin America. It stood out for its durability, its multiparty panorama reminiscent of European systems, and its inclusion of three poles clearly defined by ideology and class: a conservative Right based among the economic elites, a reformist Center rooted in the middle strata, and a Marxist Left anchored in the working class. Although the electorate evolved toward the left during those decades and many actors remained independent, the persistence of the three ideological tendencies made flexible coalitions and compromises essential to the system's survival.

The 1970 triumph of Socialist Salvador Allende Gossens as the presidential candidate of the Popular Unity (UP) coalition with 36 percent of the vote was, in many respects, a predictable outcome of one more multicandidate race in Chile. Many other presidents had been elected with pluralities short of a majority, though never with such a sweeping program to elevate the working class. Rather than any sudden change in political orientation, Allende's victory reflected decades of patient building by the leftist parties, especially the Socialists (PS) and Communists (PC). Nevertheless, the democratic election of a Marxist chief executive sent a shock wave around the globe.

Allende's ascension also marked the culmination of decades of expansion of the government's role in the economy and society. Since the 1930s, Chile had been a Latin American leader in state capitalist development, stressing simultaneous import-substituting industrialization and welfare programs for organized workers. Now the UP went much further in expanding the scope of state activities. In order to create state socialism, the government expropriated the major means of production and promoted massive redistribution to the rural and urban working class. That process accelerated under the impetus of the mass mobilization of workers, which exceeded government expectations and controls. The UP's attempt to use liberal-democratic institutions to propel radical social change generated severe economic dislocations and rampant inflation. Class conflict escalated, and political divisions polarized.

Backed by the United States, centrist forces—the Christian Democrats (PDC)—joined the rightists—the National Party (PN)—in an alliance against the UP's socialist project. In the showdown midterm congressional elections of March 1973, the nation divided between 44 percent for the government and 54 percent for the opposition. As the stalemate between the executive and the legislature continued, the UP's adversaries consolidated plans for a military solution. On September 11, 1973, President Allende died defending his government—socialism and democracy—against the lethal coup d'etat led by General Pinochet.

Consolidation of Dictatorship, 1973–1981

For nearly a decade, Pinochet reigned without significant challenge. The keys to his success were massive repression and economic innovation. Like the leaders of other bureaucratic authoritarian regimes, Pinochet relied on a coalition of capitalists, technocrats, and, above all, the military. In this volume, Arturo Valenzuela details the construction of a unique system of one-man rule, giving the president iron control over both the government and the armed forces. Despite their seventeen years in power and their rejection of civilian authority, military officers always insisted that they were not engaged in partisan political deliberations. With few exceptions, the military steadfastly obeyed Pinochet and resolutely refused to negotiate with the opposition. What had been a virtue in the democratic regime—the separation of the military from civil society and politics—now became an obstacle to redemocratization.

While destroying democratic institutions and forces from 1973 to 1975, the junta also clamped down on social organizations, especially those representing the working class. The armed forces killed, imprisoned, tortured, and exiled thousands of Chileans. The military suppressed, dismantled, and purged not only political parties but also publications, unions, schools, and other bastions of the democratic opposition. Even such privileged constituencies as university professors and students encountered serious limitations on their traditional ability to voice opinions of national, or even institutional, relevance. Not only most leftists but also some centrists were silenced and driven underground. Meanwhile, the right voluntarily suspended all public political activities.

During the 1970s, the Roman Catholic Church provided the principal shelter for those who were abused and disenfranchised by the dictatorship. Although not officially in opposition to Pinochet and frequently divided, the Church became a haven for human rights organizations and other democratic forces. It also furnished some assistance to the poor, who had been abandoned by the government's cutbacks in social services. The military regime viewed such activities with distrust, if not hostility. It launched a campaign of harassment against the Catholic Church that deeply polarized the citizenry and especially the political right. The Church withstood the attacks and defended its Vicariate of Solidarity, founded in 1976. The

Vicariate, which provided legal assistance to victims of repression, became a symbol of resistance against the regime.

Once the military had demobilized the polity and society, the regime began implanting its vision of a new order. It set out to replace not only democratic with authoritarian politics but also statist with market-driven economics. A new cadre of technocrats—dubbed the "Chicago Boys" because many were trained at the University of Chicago—designed those laissez-faire economic policies. From 1977 to 1981, their neo-liberal model fostered dramatic growth, particularly of nontraditional exports, consumer imports, and foreign loans. That approach, however, also entailed grave social costs, especially in terms of unemployment and income distribution. It was perhaps no accident that the main victims of the economic "miracle" were also the main political enemies of the regime, the urban workers. Some traditionally protected segments of industry, agriculture, and the middle class also resented the enrichment of an entrepreneurial elite at their expense.

As Pinochet solidified his system of authoritarian capitalism, he held his first plebiscite in 1978. In response to international criticisms of widespread human rights atrocities, he called for a "yes" or "no" vote in defense of his authority to forge a new institutional order. The government totally controlled that referendum and claimed a 75 percent victory.

The regime had its authoritarian constitution ratified in another noncompetitive plebiscite in 1980. Convened at the height of the economic boom, that election had no safeguards for participation by the opposition, in contrast with the 1988 referendum. According to the government, 67 percent of the voters approved the new charter, which included transitory articles to maintain Pinochet's authority through the 1988 plebiscite, when his mandate could be renewed for another eight years. Thereafter, the charter's permanent articles provided for a "protected democracy" under the tutelage of the armed forces, partly through their control of a National Security Council to oversee the rest of the government. It aimed to depoliticize society permanently by maintaining tight restrictions on individual liberties. Under this constitution, Pinochet intended to perpetuate his rule until at least 1997.

The imposition of a new institutional order stood in stark contrast to the disarray of opposition forces. During the period 1973–81, the harsh repression of party leaders and the rank and file prevented any effective counterattack on the regime. At the same time, longstanding political differences among the parties also blocked any coherent opposition strategy. Politicians not only disagreed across party lines but also feuded within their own parties. They especially quarreled among themselves and with the regime over the future role of Marxist organizations. As the government's economic and political models reached the apex of their success, the opposition appeared intimidated, fearful, fragmented, and impotent. At the start of the 1980s, no one would have predicted the opposition's takeover in the 1990s.

Crisis of Dictatorship, 1982–1988

From 1981 to 1982, the invincibility of the Pinochet regime was shaken by a severe economic crisis, which ignited social protests. In contrast with the rest of the hemisphere, however, the disaster of depression and debt in Chile did not topple the dictatorship. As Eduardo Silva explains, the government responded by adjusting the free-market model while retaining most of its key elements. By 1985, the economy was recovering, but numerous poorer and even middle-class Chileans were left behind. As a result, partisans of Pinochet cited economic growth as one of their main reasons for supporting him in the 1988 plebiscite, while his opponents pointed to the social costs of the extremely unequal distribution of benefits. The successes and failures of the open economic model provided crucial issues, constraints, and opportunities for the transition.

In the wake of the economic crisis and readjustment, cracks appeared in the previously firm foundation of regime loyalists. A few economic elites expressed dissatisfaction. A small but vital democratic right reappeared and promoted liberalization, which gradually expanded the space for political expression and activity from 1983 to 1989. Most important, some leaders of the navy, air force, and national police (*Carabineros*) became increasingly discontented with Pinochet's continuation in power, even though the army remained steadfast.

During nonrevolutionary transitions from authoritarianism to democratization in other countries, the disaffection of some members of the ruling coalition has usually proved crucial. In comparative terms, few Pinochet partisans deserted the regime. The government did not intend for liberalization to evolve into unfettered democratization. The 1988 plebiscite was designed to consecrate and prolong, not to terminate, an authoritarian regime. Although enough "soft-liners" emerged among supporters of the dictatorship to make a limited transition possible, they did not negotiate any major reforms for democratization until after Pinochet lost the plebiscite. A key question for redemocratization was how the business magnates and the armed forces could be accommodated in a post-authoritarian political order.

Despite economic upheavals and their increasing willingness to tolerate the opposition, most business executives clung to the regime. The concentration of income during the Pinochet years left the capitalists much stronger than their former nemeses among labor and the left. Property owners were well positioned to negotiate over future political and economic policies. Guillermo Campero argues that entrepreneurs, like other social actors since the 1982 crisis, have become more assertive and less subservient to political parties than they were in the past. Despite their vaunted unity and confidence, however, the capitalists have also been vulnerable to divisions. To join in a transition to a durable democracy, they will have to be convinced that their basic interests can be protected under majority rule without recourse to military intervention. The new civilian government will face the dilemma of how to maintain the essentials of the free-market model to placate the upper class while addressing accumulated social demands from the underprivileged majority.

At least as difficult will be restoring the armed forces to a more apolitical role. The armed services have tried to carve out significant prerogatives—such as the National Security Council to monitor presidential decisions—to project their tutelage into the future. They do not feel defeated or disgraced. Moreover, the top officers have indicated that they intend to use their continuing leverage to preserve their institutional integrity and hierarchy, to defend some of the authoritarian principles of the 1980 constitution, to prevent a repetition of the Popular Unity government, to prohibit retribution for past human rights violations, and to uphold the privatization of the economy. In short, elements within the armed forces will try to make the transfer of real power to civilians in the 1990s as limited and as gradual as possible. Unless the privileges and demands of the military can be reduced, Chile could remain a constrained and tentative democracy.

An attendant problem will be easing out Pinochet himself, who refused an invitation in December 1989 by then President-elect Patricio Aylwin to step down as commander-in-chief of the Army. Although Pinochet's support has been shrinking since 1982, a significant minority of Chileans still back him and his view of limited democracy.[3] Augusto Varas describes the decline of legitimacy and the fragmentation of support for Pinochet and the military regime since the early 1980s. The civilian government will need to translate those anti-authoritarian attitudes into a popular commitment to and a military acceptance of democratic rule. Perhaps the most delicate problem will be the simmering demands for justice for years of flagrant human rights abuses, including "disappearances" and murders. Despite the armed forces' authoritarian inclinations, their continued espousal of nondeliberative "professionalism" under Pinochet and their devotion to the 1980 constitution may allow for their extrication from overt political involvement. Such a reorientation might be possible if noninterventionist commanders-in-chief can be appointed, if obedience can be transferred to a civilian president, and if the constitution can be democratized without sacrificing the military's loyalty to it.

Another traditionally conservative group, women, turned against Pinochet during the 1980s, and a majority ultimately voted "no" in the 1988 plebiscite. Similarly, although Patricio Aylwin received fewer votes from women than from men in the 1989 presidential election, female support for him was higher than the combined female ballots for the rightist candidates, Hernán Büchi and Francisco Javier Errázuriz. María Elena Valenzuela analyzes the military regime's ideological attempts to court female support, which was undercut by prejudicial economic policies. Ironically, by closing down standard political channels, the dictatorship fomented fresh social movements in favor of democracy and uncontrolled by traditional parties. Like other neglected social sectors, women struggled to incorporate their own demands into the broader campaign for democratization. As the political parties assumed more and more control of the process through the plebiscite and beyond, women's groups—like activists among workers, *pobladores* (shantytown dwellers), human rights organizations, and so on—worried that their particular concerns would increasingly be subsumed under partisan political objectives. As during transitions from authoritarianism elsewhere, the relative weight of new social movements seemed likely to fade as regular democratic institutions—especially political parties—began to reassert themselves.

The resurrection of democratic forces in Chile began with the mass demonstrations of the early 1980s. Previously established social actors—like labor unionists and students—overcame fear and recaptured a voice in national affairs. Less institutionalized groups—notably slum-dwellers and women—created novel forms of survival, organization, and expression. Although these social movements initially took the lead in challenging the dictatorship, their activities soon became subordinate to the rejuvenated political parties. Difficult negotiations lie ahead over the roles and pent-up demands of these mobilized social groups in relation to the emerging democracy and its party leaders.

That social activism erupted with the protests of 1983–86. Confrontations with the military regime were spearheaded first by the labor movement and then by workers in the urban shantytowns (*poblaciones*). As slum-dwellers came to dominate those sometimes violent street demonstrations, the middle-class opponents of the dictatorship backed away from participation. Among many union and shantytown organizations, political affiliations from the pre-Pinochet period proved to be fairly durable. The Christian Democrats had made significant gains among unionists, however, and the Communists had gathered support among *pobladores*.

As Alan Angell points out, the working class had been so divided and weakened—both economically and politically—under Pinochet that its mobilization could not bring down the regime. Even more remarkable than labor's debilities, however, were the survival and revival of a workers' movement that had been the primary victim of the dictatorship. Although they were back on the political stage after the devastation of the 1970s, laborers still had to rebuild their organizations and renegotiate their ties with political parties in order to play a major role in the future. They strongly backed the "No" in the plebiscite and supported Aylwin in the presidential contest. They hoped that a progressive elected government would revitalize union rights and reinvigorate welfare programs. Until such reforms could be carried out, workers were bargaining with their adversaries from a position of weakness.

The oppression of the Pinochet years affected workers' political roles in contradictory ways. For most, especially in the trade unions, those defeats lowered expectations and demands in favor of a quest for security and survival. For others, especially the young and jobless in the *poblaciones*, deprivations bred desperation and mounting radicalism. Some shantytown dwellers, however, benefited from government programs and supported Pinochet. The Aylwin administration has vowed to move quickly to reintegrate all types of workers into national life, and the new regime will seek to reconstruct legitimate, harmonious, productive relations between the state and society.

Although still an important resource for the poor and oppressed in the 1980s, the Catholic Church backed away from its role as a shield and as a spokesperson for the opposition, ceding the political stage to the unchained political parties. Even though it was no longer in the forefront of the battle, the Church remained an ally of the transition, pressing for the unity of democratic forces and for the honesty of the plebiscite. So long as the transition kept on track, the Church assumed an increasingly neutral stance.

Continuities and changes also characterized other vital areas of political and cultural life. While some students became more radical, others abandoned much of the revolutionary rhetoric of the 1960s to concentrate on limited goals in an effort to regain control of their institutions in the 1980s. By 1987, they had managed not only to elect their own representatives for a variety of student organizations nationwide (dominated by the opposition) but also to oust the unpopular rector of the University of Chile, the leading public institution of higher education. This last event was most significant in that Pinochet intervened in order to mollify students, in an unprecedented reversal of his highly authoritarian university policy. Although demands by students and faculty —like the grievances of labor—were largely corporate in nature, their activism helped propel the drive for political participation and meaningful citizenship in all areas of national life.

As university students pushed for democratic procedures within their own institutions, intellectuals and artists emerged as complementary forces in the revival of freedom and openness. Various social science research centers, which evolved during the 1970s as shelters for persecuted academics, blossomed during the 1980s as influential think tanks that generated data, criticisms, and strategies against the military regime; their polling and planning proved to be crucial to the opposition's victory in the plebiscite.[4] In the literary field, José Donoso, Jorge Edwards, and others wrote compelling fiction that spoke directly to the consequences of authoritarianism for Chilean life. Theater—whether on the stage or in the streets—became once again a vehicle for social commentary, producing stinging critiques of the government's practices of persecution, torture, and exile. Even the strident tones of the popular rock group Los Prisioneros rallied youth to the ideals of liberty. From many quarters, an opposition culture took shape just as political parties sought to pull together their own forces to rebuild a democracy.

Amid the remarkable resurrection of civil society, equally impressive were the tenacity and resilience of the suppressed political parties. The parties had reached a low point by the end of the 1970s, suffering from General Pinochet's draconian measures and disdainful warnings against "petty politicians." Nevertheless, they resuscitated a vibrant political culture after the protests of the mid-1980s. On the surface, it seemed that the dictatorship had largely frozen the political landscape, whose configurations from right to left looked strikingly like those in 1970.

The three party clusters still prevailed by the end of the 1980s, although with altered nomenclature and electoral portions. The National Renovation (RN), the Independent Democratic Union (UDI), and the National Advance (AN) dominated on the right; the Christian Democrats (PDC) prevailed in the center, and the more moderate Socialists (PS) in the Party for Democracy (PPD) vied with their more militant brethren, the Communists (PC), and the Movement of the Revolutionary Left (MIR) in the Broad Party of the Socialist Left (PAIS) for control of the left. In this collection, Manuel Antonio Garretón establishes that those seeming political continuities masked profound changes that evolved during the long apprenticeship of redemocratization. For example, the right developed recalcitrant authoritarian elements, the Christian Democrats and "renovated" Socialists hammered out new understandings on a temperate reform agenda, and the traditionally gradualist Communists endorsed more radical strategies. The political learning process analyzed by Garretón culminated in the 1988 plebiscite and its aftermath.

By 1988, the regime had lost support not only internally but also externally. Most important was the switch in the Reagan administration's policy from improving relations with dictators to promoting takeovers by democrats. As Carlos Portales argues, those international forces exerted far less influence than domestic factors, but they did provide significant leverage at the margin. Foreign actors carried some weight in a situation where the two sides within Chile were fairly evenly matched. It may be noteworthy that the distribution of preferences between government and opposition was almost exactly the same during the United States interventions in 1973 (44 percent versus 54 percent) and 1988 (43 percent versus 55 percent).

During the 1980s, the United States took more restrained action on behalf of the opposition than it had under Allende, settling for an effort to prod rather than capsize Pinochet. It proved easier to bring down a democratic than a dictatorial government. At times, fears of a Marxist resurgence tempered United States enthusiasm for unbridled democratization. Throughout the struggle for democracy, the United States and some Western European countries struck a delicate balance between their praise for the economic model and their criticism of the dictatorship. It remains to be seen to what extent the Western powers will support Chilean democracy regardless of its ideological and programmatic content.

Washington hailed the consistent and carefully calibrated effort by the United States to nudge the dictatorship along the path to democratization as a model of success. If the Chilean transition stays on course and if the Cold War continues to thaw, then foreign diplomatic influence seems likely to diminish during the years ahead. Such a diminution will be welcomed by most Chileans, who have applauded external support for democracy in general but who oppose intervention on behalf of any partisan group in particular.

The 1988 Plebiscite

On August 30, 1988, the commanders-in-chief of the four branches of the armed forces named Augusto Pinochet to run for an eight-year presidency in the October 5 plebiscite. To legitimize that process, the ruling junta conducted a reasonably fair election. The military insisted on ample registration, which enrolled 92 percent of eligible voters. The junta also lifted the repressive State of Exception, allowed virtually all exiles to return home, and granted both sides fifteen minutes a day on television during the four weeks of the campaign. The voting itself was fraud-proof, with opposition and foreign observers at every transparent ballot box.

The either-or structure of the plebiscite allowed a socially and ideologically diverse center-left coalition to cohere around the main point they agreed on: "No" to Pinochet and his regime. Their conciliatory campaign dispelled fear and persuaded citizens they could vote "No" with impunity. By contrast, Pinochet's appeals to fears of a return to the conflicts under Allende evoked insufficient resonance after fifteen years. Following his defeat by 55 to 43 percent in the yes-or-no referendum, Pinochet was supposed to hand over the government to an elected administration on March 11, 1990. Because the armed forces demanded adherence to their constitution and timetable, they accepted those electoral results.

The 1988 plebiscite moved Chile from an autocracy to a liberalized autocracy. The most ardent supporters of Pinochet and his constitution hoped to stop that process at a limited democracy. Meanwhile, the opposition—with momentum on its side—struggled to push on to full democratization. After hard bargaining, the government and the opposition agreed to some changes in key undemocratic provisions of the 1980 constitution. Approved in a consensual plebiscite in July 1989, those reforms expanded civilian representation in the National Security Council; softened restrictions against parties espousing "totalitarian" ideas; increased the number of elected senators from twenty-six to thirty-eight (out of forty-seven); prohibited the suspension of habeas corpus under States of Exception; and, most important, eased the process for amending the constitution. At the same time, the tenure for the president inaugurated in 1990 was reduced to half the regular eight-year term.

The Elections of December, 1989

The results of the 1989 contests suggested that the 1988 plebiscite had been a "realigning" or "founding" election. As had been expected, Chileans voted massively on December 14, 1989, to replace the military government with a democratic civilian administration. Patricio Aylwin, a veteran politician who had led the senate against Allende but who had also captained the coalition for the "No" vote against Pinochet's regime, captured the presidency with 55 percent of the votes. He triumphed as the nominee of the continuing seventeen-party center-left alliance dominated by his own Christian Democrats and moderate Socialists. He also received support from Communists and other leftists. The three-way race produced a disappointing 29 percent for Hernán Büchi, the candidate of the government and of most rightist parties, and a surprising 15 percent for Francisco Javier Errázuriz, a maverick entrepreneur-turned-politician.

Although replicating the general contours of the 1988 plebiscite, the 1989 elections also revealed some profound changes from 1973. At least for the moment, one legacy of the authoritarian years was a stronger right, an enduring center, and a weaker left. In the lower house of deputies, the three camps reflected the trends in the 1988 plebiscite and the 1989 presidential balloting. The right claimed 40 percent of the deputy seats, the centrist Christian Democrats 33 percent, and the left (from the most moderate socialists to the most radical groups) approximately 22 percent. In the senate, the Aylwin coalition also won 56 percent of the elected seats but only 47 percent of the total, because the constitution gave seats to nine conservative senators who had not been elected.

The poor showing of the left, especially the Marxists, constituted the major surprise of the 1989 congressional elections. Although a handful of left-wing Socialists won election as deputies and senators, no one from the Communist Party netted a seat. By contrast, the moderate leftists—mainly "renovated" Socialists—represented by the PPD elected four senators and seventeen deputies. In the wake of those results, the Socialist Party reunited. Meanwhile, the Christian Democrats placed forty in the house and thirteen in the senate, compared to twenty-nine in the house and five in the senate for their closest rival, National Renovation. The voters rejected extremes on both the right and the left. They also spurned candidates closely associated with either the Pinochet or Allende years.

As a result of the elections, Aylwin controlled a majority in the house (70 out of 120 seats) but not the senate (22 out of 47 seats). Therefore, his government will need unified support from his own diverse coalition as well as some agreements with the right. Respecting Aylwin's electoral mandate, his coalition gave him a free hand to name his initial cabinet. He placed Christian Democrats in nine of the twenty positions and appointed Socialists, Radicals, Social Democrats, and others to the rest.

Claiming to have accomplished its mission of returning Chile to a sanitized democracy, the government of Pinochet moved to cooperate with its successor. It quickly acknowledged the results of the 1989 elections, in contrast with its slowness to accept the outcome of the 1988 plebiscite. Pinochet invited Aylwin for discussions at the presidential palace and instructed representatives to orchestrate a smooth transition with the winning camp. At the same time, the dictatorship continued its attempts to extend its legal and institutional influence into the future while setting limits on the freedom of action of the next government. By the beginning of 1990, although remnants of authoritarianism remained, most Chileans looked ahead to the democratic takeover with calm and confidence.

The Future

The civilian government inaugurated in 1990 will have to carry forward and consummate the transition to democracy, but consolidation will take time. The scope and rapidity of the transition will depend on how skillfully the Aylwin coalition can expand its power and the people's sovereignty. The strong electoral mandate should help the new administration further reform the constitution, reduce the political authority of the military, persuade the capitalists to cooperate, and address the socioeconomic grievances of millions of Chileans. In comparison with other recent Latin American transitions from right-wing authoritarianism to democratization, Chile is unusual in that the first elected government represented not only aspirations for political democracy but also the people's desire for social reform.[5]

According to Felipe Larraín, the economic challenge for a democratic government was to sustain the momentum of a market-powered system while redistributing more goods and services to the neglected majority. Achieving equitable growth sufficient to dissuade the rich and poor from extreme alternatives is a daunting task. Most other recently installed democratic governments in Latin America have not had enough resources to carry out significant social reforms, so they have often given their people "political goods" in lieu of "economic goods."

Fortunately, Chile's new administration took office with far healthier economic underpinnings than most of its neighbors. Moreover, a broad consensus prevailed from right to left on the need to retain macroeconomic stability and a vibrant private sector. At the start of 1990, the debates in Chile ranged over the tradeoffs between increasing investment and reducing poverty and among alternative policies to achieve superficially common objectives. The Aylwin government sought to resolve those dilemmas while containing inflation.

Although democratization seemed to be on track at the beginning of the 1990s, troubling questions still hung over the political horizon. Can the right fully resuscitate its historic democratic avocation, will its authoritarian segments fade in significance, and will it continue to participate in a majoritarian electoral system that renders its capturing of the presidency unlikely? Can the Christian Democrats mute their desire to be the single dominant party and continue to forge working coalitions with their rivals? Can the Socialists reconcile their more "social democratic" and more "Marxist-Leninist" tendencies? Can the Communists shed their insurrectionary dreams from the struggle against the dictatorship, rejoin the electoral arena on terms acceptable to the other parties and the armed forces, and retain their social base? Can the numerous minor parties and independents be absorbed into the predominant political organizations? And can a multiparty system founded on sharp social, ideological, and clientelistic cleavages become more pragmatic and incremental so as to avoid the mistakes and polarization of the past? The clues to these questions can be found in the hopeful developments of the last decade.

Whatever the pace of change in the 1990s, the 1980s witnessed the termination of the longest lasting and, in many respects, the most radical government in Chilean history. Through the transformations and transition examined in this anthology, Chile's unusual authoritarian regime ran its course. Even in the highly unlikely event of a reversion of the accelerating democratization unleashed by the 1988 plebiscite, it would be extremely difficult to reinstate the former Pinochet system in its entirety. Even most supporters of the dictatorship came to favor some change. That consensus for moderation was demonstrated when 86 percent of the voters approved the constitutional reforms in the 1989 referendum.

At the beginning of the 1990s, the politics of compromise superseded confrontation. In contrast with some other Latin American cases of democratization, Chile's prospects appeared to be optimistic. Seemingly favorable conditions prevailed both because the economy was robust and because the transition entailed a return to deeply rooted values and institutions. A noble democratic tradition was revived and, we hope, strengthened out of the painful experience of authoritarianism.

Notes

1. The authors wish to thank Manuel Antonio Garretón, Brian Loveman, and Augusto Varas for comments on an earlier draft of this introduction. For details on the 1988 plebiscite, see Paul W. Drake and Arturo Valenzuela, "The Chilean Plebiscite: A First Step Toward Redemocratization," *LASA Forum* 19 (Winter 1989): 18–36.

2. J. Samuel Valenzuela and Arturo Valenzuela, *Military Rule in Chile: Dictatorship and Oppositions* (Baltimore, 1986).

3. On the difficulties that democracies face in whittling down the autonomous powers of the armed forces, see Alfred Stepan, *Rethinking Military Politics: Brazil and the Southern Cone* (Princeton, 1988); and Augusto Varas, ed., *La autonomía militar en América Latina* (Caracas, 1988).

4. After the 1989 elections, many of those intellectuals rose from the opposition to powerful posts in the incoming democratic government.

5. On the dangers of transitions from authoritarian rule stopping short of full democratization, see Guillermo O'Donnell, Philippe Schmitter, and Laurence Whitehead, eds., *Transitions from Authoritarian Rule: Comparative Perspectives* 4 vols. (Baltimore, 1986).

Part I: The Regime's Supporters

Arturo Valenzuela

The Military in Power: The Consolidation of One-Man Rule

Few Chileans could have imagined on September 11, 1973, that the military dictatorship arising from the destruction of Chile's democracy would become the most durable and revolutionary government in the nation's history. Nor could anyone have predicted that General Augusto Pinochet Ugarte, the somewhat loutish and obedient military man whom President Salvador Allende had believed loyal to the constitutional government, would govern longer than any other Chilean president while accumulating a degree of power rare in the annals of modern dictatorship. From one of the most democratic and politically mobilized countries in the world, Chile became one of the most autocratic, and its authoritarian regime would outlast the "bureaucratic authoritarian" regimes that dominated South America during the 1960s and 1970s.

Like its neighboring counterparts, the Chilean regime was exclusionary.[1] Through harsh and repressive tactics, exceptional even on a continent accustomed to violence and unconstitutional seizures of power, Chile's new rulers sought to put an end to the participatory politics, mass mobilization, and political confrontation that had reached unprecedented levels in the final days of the Popular Unity government. Where for generations parties and interest groups had dominated the political process, the military authorities sought to govern "without politics," appointing men in uniform or other trusted advisers to posts ranging from cabinet officers to university presidents, from ambassadors to presidents of public corporations, governors, and mayors. For years the strong-armed tactics of the regime—including exile, internal exile, imprisonment, and assassination—kept political leaders and leaders of civil society at bay.

In charting major policy initiatives, the new rulers relied heavily on technicians and experts to unlock the secrets of "efficient" administration and to change the physiognomy of the nation's social, political, and economic life. They proceeded to dismantle much of the publics role in the economy, deliberately eschewing the notion that the state is responsible for implementing economic and social policies for the common good. The goal of the government of the armed forces was to develop the economy and to purify Chilean politics by creating state institutions and citizens impervious to the demagogic appeals of political leaders and parties inspired by foreign ideologies.

Although the military government shared some characteristics with other Latin American dictatorships of the time, the salient differences appear to be more important than the similarities. Unlike Peru, Brazil, Uruguay, and Argentina, where military officials selected chief executives on a periodic basis after considerable intrainstitutional bargaining, power in Chile became centralized to an unusual degree in the hands of the commander-in-chief of the army, who remained president throughout the entire period.

Yet, the preeminence of Pinochet as ruler did not mean that the Chilean regime was a personalistic dictatorship. Pinochet wielded more power than any other leader in Chilean history and provided a degree of coherence and stability to the Chilean regime, but his power was not arbitrary or absolute. Ultimately, Pinochet was limited by the very institutions that gave him power—the armed forces and the state—institutions that were subject to the framework of a highly regularized legal process and that responded to a greater or lesser degree to the press of broader societal forces. It is these constraints that led to the downfall of his secret police and prevented him from adopting a more authoritarian constitution. This in turn forced Pinochet to agree to a political opening that led to his ignominious political defeat on October 5, 1988, and forced him to accept the negative verdict of the electorate in a plebiscite that had been carefully planned to perpetuate his rule until his death.

Although the armed forces in Chile constituted the fundamental pillar of the regime, as they did in neighboring countries, the military as an institution did not participate directly in the decision-making process. In sharp contrast with Uruguay, where the Consejos de Generales and the Consejo de la Nación (dominated by high-ranking officers) openly debated policy options, or in Brazil, where generals debated the merits or demerits of alternative military candidates for the next presidential term, in Chile only the commanders of the other three services shared Pinochet's role in the policy process. A clear separation developed between the military as institution and the military as government, one that was made possible by the strong traditions of discipline and hierarchy in Chile's armed forces. Yet, this disjuncture did not create fundamental conflicts between the two roles, because Pinochet was successful in consolidating power, both as the final authority in the armed forces and as president of the Republic.[2]

Paralleling the separation between the military as government and the military as institution was the continued separation of Chile's military and civilian worlds, which was accentuated by the regime's successful efforts at political demobilization. Although prominent civilians on the right had considerable influence on public policy and access to military decision-makers, the state developed an unprecedented degree of autonomy from organized civilian interests and pressures. The regime was thus able to implement its constitutional formula as well as its far-reaching social and economic policies with minimal concern for the reaction of affected groups. Only in Chile was a military regime able to fulfill its strategy of sharply reducing state intervention in national life and spurring the growth of a dynamic export economy.

The shift to radical free-market doctrines may not have been the result of an inexorable logic of underlying social and economic forces aided and abetted by outside powers. In Chile, there was no coherent demand for a "deepening of industrialization," and such a "deepening" did not occur. Nor was the military committed prior to the coup to an economic experiment of low tariff barriers and an export-oriented growth strategy based on the theory of comparative advantage. Political developments during the first two years of military rule, including the character of the political support for the regime, the weight of key advisers, and the ambitions of Pinochet himself, combined with the critical state of the economy to tip the balance of economic choice away from a statist or developmentalist model to a neo-liberal one.

Just as the coup was not inevitable, but was the result of growing polarization and the failure of leaders to reduce tensions and preserve democratic institutions and practices, so the adoption of free-market economic policies resulted from a series of conscious choices that created their own dynamic, leading to the consolidation of a particular set of anti-statist policy options. In time, these options strengthened the regime's position by contributing to the disarticulation of organized groups schooled in the politics of a far more statist society.[3]

It would be a profound mistake, however, to attribute the durability and success of the Chilean regime to the dominance of its leader, the character of military rule, or the policy successes of its planners. Although these factors are basic to an understanding of the nature of the Chilean regime, the regime's longevity can only be explained by reference to the profound crisis of Chilean society that led to the regime's establishment in the first place. The comparative study of authoritarianism must consider the circumstances surrounding the previous regime's breakdown and the weight of the historical memory of those events as critical variables in judging the new regime's characteristics and durability.

Unlike other military regimes that came to power in Latin America because of the perceived inefficiency, corruption, or demagoguery of civilian regimes, Chile's military coup took place in a nation sharply divided on class lines. South America's most powerful Marxist parties had captured the presidency and were committed, despite majority opposition in the Chilean parliament, to implementing a socialist order. Chile's upper classes, a substantial proportion of the large middle class, and even many working-class citizens who identified with opposition parties, believed they were profoundly threatened by the policies of the Popular Unity government and by the climate and rhetoric of confrontation, violence, and disorder that resulted from the escalating clash between government partisans and opponents.

This sentiment gave the Pinochet regime a bedrock of popular support, which quickly came to the regime's defense during its moments of weakness. The failure of the protest movement in the early 1980s, during a time of severe economic recession, had less to do with Pinochet's survival skills than with the unwillingness of large sectors of Chilean society to risk the demise of the regime, which they feared might return the left to power. The profound divisions among civilian sectors and the continued fear of the left are critical ingredients in comprehending the degree of state autonomy and, by implication, the regime's strength.

From Coup d'État to a Foundational Regime: The Military in Power

The coup that brought the Chilean military to power was an ad hoc affair, a gradual process of escalating discontent within the services. Military conspiracies were encouraged by increasingly frantic civilians who challenged officers to protect "national security" by disassociating themselves from a government they saw as intent on establishing a revolutionary Marxist regime.

The highly professional Chilean military, with no real tradition of direct involvement in politics, proceeded against the Popular Unity government as if it were occupying enemy territory. The military and its supporters perceived government officials, party and union leaders, and thousands of UP militants as "foreign" foes who had to be defeated. For the first time in generations, the Chilean military went to war; for the first time in the nation's history, a united military assumed the reins of the state, dispensing with institutions, political parties, leaders, and followers.[4] The ferocity of the military's action was spurred by a lifelong socialization in the art of warfare, a powerful fear that Popular Unity supporters had the capacity to resist militarily, and, perhaps more to the point, a fear that enlisted men and even officers might be more loyal to the legitimately constituted authorities than to their superiors. Ironically, the left had encouraged this fear through its rhetoric before the coup. Slogans such as "the people united will never be defeated" were accepted as true, not only by much of the left but also by the military, which feared that the Popular Unity was creating an insurrectionary force capable of challenging the armed forces at its own game. Although resistance proved to be minimal even in strongholds of the left, the logic and momentum of war prevailed, transforming one of the most civilized and tolerant countries of the world into a nation characterized by widespread abuses of human rights.[5]

Throughout the nation, former officials of the Popular Unity government, as well as party leaders and activists associated with Allende's governing coalition, were harassed, fired from their jobs, arrested, imprisoned, or executed. The newly formed military junta outlawed the Popular Unity parties and confiscated their assets; declared other parties in "recess"; disbanded the labor federations; dissolved Congress; removed elected local government officials and replaced them with junta appointees; prohibited or censored newspapers, magazines, and radio stations; and banned books and films. Military authorities severely restricted all political activities and public meetings. Private organizations, ranging from business and professional organizations and nonprofit research organizations to small-town protestant churches, had to obtain permission from military commanders to elect officers and conduct business.

Despite the trauma and terror inflicted on so many citizens, the junta had widespread support in Chile's sizable middle and upper classes, where many were convinced that the military had liberated the nation from the threat of a Marxist tyranny that would have destroyed their way of life. Others, including many poor Chileans, were simply relieved that the ever-present political rhetoric, the marches and rallies, the confrontations and incidents of street violence had come to an end. Although consumer prices rose sharply with the lifting of price controls, many Chileans were pleased that once again the stores were stocked with goods and that the country had returned to "tranquility."

Most supporters of the regime, as well as many apolitical Chileans, were not aware of the extent of official repression, which gradually expanded from the jurisdiction of the armed services to a network of intelligence organizations, including the Dirección Nacional de Inteligencia (DINA), which soon became a law unto itself. Others were willing to tolerate human rights abuses as a necessary evil in the war against subversion and, paradoxically, because emergency measures were the "law" and Chileans prided themselves on being law-abiding. This attitude prevailed in many spheres of Chilean society, including the legal profession and the judiciary. Although nominally independent of the executive, the Chilean judiciary abdicated its role of protecting individual human rights from abuses by agents of the government.[6]

With cold professional efficiency, the military undertook the task of demobilizing Chile's highly politicized society. But the commanders of the armed forces were unprepared for their most important challenge: governing a shattered country. Aside from a commitment to vague notions of national security, they had, in the words of former air force commander and junta member Gustavo Leigh, "no program, no plans, nothing."[7] Nor did they have a clear notion of how a military government should be organized. Unlike a number of its coup-prone neighbors, Chile had no precedent for military rule within memory; its officers, who had traditionally been subordinated to civilian authority, were well-versed in warfare but singularly unprepared for governance.

During the weeks and months after the coup, Chile's military rulers repeatedly stressed two themes, both of which proved to be short-lived. First, they argued that the regime would be temporary and aimed at restoring institutional traditions that had been undermined by the Marxist experiment. Second, they stressed that the government would be a collegial effort, under the joint responsibility of the commanders of the army, navy, air force, and *Carabineros*, Chile's para-military police.

From the outset, the junta emphasized that its "historic act" was based on the premise that the Allende government had violated the 1925 constitution and that the military had a mission to restore the laws of the land. In early statements and documents, the junta repeatedly sought to justify the coup by referring to the nonbinding resolution adopted by the Chamber of Deputies on August 22, 1973. The first law approved by the junta—Decree Law No. 1 of September 11, 1973—stated that "the armed forces had taken power with the patriotic commitment to restore the fractured Chilean values [*chilenidad*], justice and institutionality." Bando (Directive) No. 5 of the same date stressed that the junta had deposed the Popular Unity government because it had become "flagrantly illegitimate," "immoral," and "non representative of the broad national sentiment," echoing the language in the Chamber of Deputies resolution. The directive added that the junta would hold power "for only that lapse which circumstances require."[8]

The coup had been a negotiated effort among the service branches; the principal initiative came from the navy and air force, with the army joining at the last moment. At first, the new government mirrored this relationship, with commanders of each military branch staking out co-equal positions. At the swearing-in ceremony for the junta, General Pinochet noted that

there was, in reality, a gentlemen's agreement. I have no pretension to direct the Junta while it lasts. What we will do is rotate. Now it is me, tomorrow it will be Admiral Merino, then General Leigh and after General Mendoza. I don't want to appear to be an irreplaceable person. I have no aspiration but to serve my country. As soon as the country recovers, the junta will turn over the government to whom the people desire.[9]

Meanwhile, the four-man junta would exercise all of the nation's executive, legislative, and constituent powers. The conservative Chilean judiciary and the comptroller general were permitted to retain their nominal autonomy on the assumption that they would continue to simply interpret and apply the law as adopted by the new law-making authority.[10] Top officials in the professional staff of the Congress and in the comptroller general's office proceeded as if nothing significant had happened to disrupt Chile's constitutional processes. Congressional staffers would prepare reports for the "new legislature" as they did for the old, and employees of the comptroller general's office would continue to ensure that government decrees were consistent with laws in force and that new legislation conformed to constitutional requirements. The legitimacy of the junta was not an issue, except with the relatively small number of staff members who were fired because of their political sympathies with the left.[11]

The original character of the military regime changed quickly. As the logic of repression escalated and as more elements of the civilian elite were replaced by armed forces personnel, it soon became apparent to high-ranking officers that their mission could not be fulfilled by a brief interregnum that would lead to the restoration of the old order. Emboldened by their takeover of key positions throughout the state apparatus and encouraged by their military staffs and a small group of ad hoc civilian advisers, these military men began to redefine their role as all-encompassing, aimed at purifying and transforming the very foundations of Chilean politics.[12] They blamed the nation's problems not only on the Allende government but also on decades of civilian democratic rule. As they saw it, the fault was in the institutions and political procedures that had served selfish and demagogic purposes and that proved to be incapable of defending the country from a "Marxist threat." As the saviors of the nation, Chile's professional soldiers came to see themselves as a special breed, rising above competing and parochial interests and maintaining the front line against foreign totalitarian doctrines.

As early as October 8, 1973, through Decree Law No. 77, the junta embarked on a campaign to "extirpate Marxism from Chile." Not content with having outlawed Chile's leftist parties, the junta declared that its "mission" entailed

reconstructing the country morally and materially towards economic development and social justice, giving life to new institutional forms which would permit the reestablishment of a modern democracy cleansed of the vices that favored the actions of its enemies.[13]

On October 25, an informal group of conservative experts in constitutional law was established by decree as a constitutional commission charged with "reconstituting, renovating the fundamental institutionality of the Republic."[14]

The junta's low regard for Chile's constitution was apparent in the repeated adoption of decree laws that openly contravened that document's basic provisions. The disparity between junta legislation and the fundamental law of the land was such that on December 4, 1974, the junta was forced to come to terms with its "unconstitutional" character by adopting Decree Law No. 788. The law vividly illustrated the extent to which the junta considered itself to be the repository of the national will. It stated that

all decree laws dictated to date by the Governmental Junta which are contrary, or in opposition to, or different from any precept of the Political Constitution of the State, have had and have the character of modifying norms, either expressly or tacitly, partially or totally, of the corresponding precept in the Constitution.

With the stroke of a pen, the four-member junta abandoned the principle of a written constitution anchored on popular sovereignty by making it clear that any of its laws took precedence over the constitution and automatically amended it.[15]

The gradual shift from a definition of the armed forces as moderators of Chilean politics to forgers of a new national reality was encouraged by military hardliners who came to be identified with the security forces and by a handful of civilian advisers who espoused a deep anti-communism and held jaundiced views of traditional Chilean political practices. Although Christian Democrats and National Party members, along with leaders of the business federations, had led the political opposition to the Allende regime, the military commanders soon made it clear that they intended to put considerable distance between themselves and the "traditional" party and interest group elites.[16] Junta leaders came to rely heavily on "non-partisan" advisers and technocrats for drafting decree laws, formulating policy, and defining the general principles of the regime. The corporativist tone of many early speeches and declarations reflected the Catholic integrist tendencies of influential advisers such as Jaime Guzmán, a young professor of law at the Catholic University and a founder of the conservative and nonpartisan "gremialista" movement in that university.[17] Later, this corporativist language would be superseded by the free-market rhetoric of the economists and technocrats who would become the architects of the regime's economic and social policies and who would give the regime its most articulated political philosophy.

economists

Pinochet and the Consolidation of Personal Rule

The redefinition of the military regime as foundational coincided with the gradual emergence of Pinochet as more than "first among equals." Many observers and early advisers to the junta were convinced that General Gustavo Leigh Guzmán, the air force commander, would become the strongman of the regime. He was far more articulate and polished than Pinochet, and he relished taking the initiative in government pronouncements. Whereas Pinochet had joined the coup at the last moment, Leigh had been an early instigator of the conspiracy, a role that gave him considerable prestige in military and civilian circles.[18]

But Pinochet had far greater cunning, determination, and ambition. A single-minded, even ruthless military man, Pinochet soon understood the degree to which much of Chilean society had been traumatized by the Allende experiment. He became convinced that his was a holy war against communism, a divinely inspired mission that would forever elicit the gratitude of his people. From the outset, Pinochet believed that he was a marked man, engaged in a deadly struggle for survival in which he would have to resort to the most extreme measures to come out alive and protect his family and closest associates. Pinochet was an authoritarian figure who had been deeply influenced by the strict Prussian training of the Chilean army, with its exaggerated stress on hierarchy and discipline. He had little sympathy for Chile's democratic traditions.[19]

Pinochet surprised both his friends and enemies by exhibiting far more skill than his rather simple demeanor suggested. Under his repressive rule, the political arena was dramatically reduced. The politics of parties, of the press, of clashing forces and interests disappeared and were replaced by the politics of a few hundred individuals who were given privileged access to the corridors of power. In an environment of committees, cabals, and conspiracies, Pinochet was a master tactician with a keen sense of how to use his considerable resources to outwit opponents both inside and outside the government. Above all, he learned how to assert his authority over the army, the institution that would become the fundamental pillar of the regime.[20]

Ambition, political acumen, or a sense of mission, however, are not sufficient to explain how a dictatorial figure emerged in a country with a long history of republican and representative rule. Above all, Pinochet's rise to preeminence was symptomatic of the degree to which many powerful and not so powerful Chileans wanted a respite from politics and social unrest and their willingness to put their trust in a military strongman.

Pinochet's rise to power was aided by three factors, two of which are directly related to Chile's tradition of democratic governance. First, he benefited from the traditional commitments to discipline, hierarchy, and respect for authority that had been a hallmark of the Chilean armed forces for generations. Pinochet was able to ensure that the military, which had started to become fragmented and politicized under the Popular Unity government, returned to traditional professional commitments and an undivided loyalty to governmental authorities. Second, Pinochet and his advisers successfully drew on Chile's strong historical tradition of respect for the rule of law and a constitutional framework of presidential government. Third, the junta president received indispensable help from a large network of staff members, advisers, and technocrats, who provided him with information, tools of coercion, and a governing program. Among these "internal supporters" was the dreaded secret police, whose work on Pinochet's behalf gave him a clear edge over potential rivals during the early years.

An "Apolitical" Military:
The Basic Pillar of the Regime

Ironically, one of Chile's strongest political traditions, a military establishment accountable to constituted authority, was at the center of Pinochet's successful rise to power. Chile's military, especially the army, is a very hierarchical organization with strict canons of discipline and an unusually strong esprit de corps. Pinochet, making skillful use of his positions as commander-in-chief and later president of the junta and the country, outmaneuvered his rivals and ensured that the armed forces remained loyal to the regime by adhering to their traditional professional and apolitical posture.

Pinochet's task was not easy. During the Popular Unity years, the armed forces broke, for the first time in living memory, with the tradition of subservience to civilian authority. The break implied an unprecedented degree of politicization of the officer corps. The coup occurred only after commanders who were loyal to the constitutional government were either forced to resign or, as in the case of the navy, neutralized by subordinates intent on resolving the country's crisis by force. The pro-coup officers carried the day, and the services followed through in removing the Popular Unity government by force.[21]

During the early days of the new regime, Pinochet was in a relatively weak position with respect to the army, his own institution. He had joined the conspiracy at the last moment, only after realizing that he could no longer count on the support of a majority of his generals for a policy of continued military neutrality.[22] Key army generals who promoted and carried out the coup, including Manuel Torres, Oscar Bonilla, Pedro Palacios, Sergio Nuño, and Sergio Arellano, had considerable influence after the coup and spoke freely on policy matters. Bonilla, named minister of the interior a week after the coup, soon became one of the most visible and important figures of the regime, and Arellano, as commander-in-chief of the Santiago Garrison, was a force to be reckoned with.[23] During the days after the coup, high-ranking officers in all services became personalities. In the absence of political parties as channels for communication and representation, individuals and groups began to approach prominent officers to serve as intermediaries with government authorities.

Shortly after the coup, Pinochet moved to assert his command. On September 21, 1973, the junta adopted Decree Law No. 33, a measure designed to stave off insubordination by army officers who might be loyal to the Allende government. The law gave Pinochet, as commander-in-chief of the army, exclusive powers for one year over the promotion and retirement of army officers, powers that had historically been vested in the Council of Generals and the president of the Republic.[24] Pinochet shrewdly used his new powers to systematically neutralize and retire those officers who had engineered the coup, such as General Baeza and General Torres, and to promote officers who had proved their loyalty to Pinochet and his predecessor, General Prats. In so doing, Pinochet removed most of the generals in his generational group, who were those most likely to challenge his authority. A key turning point came in July 1974, when Pinochet removed General Bonilla from the Ministry of the Interior and placed him in the Ministry of Defense, thus removing his most important rival from a visible policy role. Three generals identified with the coup were retired from the army during the first year, and all but one were no longer active within three years. Prized promotions went to generals who served directly on the president's staff or in the intelligence service, including César Benavides, Julio Canessa, Santiago Sinclair, Manuel Contreras, and Humberto Gordon.[25]

While Pinochet was purging the service of any potential rivals, he was also reinforcing his personal power by substantially expanding the corps of generals. This gave younger officers, whose careers depended on their loyalty to Pinochet, greater hope that they might attain the highest rank. In 1973, the Chilean Army had twenty-five generals; by 1985, it had fifty-two, all of whom were several "promotions" younger than their commander-in-chief. On achieving the rank of colonel, officers were expected to submit a letter of resignation to the commander-in-chief, which was kept on file and could be used at any moment to retire the individual in question. Pinochet had the final say over promotions above the rank of colonel. Furthermore, after the adoption of Decree Law No. 1639 of December 30, 1976, army generals could be kept in service beyond their obligatory retirement date by being promoted to the prestigious, newly created ranks of major general and lieutenant general. Pinochet reserved the post of captain general for himself, giving symbolic weight to the enormous age differential between himself and his army peers as he remained in the post of commander-in-chief years after normal retirement. Major generals and lieutenant generals owed their careers exclusively to Pinochet's judgment.[26]

Furthermore, military government meant that officers of all services could aspire to governmental positions. Provincial and departmental governors, the highest ranking political authorities outside the capital, were drawn from the services. Officers also held key posts as heads of state corporations, university presidents, undersecretaries, and cabinet ministers. Ambassadorial posts were reserved as special rewards for loyal officers or as inducements to keep officers in line who were thought to be less than loyal. Even generals who were somewhat independent of their commander-in-chief were offered embassies or financially rewarding opportunities before or after retirement. From 1973 to 1986, 56 of 118 cabinet-rank officials were military men, almost half of them from the army. During the same period, 47.5 percent of all ambassadorial positions (111) were occupied by military men, with the army representing nearly half.[27] As late as 1988, 40 percent of the 174 high-ranking officials, including ministers, undersecretaries, and agency heads, were military men, with the army obtaining 25 percent of all appointments.[28] For the first time in Chilean history, military men, who civilian elites had often viewed with contempt, became important community and public figures.

This privileged treatment implied important increases in fiscal spending for defense. In the period 1964–69, 2.7 percent of Chile's Gross National Product went for defense. Between 1973 and 1974, military expenditures increased 30 percent in real terms. Between 1980 and 1984, military expenditures had risen to 4.6 percent of GNP, not including expenditures for the secret police and a 10 percent allocation from copper profits for defense. It is instructive, however, that the bulk of the increase did not go to buy military equipment, but to personnel increases (from 90,000 military men in 1973 to 120,000 in 1986), salaries, and military pension plans.[29] Between 1969 and 1979, public expenditures for nonmilitary personnel increased 19 percent; public expenditures for personnel in the defense sector increased 170 percent.[30]

Although the widespread appointment of officers to government posts helped cement the loyalty of the armed forces to "their" government and president, it is important to remember that the armed forces in Chile did not govern as an institution. Officers took leaves of absence from their institutional duties in order to take on government assignments. Upon joining the government, however, they no longer took orders from their military superiors but from their superiors in the government. They served the government as individuals, not as representatives of their service. Moreover, Pinochet's practice of placing officers from different branches of the military in the same ministries—naming a cabinet secretary from one branch and an undersecretary from another—isolated officers from their peers and served as an effective deterrent against politicization of particular services. Finally, only a small group of active-duty officers had lengthy careers in government service, mainly on Pinochet's staff. Most were quickly rotated out and back to institutional responsibilities. Cabinet officers with the longest terms of service were in-

variably civilians or retired officers. The position of regional intendant was particularly short-lived, lasting on average about a year and
a half.[31]

At the same time, military officers remained apart from civilians,
rarely interacting with them except in official ceremonies. Even
prominent government figures on the right often wondered what
military leaders in government felt or thought about key issues. The
powerful socialization experience of military service in Chile made
it difficult for civilians to build bridges to military leaders, even
when working for the same government. Indeed, excessive social
contact of officers with civilians was severely sanctioned by military authorities.

While military men in government jobs made daily management
decisions, important policy decisions were made by Pinochet with
the support of his large and experienced presidential staff, his ministers and advisers, and, at times, the junta. Policy questions were not
discussed within the services or in the Council of Generals.[32] Early
efforts by high-ranking officers to have the Academia Superior de
Seguridad Nacional (ASUSENA)—later the Academia Nacional de Estudios Políticos y Estratégicos—generate policy options for the government did not succeed.[33] With a few exceptions, such as Admiral
Patricio Carvajal and General César Benavides, most military officers served in the less important and more technical ministries. After Pinochet's ascendancy, the key ministries of Interior, Finance,
Economics, Justice, and Education were staffed primarily by civilians, with Minister of Justice Mónica Madariaga and Finance Minister Sergio de Castro holding their positions the longest. In part, this
turnover occurred because military duty was a requirement for promotion and officers needed to return to professional pursuits to ensure advancement. But it was also clear that the president would not
tolerate a military officer who projected himself too strongly as a
public figure, and he discouraged the rise of officers who exhibited
intellectual and leadership qualities, such as former commanders
René Schneider and Carlos Prats. Talented officers like General
Luis Danús and General Gastón Frez, known for their disagree-
ment with many government policies, particularly in the economic sphere, and officers with strong characters and intellect
like General Horacio Toro were soon relegated to minor or distant
government and military posts or they were forced out of the institution. Except for the early administrative reforms of Colonel

Canessa and the legal work of key aids such as Fernando Lyon, most important policy innovations were conceived and carried out by civilian officials.

Pinochet and the Weight of Presidentialist Tradition

It was not simply the Chilean tradition of military obedience that contributed to the emergence of the most powerful and durable chief executive in Chilean history. Pinochet's rise to power was also aided by the strong attachment of Chilean elites, and the public at large, to a presidential form of government and their respect for legal formalism. The single most important step in Pinochet's political career was his designation as the "first" president of the junta. From the outset, cabinet ministers and government functionaries reported to the junta president rather than to the junta as a group. Schooled in the lines of authority and the procedures of a presidential regime, government officials were uncomfortable with the cumbersome practice of reporting to a plural executive. Aides also despaired at having to deal with the demands of a protocol-conscious military; it was not a simple task to find doors wide enough so that all junta members could walk through them at the same time.

Even as the junta was issuing decrees that contravened the 1925 constitution, Pinochet and his governmental experts and advisers approached the task of building the governing institutions of the military regime within the framework of that constitution, with its clear separation of powers among executive, legislative, and judicial organs of government. Ministers and government officials proved to be ready allies. They feared that the junta's early disorganization and lack of direction were endemic to a plural executive and would undermine the effectiveness of the regime. In eloquent arguments before the junta, and with the clear support of Pinochet, a small group of jurists and constitutional experts persuaded junta members that Chile required clear presidential authority. Ironically, Chile became a uni-personal dictatorship partly because influential Chileans close to the new authorities were too faithful to the constitutional and legal traditions, if not practices, that had evolved under democratic rule. As General Leigh stated, "We broke away from the Constitution, but as soon as we came to power we had to conform to the same Constitution. Pinochet clung to all of the attributions of the constitutional Chilean presidency. Our mistake was not to be more revolutionary."[34]

The turning point in Pinochet's consolidation of executive control came nine months after the coup with the adoption of Decree Law No. 527 of June 26, 1974, which approved the Statute of the Governmental Junta. The law specified that the junta had constitutional and legislative powers but that "executive power is exercised by the President of the Junta who is the Supreme Chief of the nation." Although Pinochet's legal advisers deliberately chose the title to distinguish it from the traditional title of President of the Republic, the other military commanders were displeased with the initiative. At a stormy meeting of the junta, they finally relented, persuaded by the argument that the statute was nothing more than a technical change necessary for the proper administration of a country whose legal corpus was designed for a presidential regime with a clear separation of powers. To safeguard its rights, the junta insisted that Article 10, which listed the special powers of the junta president, include language calling on the president to obtain the junta's "approval" for cabinet nominees and to "hear" the junta on other matters, such as the appointment of judges.[35]

To the consternation of the other junta members and even some of the general's civilian advisers, however, Pinochet used Decree Law No. 527 to claim the symbolic and ceremonial trappings of the Chilean presidency. Shortly after the law was adopted Pinochet held a "swearing-in ceremony" in which he had the president of the Supreme Court invest him with the traditional ceremonial sash of the presidency.[36] But the new Supreme Chief was still not satisfied. Five months later he asked his chief legal aide, Mónica Madariaga, to draft a bill changing his title from Supreme Chief of the Nation to that of President of the Republic, on the grounds that most of the country's legislation referred to that office when referring to the executive branch. Already on the defensive, the junta approved the change through Decree Law No. 806 of December 17, 1974. It was not long before Pinochet was making all cabinet, judicial, and ambassadorial appointments on his own authority, ignoring the ambiguous provisions of Decree Law No. 527 that he "hear" or act with the "agreement of" the junta, thus eroding the remaining jurisdiction that other junta members claimed over particular ministries.[37] By mid-1975, the Economic Council under Merino, the Social Council headed by Leigh, and the Agrarian Council led by Mendoza were phased out. Initiatives for new rules, regulations, and government reforms shifted to the ministries and to the junta staff, who had become de facto members of Pinochet's staff. In most cases, the ministers brought proposed legislation directly to the president, who would decide whether or not to bring the matter to the attention of the junta. Ministers would then defend their proposals before the junta with far more knowledge and information than was available to junta members.

The constitutional experts failed to recognize that the junta could not be a counterweight to the executive in the same way that Congress had been under democratic procedures. This was particularly the case because Pinochet, while gaining executive authority, remained a junta member, and junta business could only be transacted by unanimous agreement of its members. This provision effectively gave Pinochet veto power over any junta action that might be directed at trimming the president's broad interpretation of his powers.[38] The junta became a weak legislature beholden to executive initiatives. Its diminishing role was reinforced by a reluctance and inability to seek out and respond to the interests of societal groups affected by government policy. By operating with little direct contact with civilian organizations, the junta was unable to build constituency groups that might have provided a countervailing force to the dictatorial ambitions of the executive. The closed nature of Chile's exclusionary authoritarian regime played directly into the hands of Pinochet and those elements in the regime who supported dictatorial rule.

Tensions between the junta and the president became serious in late 1977 when the United Nations voted overwhelmingly to condemn Chile for human rights violations. Pinochet responded by proposing a symbolic referendum on January 4, 1978, which would call on citizens to "endorse President Pinochet in his defense of the dignity of Chile, and reaffirm the legitimacy of the Government of the Republic to head in a sovereign way the country's institutional process."[39] Leigh and his advisers interpreted this as a brazen attempt by Pinochet to gain political legitimacy directly from the Chilean people rather than from the junta, a legitimacy that would help him curb the junta's powers. Both Leigh and Merino opposed the presidential initiative, and Pinochet called the plebiscite by executive order. When the comptroller general rejected the order as unconstitutional, Pinochet simply forced him to resign and had a slightly revised text approved by his more pliant successor. The plebiscite, engineered with massive government publicity in an atmosphere that intimidated opposing sentiment, was overwhelmingly approved by the voters.[40]

Leigh persisted in his criticisms of Pinochet's growing dictatorial powers. In a memorandum sent to Pinochet on May 16, 1978, Leigh called for an end to the military government within five years and the immediate incorporation of citizen groups into the policy-making process. He also advocated a modification of Decree Law No. 527, which would bar the president from voting in the junta. Decree laws would be approved by the other three commanders as a majority of the junta members. Pinochet would be given the power of veto, which could only be overridden by a unanimous vote of the three junta members. Finally, the air force general argued that a new constitution was not necessary. According to Leigh the 1925 constitution had served the country well and needed to be amended only slightly in order to meet new realities.[41]

These demands proved to be too much for General Pinochet. When Leigh presented some of these views to an Italian newspaper, Pinochet found an excuse to try to discredit Leigh as a detriment to the armed forces and the military government. On July 24, 1978, when Leigh went to his office at the Ministry of Defense, he found it surrounded by paratroopers. In a development that took him totally by surprise, he was summoned before the other members of the junta and asked to sign a decree approving his retirement. When he refused, the other junta members signed an order retiring him on the grounds of disability: the order was carried out with a decree from the Ministry of the Interior. Pinochet obtained a signed declaration from all cabinet ministers that sharply questioned Leigh's judgment and patriotism. The atmosphere in Santiago was tense as Pinochet made clear his determination to use force if necessary to persuade Leigh and the air force to capitulate to his demands. The air force backed down, although Pinochet retired eight generals and eleven others resigned in solidarity with Leigh before General Fernando Matthei was found willing to assume the post of air force commander and junta member.[42] In risking an open military confrontation, Pinochet demonstrated that he would stop at nothing to consolidate his authority. With Leigh's departure, Pinochet could turn more comfortably to creating a new constitutional order that would ratify the new power relations and provide a juridical base for projecting the regime into the future.

Military and Civilian Advisers,
Secret Police, and Technocrats

A nonpolitical and obedient military combined with a tradition of presidential rule made Pinochet's rise to power possible. His success in achieving that goal, however, depended on his ability to control information, make key appointments, take policy initiatives, and wield instruments of coercion. It is difficult to overestimate the importance of staff, advisers, technocrats, and intelligence operatives in this process.

During the first chaotic weeks after the coup, Chile's military commanders felt overwhelmed by the demands of government and daunted by the complexities of the nation's legal and administrative practices and its serious economic crisis. This permitted both military and civilian experts to gain a relatively free hand in pressing for their conception of what the military regime should be. Pinochet, with years of experience in a large professional bureaucracy, understood the importance of staff better than any of his colleagues. One of his first acts was to offer the junta an advisory group from the army high command and to ask the other junta members to complement its staff by naming officers from their services to its ranks. The group was headed by an army officer who reported directly to Pinochet, however, and the other commanders failed to keep close ties to their own subordinates on the advisory group. Army officers headed the Junta Advisory Committee (COAJ), which was set up along military lines and was primarily responsible for keeping track of decree laws that emanated from the junta. Army officers also headed the Commission for Administrative Reform (CONARA), which was organized to study administrative reforms in such areas as regionalization and local government.[43] Occasionally, both CONARA and COAJ turned to civilian authorities for help on particular projects. Soon most experts and advisers, in groups or as individuals, were gravitating to the president of the junta, providing him with critical information that he used to take a series of initiatives. General Leigh, when asked what power he had as a member of the junta in the early days, noted ruefully that "as advisers, courtesans, etc. . . . began appearing, we the other members [of the junta] were systematically displaced until we had no say at all in executive matters."[44]

An important turning point came in 1974, when Pinochet gave newly promoted army General Sergio Covarrubias the mission of building a broader general staff. Decree Law No. 528 had created cabinet-level staffs for each junta member. Covarrubias, with the help of an executive order, centralized the flow of information into the office of the junta president. By 1977, demonstrating his growing personal authority, Pinochet had transformed that staff into the Estado Mayor Presidencial (Presidential Staff) to coordinate the work of ministries and other advisory groups, review legislation, and manage the presidential office. General René Escauriaza, Covarrubias' successor, moved a step further in planning the creation of a cabinet-level position for the presidential staff. In 1981, when Pinochet assumed the presidency within the framework of the 1980 constitution, CONARA and COAJ were combined. In 1982, both were incorporated into the Estado Mayor Presidencial, leading to the creation of the cabinet-level office of the Secretaría General de la Presidencia under General Santiago Sinclair. Although the staff set up by the executive under army jurisdiction played an essential role in governance, it mainly performed the managerial and technical functions of day-to-day administration and coordination. Important policy thrusts and innovations, as well as the more coherent definitions of regime ideology, often came from influential ministers and other staff members, sometimes working within the framework of formal advisory bodies and sometimes acting informally as individuals or small groups.

It is not easy to detect clear patterns or regularities in the staffing structure of an authoritarian regime. The very absence of regime institutionalization and the highly arbitrary nature of personal rule meant that these structures were often ad hoc; they were dependent on personal access to leaders in the presidential bureaucracy or to junta members or its president (or members of his family, especially First Lady Lucía Hiriart de Pinochet). Furthermore, these advisory structures changed as the regime evolved and faced different challenges. Thus, as the country moved away from a concern for "internal war" to a concern for societal "modernization," and away from unstable collegial rule to personal dictatorship, both the organization of governance and the particular groups and individuals with influence and access to power changed.

Despite these reservations, it is possible to identify three distinct groups that played critical roles in the evolution of the Chilean military regime: the civilian political and legal advisers, the secret police, and the technocrats. In most respects, these groups were dissimilar in their visibility, their functions, their degree of coherence, and the nature of their access to presidential authority. They also had different agendas and objectives. All three groups, however, played prominent roles in the internal struggles of the regime and were key actors in the central struggle between the *duros*, or hard-liners, who believed in the continuation of repressive policies and the institutionalization of an authoritarian formula for governance, and the *blandos*, or softliners, who advocated liberalization, gradual increases in societal participation in policy-making, and an eventual return to liberal democracy.

Informal and secret advisers played a leading role during the first five years of the regime. After 1978, by which time many of the regime's perceived "enemies" had been eliminated and Pinochet had consolidated authority, power became more formalized, with the National Planning Office (ODEPLAN) and cabinet ministers assuming the primary responsibility for designing policy initiatives. The final formalization of the regime came after the 1980 constitution was adopted, Pinochet had moved into the Moneda palace, and the Secretaría General de la Presidencia had been created. This shift coincided with the entry of a large number of civilians into ministerial ranks.

LEGAL AND POLITICAL ADVISERS

For the most part, the legal and political advisers were the least cohesive group in the new regime, achieving influence as individuals or informal cabals. They were most prominent during the early years of the regime and during key periods of rule-making, such as the period before the 1980 constitution was enacted and the period leading up to the 1988 plebiscite, when a series of laws had to be adopted in order to implement the provisions of the constitution. Although dozens of people collaborated with the authorities in defining the regime's changing legality, first as informal advisers to the junta and later as members of presidential advisory groups and junta legislative committees, a few individuals and groups stood out above the rest.

These groups and individuals were significant because they represented different tendencies within the ranks of the regime's supporters. Some represented the parties of the right and traditional business elites, who favored a return to democratic practices in which the rightist politicians would once again have positions of prominence. Others represented a "new right" committed to free-market economic policies and an abandonment of past democratic practices through the structuring of new parties and more "modern" political institutions. Still others came from the authoritarian right; they were strong supporters of military and one-man rule and were highly critical of liberal democracy. This group was linked to elements of the armed forces and the secret police.

Pinochet became a skillful and wily executive, often pitting one advisory group or adviser against others or commissioning the same task from different individuals without telling them so. By retaining the services of advisers and influentials from different factions and ideological camps, Pinochet was able to coopt potential critics and obtain support from different quarters for different measures. More important, he was able to insulate himself from a close identification with any group, improving his own distance and autonomy from political forces. Pinochet's own authority was clearly enhanced by keeping all options open and positioning himself as the fundamental arbiter of the contradictory advisory channels entering the formal and rigid administrative structure of his military staff.

The most visible of the formally constituted bodies advising the junta was the commission appointed to begin drafting a new constitution. For several years, however, Pinochet and his advisers refused to give the constitution a clear go-ahead, believing that such a document would force them to define an end to the regime and to specify prematurely the outlines of a new political order. The commission, headed by conservative jurist Enrique Ortúzar, became an advisory body that drafted laws and reviewed the legal soundness of proposed legislation, to the consternation of some constitutional law experts.[45]

An even less direct and decisive role was played by prominent figures appointed to the Council of State, a high-level advisory body created to give the regime a degree of legitimacy and to act as consultant on important constitutional questions. The council, whose members came from various walks of life, included two of Chile's three living presidents. The most important role of the Council of State was revising the final draft of the 1980 constitution.

More important than these formal bodies were informal advisory groups and individuals. During the early years, a "political committee"—consisting of conservative civilians Jaime Celedón, Gastón Acuña, Eduardo Boetch, Sergio Rillón, and Federico Willoughby—prepared advisory reports for military staffers. The only female staff member of note was Mónica Madariaga, a close adviser who rose to prominence because of her family's ties to Pinochet. Madariaga, an intelligent and skillful legal expert who had worked in the office of the comptroller general, thought of herself as Pinochet's chief "legal plumber." At the president's personal request and in coordination with the presidential staff, she often banged out key legislation on her manual typewriter. She would then lobby before the junta, stressing the "technical" nature of the legislation and the urgency of its adoption. Pinochet rewarded her by naming her minister of justice and later ambassador to the OAS.[46]

In addition to the civilian staff members who worked directly with the junta and executive advisory bodies, Pinochet's top staffers occasionally relied on the advice of prominent conservative party leaders. Much to Leigh's chagrin, General César Benavides as minister of the interior announced in 1976 that the government was consulting the Asesoría Política (ASEP) for political advice on sensitive issues such as the expulsion from Chile of the leader of the Christian Democrats. The small group of former leaders of the National Party and Democracia Radical included former senators Francisco Bulnes and Angel Faivovich and lawyers Hugo Rosende and Miguel Schweitzer. It reported to General Covarrubias and General Escauriaza until civilian ministers were appointed to the ministries of interior and justice in 1978. At that point, ASEP became more of a resource for Minister of the Interior Sergio Fernández.

The most influential civilian adviser during the first years of the regime represented a very different tendency in Chilean rightist politics. Jaime Guzmán, the brilliant and devout young constitutional law professor from Catholic University, was skeptical of the traditional parties of the right, which he saw as responding to the same demagogic impulses of a corrupt democracy in which leaders stumbled over one another to promise the impossible. Coming from the "gremialista" movement at Catholic University, he initially favored a more corporativist model of society, such as that followed in Franco's Spain, where representation would be channeled through organized groups defined by the workplace rather than through political parties. Some of the early statements of the regime's political philosophy, including the Declaration of Principles, reflect his views. Guzmán began his government service as an adviser to Leigh, but he soon moved closer to Pinochet as he watched the army general become the leader of the military government. Particularly during the period between the coup and Leigh's ouster in 1978, Guzmán enjoyed direct access to the president and advised him on most important political and governmental initiatives. Guzmán wrote statements and speeches, advised the junta president on cabinet changes, and argued for abandoning the collegial form of rule and was instrumental in drafting the foundational documents of the regime.

While serving the regime, however, Guzmán underwent an important philosophical transformation. He shed his long-held Thomistic views in favor of Frederick von Hayek's vision of society. Guzmán now believed that free-market economics could modernize Chilean politics and make parties and ideologies a thing of the past, obviating the need for corporativist solutions. Working closely with top aids in the Estado Mayor Presidencial, Guzmán played a key role as one of the most effective supporters of the policies of "free market" technocrats in the bitter internecine battles against the more statist designs of the "nationalist" supporters from the far right. He was also influential as a member of the constitutional drafting commission, pushing for a form of "protected" democracy and resisting pressures for an early transition to democratic rule or for a permanent authoritarian formula for the country's future governance. This battle culminated in 1977, when Pinochet defined the broad outlines of a new constitutional order and set a specific timetable for the return to civilian rule.[47]

Another key civilian player was Sergio Fernández, a little-known lawyer who was appointed minister of labor in March 1976. Fernández' appointment was a clear rebuff to the work of outgoing Labor Minister Díaz Estrada, an air force officer who had attempted to establish good relations with unions, much to the chagrin of those economic advisers who were advocating free-market policies. With Fernández' entry into the government and the appointment of Madariaga to the Ministry of Justice, the influence of the old-line political leaders in ASEP clearly waned. Unlike Guzmán, who worked behind the scenes, Fernández became one of the most visible civilian leaders of the military regime, serving as its first civilian minister of the interior in 1978. He occupied the post on two separate occasions, the last time as the head of Pinochet's losing plebiscite campaign in 1988.

As minister of the interior, Fernández helped draft the final text of the 1980 constitution. Upon leaving the ministerial post, he took over the leadership of the commission charged with drafting the constitution's enabling laws. Like Guzmán in an earlier period, Fernández played a critical role in championing the free-market policies of the economic team and was an important protagonist in the internal power struggles between supporters of free-market and statist policies. On leaving the government, he joined Guzmán's Unión Democrática Independiente (UDI), the party identified with the regime's neo-liberal economic advisers.

To the conservative party advisers and the neo-liberal group represented by Guzmán, Fernández, and the economic technocrats must be added other civilian advisers of a more "nationalistic" or authoritarian tendency. These advisers remained in the wings of the military regime, occupying various advisory posts on junta legislative commissions and other bodies, but never achieving the influence they hoped for. Strongly critical of the economic technocrats and the traditional political elite, they argued for a permanent authoritarian solution and were unabashedly pro-Pinochet. Although they successfully provided support for a hardline posture in the political field during the mid-1970s, they lost key battles in the economic sphere. The most prominent figure in this camp was Pablo Rodríguez Grez, the founder and former leader of the ultra-right Fatherland and Liberty (Patria y Libertad) movement, which played a prominent role in fomenting violent opposition to the Allende government. Rodríguez was often rumored to be in line for the minister of the interior post whenever the demise of the Chicago Boys was predicted. He had close ties to Pinochet and to elements of the army, particularly the secret police, where the real strength of "nationalist" sentiment was located. Rodríguez often argued for a large "civic-military" movement of support for Pinochet and the armed forces, a movement that was begun on several occasions with encouragement from Pinochet and elements in the secret police. Civilian support for the movement was weak, however, and other advisers, particularly those associated with the economic team, adamantly opposed the creation of a political movement with "fascist" connotations, which they saw as threatening free-market economics. Pinochet himself was persuaded that such a movement could get out of hand and could reduce his capacity to manage the political process. Army officers may have shared the nationalist's statist views, but they were also concerned about the political ramifications of the ultra-right civilians.[48]

THE SECRET POLICE

Formally authorized by Decree Law No. 521 of June 18, 1974, the Dirección Nacional de Inteligencia (DINA), Chile's secret police, was actually created by the junta in November 1973 to coordinate the intelligence activities of the military services and to spearhead the clandestine war against those who opposed the regime. Quickly realizing the potential power of such an organization for his own purposes, Pinochet moved rapidly to establish control of the new organization.[49] Although the DINA included officers from all the services, Pinochet ensured that the director was an army officer who reported directly to him. General Leigh, after objecting to the junta's inability to control the organization, withdrew air force officers from participation. The DINA, closely monitored by the junta president, became a feared and shadowy organization that operated at the margins of the law. Moreover, it became a crucial resource for Pinochet in his drive to consolidate personal power.[50]

Employing military officers and right-wing civilians, including former members of Patria y Libertad, the DINA embarked on a "dirty" war to destroy any militant opposition to the regime that had survived the initial wave of arrests, deportations, voluntary exile, and executions after the coup. The DINA was responsible for the disappearance and presumed death of hundreds of individuals who were arrested by armed men in civilian clothes, usually operating at night under the cover of the curfew.

In 1974, most of the disappeared were members of the Movement of the Revolutionary Left, whose national leaders were killed in a series of "armed confrontations." The following year, the security forces targeted the Socialist Party and in 1976 the Communist Party. Of 108 people who "disappeared" in 1976, 78 were Communist leaders, including many members of the party's Central Committee. The Vicariate of Solidarity documented the disappearance of 668 persons from 1973 to 1978 following arrests by security forces.[51]

After concentrating on destroying opposition to the military government, the DINA soon spread its activities abroad. Political moderates in exile were targeted for assassination because of their role in influencing international public opinion against the military regime. The DINA established extensive contacts with right-wing terrorist groups and foreign intelligence organizations. It was implicated in the brutal assassination of General Carlos Prats in Argentina in September 1974 and in the death of Orlando Letelier,

Allende's former foreign minister, in the streets of Washington in September 1976. It may also have been responsible for the earlier assassination attempt in Rome of moderate Christian Democrat Bernardo Leighton, one of Chile's most respected political leaders.

The DINA's activities also expanded into state agencies and the military institution itself, until it had become a powerful political force. Even high-ranking officers and cabinet members came to fear the ubiquitous intelligence officers who monitored their actions and words and who brought them to the attention of their superiors and Pinochet himself. Generals Bonilla, Lutz, and Arellano were appalled at the increasing power of the DINA, which was headed by a lower-ranking officer who seemed to have more authority than they did. Bonilla clashed directly with Colonel Manuel Contreras, the DINA head, when he discovered the extent of the DINA's power and the nature of its underground activities. Shortly after Bonilla attempted to curb Contreras' power, at a time when he was also opposed to the expansion of Pinochet's authority, he was transferred out of the politically sensitive Ministry of the Interior and placed in the Ministry of Defense. The DINA received legal sanction through Decree Law No. 521. A year later, Bonilla died in a mysterious helicopter accident.[52]

By 1976, under Contreras' direction, the DINA had mushroomed into a vast organization with numerous departments, including counter-intelligence, internal government, psychological warfare, and economic policy-making. The DINA, concerned about its own budgetary independence from the junta, also set up businesses for profit, taking over fishing companies that were once in state hands. Contreras, allied with other hardliners, convinced Pinochet to adopt a series of measures that would strengthen the authoritarian and repressive character of the government. In March 1976, Pinochet restructured his cabinet, outlawed the Christian Democratic Party, and imposed broad prior censorship of publications. That year, the Communist Party leadership was decimated without arrest or trials, and Orlando Letelier was assassinated in Washington, D.C. Early in 1977, the executive drafted an amendment to Constitutional Act No. 4, further restricting basic civil rights, without consulting the Council of State, the Constitutional Commission, or the legislative committees of the junta.[53]

The growing power of Colonel Contreras so alarmed other insiders, including legal advisers and other conservative civilians close to the regime, that some began to fear that Contreras might jeopardize Pinochet's power and undermine any hope of institutionalizing the regime or creating the foundations for a future constitutional order.[54] This fear was also prevalent in military circles, whose members worried that Contreras may have overstepped the bounds of his intelligence-gathering activities. Contreras' actions were bitterly opposed by officers in charge of army and air force intelligence and the civilian investigation police, who resented and feared the growing reach of the DINA's operations. With the strong support of General Sergio Covarrubias, head of the Estado Mayor Presidencial, the *blandos* prevailed on Pinochet to define the outlines of Chile's future institutional structures and to provide a specific timetable for its implementation. He did so at a youth rally held at Chacarillas on July 9, 1977, undercutting Leigh's arguments for regime liberalization, while signaling the *duros* that the government would reject the establishment of an indefinite authoritarian regime.

The concerted efforts of Contreras' opponents within the regime finally led to the curbing of his power, aided in no small measure by growing discontent within the corps of generals who formed a special committee to examine the DINA. The anti-DINA elements were also helped by the extraordinary international outcry provoked by the Letelier case and particularly by the demand from United States prosecutors and the Carter administration that Contreras be extradited to face trial in the case. Although Chile refused to honor the extradition request, Colonel Contreras was relieved of his duties and the DINA was reorganized and replaced by the National Center for Information (CNI). The DINA was dismantled on August 6, 1977, only days before Terence Todman, U.S. Assistant Secretary of State for Latin American Affairs, visited Santiago.[55]

The Chacarillas speech was an important turning point. It marked the first time that the president had sketched out a plan for Chile's future institutions, a plan that, although it called for a restricted democracy, nevertheless accepted the legitimacy of a democratic order. The speech can only be understood as the culmination of a fierce internal struggle that came to a head in response to powerful pressures from contradictory sources: (1) those of the DINA and the regime *duros* who were unalterably opposed to liberalization and to a timetable for return to civilian rule; (2) those from General Leigh who, in his effort to curb Pinochet's monopoly of executive author-

ity, had proposed his own formula for a return to democratic practices; and (3) those from the regime *blandos,* who were convinced
that Pinochet's authority over Leigh had to be strengthened for the
military government to succeed and that the growing strength of
Contreras and the hardliners had to be resisted.

But the *blandos'* victory was less than complete. They did succeed
in helping Pinochet undercut General Leigh with policy proposals that
also undermined the position of Contreras and the *duros.*[56] But even
though General Contreras lost prominence, averting a potential takeover of the regime by the *duros,* Pinochet himself was the most important *duro* on political and constitutional matters. Once he ousted General Leigh, his commitment to the timetable spelled out at Chacarillas
quickly waned and he renewed his intentions of seeking a more permanent authoritarian option for the country. By supporting Pinochet in
his struggles with both Contreras and Leigh, the *blandos* only contributed to enhancing the president's personal power.

The 1980 Constitution

Pinochet's speech in Chacarillas on July 9, 1977, marked the beginning of a concerted effort to project the military government into the
future by creating a new institutional framework for Chile. Prior to
that date, the authorities, locked in internal disagreements, had
avoided providing an outline for a permanent constitutional formula and setting specific deadlines for return to civilian rule. The
regime had proceeded in an ad hoc fashion by explicitly or implicitly
modifying the 1925 constitution, creating a juridical morass, and
giving the impression of drift and impermanency. Four years after
the coup, with serious dissent in the junta over Pinochet's emerging
power, the regime seemed to be running out of the legitimacy it had
enjoyed during the months after the coup. At Chacarillas, Pinochet
reiterated that the "11th of September [1973] did not represent only
the overthrow of an illegitimate and failed government, but represented the end of a political-institutional regime that was de-
finitively spent, with the consequent imperative to build a new
one." Showing that he was capable of political flexibility, he called
for the implementation of a new constitution that would structure a
"protected" and "authoritarian" democracy, which would begin in
1980 with a "designated" parliament that would last for four or five
years. Subsequently, an elected parliament would designate the

president for a six-year term, at which time open presidential elections would be held.[57]

On November 15, 1977, Pinochet sent the Constitutional Commission a long memorandum outlining a series of proposals for the new constitution.[58] The commission incorporated many of those proposals into a draft that reflected substantial continuity with Chile's constitutional past but added elements further reinforcing presidential power. It completed its work in October 1978 and turned its draft over for comments to the Council of State, a consultative body that included former presidents Jorge Alessandri Rodríguez and Gabriel González Videla, who had been named to the council by Pinochet to help legitimize the regime.

The Council of State called for reactions to the text from a wide variety of social groups and institutions, the great majority of which were partisans of the regime, and submitted a substantially modified document to President Pinochet on July 8, 1980. The most important innovation of the Council of State draft, which was introduced at the insistence of Council President Jorge Alessandri, was the incorporation of "transitional articles" that provided for a specific timetable for the transition to civilian rule. The council specified that Pinochet would stay in office until 1985 but would share power with an appointed but broadly representative Congress that would generate the laws. The junta would be retained essentially as an advisory body.[59]

President Pinochet was not completely satisfied with the work of the legal experts. He had believed all along that their proposed constitution was too similar to the 1925 constitution. The president had reluctantly agreed to present a constitutional outline reflecting the work of his legal advisers at Chacarillas, but only in response to the political pressures of the moment. The general's own preference was for a far more authoritarian solution, one in which the armed forces would have an even stronger tutelage over elected officials and direct participation in the formulation of public policy.[60] But he was prepared to accept the proposed document because it would create a "protected" democracy; that is, it would bar totalitarian forces from political participation and give the armed forces some veto powers over policies injurious to "national security."

What Pinochet was no longer prepared to accept was the timetable for his own retirement, which he had articulated in the Chacarillas speech and which had later been put forward by the Council of State in its transitional articles. Having consolidated his own authority and clearly enjoying his role as Chile's most powerful figure, Pinochet no longer felt pressured to underscore his personal commitment to the liberalization of the regime. He was determined to stay in power until he died, believing that, as the living embodiment of all soldiers, he remained indispensable in his mission to rescue the country from demagoguery and communism. To that end, he instructed a small group of trusted advisers to draft a new set of transitional articles that would provide for his continuation in office until 1997. When consulted, however, prominent constitutional experts were appalled at the provision. They convinced the president that it would be difficult to obtain ratification of the constitution in a plebiscite if the document carried a provision that gave Pinochet an automatic twenty-four years in power, particularly since the permanent articles of the constitutional draft called for a nonrenewable presidential term of eight years.

In order to accommodate the general, the drafting commission agreed to a provision that gave Pinochet an automatic eight-year term, from 1981 to 1989. It then devised a formula calling for the commanders-in-chief of the armed forces (including Pinochet as army commander) to select by unanimity a single presidential candidate in 1988 to serve for eight more years, subject to ratification by plebiscite. The draft exempted Pinochet by name from the provisions in the document that prohibited presidents from succeeding themselves, thus opening the way for Pinochet to be the designated candidate for a new term. Not until 1997, under this formula, would competitive presidential elections be held.

The new transitional articles were also designed to provide constitutional legitimacy to Pinochet's dictatorial powers during the period 1980–89. They gave him complete latitude to declare states of emergency and to impose drastic curbs on individual liberties and rights without appeal to the courts. The right of habeas corpus was effectively abolished in Chile through constitutional provisions (Transitional Article 24). The new articles made an explicit distinction between Pinochet's executive powers and the junta's legislative powers. The new document removed Pinochet as a member of the junta but permitted him to retain his post as commander-in-chief of the army and to appoint his replacement on the junta—an army general who would be expected to strictly follow presidential wishes. The unanimity rule for all junta business was retained. In its permanent clauses, the constitution created a powerful executive and a weak legislature. It severely limited the notion of popular sovereignty, calling for a Senate with a third of its members non-elected (Article 45) and creating a Constitutional Tribunal with a strong military presence.

The constitution would also grant significant powers to the four commanders of the military institutions, who would be protected from removal from office for four years after being appointed (Article 93). Together with the president of the Senate, the four commanders would also sit as a new body called the National Security Council, where they would be able to admonish elected authorities should they violate "the bases of institutionality" or compromise "national security" (Article 95 and Article 96).

The constitution specified that "any act of individuals or groups aimed at propagating doctrines which affront the family, advocate violence or a conception of society, the State or the juridical order of a totalitarian character or based on class conflict is illicit and contrary to the institutional ordering of the Republic" (Article 8). Party membership was prohibited among leaders of secondary associations (Article 23). Finally, the constitutional document placed severe restrictions on the process of amendment, making it impossible for basic constitutional reform to be instituted without the consent of the powerful executive (Article 118).[61]

Few people outside the narrow circles of constitutional lawyers and government advisers were aware of the extent of the revisions that Pinochet and the junta (which ratified the changes) had made in the constitutional draft. Several prominent individuals were disturbed by the changes, including Jorge Alessandri, who resigned from the Council of State in protest but who refused to provide a public explanation for his resignation or to publicly oppose the plebiscite.[62]

As soon as the draft was finished, the government mounted a massive publicity campaign to obtain ratification of the constitution in a national plebiscite. The opposition—still fearful of official repression and hampered by limited financial resources, weak organization, and negligible access to the mass media—was unable to mount an effective campaign against the plebiscite. They were also hurt by the lack of an official alternative to the constitution and by continued rivalries and disagreements among opposition parties. The main opposition event, an anti-constitution rally in a local theater featuring former President Eduardo Frei as speaker, was marred by the chanting of Popular Unity government slogans, which government publicity skillfully exploited. According to the official results, the plebiscite was won by a margin of 67 percent. The fairness of the electoral process is difficult to judge, though there appears to have been no massive fraud. But there were no electoral registers and the ballots were counted by government authorities, so the potential for manipulating the results was considerable.[63]

Whether or not it was approved by a majority of Chileans, the importance of having a new constitution in a highly legalistic society cannot be overestimated. For better or worse, Chile had a new fundamental document, one that would be interpreted by the courts, guide the development of future legislation, and structure the basic rules and regulations of national life. It was a document closely identified with Pinochet, ratifying his ascendancy to a position of near-absolute power. It was also a document that the armed forces could identify as their own—their historical legacy for the future. Ironically, the constitution would eventually come to constrain the regime, and the transitional formula of 1989 would prove to be a much greater challenge to Pinochet than his advisers imagined in the euphoric days of 1980. The constitution gave the regime an institutional base that it had previously lacked. And it also locked the armed forces into a specific timetable for a return to civilian rule—one that would be increasingly difficult to sustain as the years went by and one which would prove to be Pinochet's own undoing.

THE ECONOMIC TEAM

The economic team consisted of a network of individuals who began their government service dealing with macro-economic policy and eventually extended their influence throughout the government, profoundly affecting social policy as well. The team shared with fervor a common conception of free-market economics, although it would be a mistake to describe it as completely cohesive. Economic policy-makers in the early years of the junta strongly emphasized the primacy of monetary and macro-economic stablization policies, whereas a group in the late 1970s paid much more attention to the expansion of neo-liberal policies to other spheres of society. The former sought to dismantle the regulatory and productive functions of the state, encouraging open competition at home and abroad. The latter sought to encourage broad-scale privatization in the social sphere, including labor relations, pension plans, and health. The team and its allies, in various incarnations, became a veritable internal political party, promoting members of the group to important posts throughout the public sector, far beyond the purely economic ministries and agencies.

The core of the team consisted of a group of economists trained and based primarily at Catholic University. Most had received graduate training at the University of Chicago, and their continued ties with the economics department at Chicago led to their nickname, the "Chicago Boys." In March 1973, with the blessing of all parties opposed to the Allende government and with the support of the Sociedad de Fomento Fabríl (SOFOFA), the powerful industrial association, the team developed an economic blueprint for a new "civic-military" regime.

As soon as the first cabinet was installed after the coup, these economists sought to "sell" their plan to the new authorities. They were aided by their close connections with officers in the navy who were actively plotting to overthrow Allende. The navy officers received copies of the team's work, which helped the navy secure jurisdiction over economic policy-making in the early discussions of the junta.[64]

Although the economic team succeeded in having one of its own, Sergio Undurraga, appointed head of the Oficina de Planificación Nacional (ODEPLAN), its radical proposals faced serious opposition from advisers close to the military who advocated less drastic economic adjustment measures and a more statist conception of economic policy. The first battle was over the team's proposal for a sharp devaluation of the Chilean currency. Hugo Araneda Dörr, a retired army captain with close ties to Pinochet and with ambitions to become the architect of junta economic policy, strongly objected to the measure. Faced with divergent proposals, the junta agreed, at Leigh's suggestion, to consult Chilean economist Raúl Sáez, one of the nine "wisemen" of the Alliance for Progress, who was then living in Venezuela. Saez strongly supported the arguments of the economic team and recommended that Fernando Léniz, an executive with the Edwards group, be appointed minister of economics. After his appointment, Léniz brought key members of the team into government service; among them was Sergio de Castro, who as minister of finance would become the chief architect of Chile's economic stabilization policies.[65]

The economic team prevailed because Pinochet and his military officers were impressed by the coherence and logic of economic models and the emphasis on the general welfare of society, one sharply opposed to the Marxist tradition but also opposed to the politics of patronage and populist appeals. This perspective dovetailed with the military's own mission to find solutions that could be understood as benefiting the nation as a whole, rather than satisfying the ubiquitous group demands that were already flooding in from supporters of the military coup. Rafael Cumsille, head of the Small Business Council and a strong supporter of the coup, called for a freeze on prices. Big business interests, which had organized in the Confederación de Producción y Comercio, also offered to help and received a strong rebuff from the military officer appointed to the Ministry of Economics.[66]

The neo-liberal economists prevailed, despite bitter opposition from business elements and from civilian and military leaders who had nationalist and statist conceptions of political authority, including the DINA and General Leigh. In early meetings with the junta, the team dazzled the members with brilliance and technical wizardry, outclassing proponents of statist formulas and conventional go-slow policies. Pinochet and his colleagues were awed by the economists' claim to scientific authority and by their arrogance. Sergio de Castro particularly impressed Pinochet, because he was bold enough to dismiss the general's objections with a quick retort. One influential former minister, who was skeptical of the wisdom of radical free-market measures, remembered that "the economic team made the rest of us feel like insects."[67] Pinochet gave the team considerable latitude and, in turn, benefited from the economists' ability to take control of the state apparatus and to propose broad-ranging reforms based on a coherent and attractive set of assumptions. From positions in ODEPLAN, the National Planning Office, the Central Bank, or the Ministry of Finance, often after a stint of study at the University of Chicago, these young technocrats slowly assumed positions throughout the bureaucracy.[68]

Although they did not share the blueprint of an authoritarian future advanced by the *duros*, the Chicago Boys shared their profound contempt of traditional politics and parties. They believed that democracy could not work well in an underdeveloped society that was buffeted by the easy and misleading solutions of demagogic politicians. Authoritarianism gave them an opportunity to impose practical formulas dic-

tated by free-market theories, unfettered by the troublesome objections of interest groups or elected representatives. Even though their
free-market policies were carried out under authoritarianism, they argued, they would promote a freer country and a more open society,
where everyone had an opportunity to pursue entrepreneurship without being "shackled" by statist and socialist policies.

According to the economists' logic, once the country had been modernized and was freer in its economic and social relations, democratic
politics would be inevitable. A modernized nation would provide such
abundance that it would undermine the ideological appeals of the left
and the populist parties to return to collectivist solutions. Voters
would become more like consumers than party militants, the young
economists believed, shopping for those parties that delivered policies
that would maximize their immediate economic interests. The old
parties would be rendered obsolete, replaced by modern, pragmatic political organizations that would be more likely to support ongoing economic and political arrangements. Only by achieving economic freedom, they imagined, would Chile be able to establish real political
freedom. Pablo Barahona, who served in several key posts, including
president of the Central Bank and minister of economics, put it this
way: "The problem is not to return to political normality, understood
as a return to the past, which would be of little use, rather it is to
change the structures such that the so-called return to normality will
mean that in this country we can generate simultaneously political
stability, social justice, and economic growth."[69]

Pinochet and key military advisers, such as General Covarrubias and General Escauriaza, gave critical support to the Chicago Boys during the early years of the regime. They soon came to
realize that the young economists offered the regime a rich ideology, one that dovetailed with their own contempt for politics and
their own hope for a future of "new citizens" who would be "sanitized" of the ideologies and programs of the past. If this could happen, the military would not have to rely so much on repression or
new laws to restructure society. Economic and social planners
would produce "modernizations" that would bring about structural transformations of profound political importance. The military men also felt more comfortable with a policy that deliberately counseled against populist rhetoric and popular mobilization, alternatives that were encouraged by the more fascist civilian elements close to the regime.

The support for the Chicago Boys also responded to more immediate political and practical considerations. In theory, Chile's new rulers had a third option beyond the radical free-market policies advocated by the Chicago Boys and the statist policies of the authoritarian right. The Christian Democrats had been as strongly opposed to the Allende government as had parties on the right, and their technicians had also participated in the economic team set up under the Edwards group. Indeed, former Christian Democratic Finance Minister Sergio Molina was brought back from Argentina after the coup in the expectation that he might become minister of economics. But the growing rift between the new authorities and the Christian Democrats soon put to rest any possibility of open and direct collaboration. Christian Democratic leader and Senate President Eduardo Frei snubbed the junta leaders at a religious mass after the coup because he objected to the closing of Congress. Christian Democrats also objected to the widespread human rights abuses and the military's intention of staying in office for an indefinite period of time. By mid-1974, the Christian Democrats had concluded that they could not work with the government and called on their leaders to resign from government positions or leave the party. Military officers of strong religious convictions who sympathized with the Christian Democrats blamed the party for leaving the government and giving the authorities no option but to listen to the Chicago Boys.

It is unlikely, however, that the Christian Democrats could have provided the regime with its economic policies over the long term. The resentment against Christian Democratic leaders, and Frei in particular, was very real among many top army officers. More significantly, Christian Democratic participation would always have been conditioned by party strategy—something that Pinochet and his colleagues would have found intolerable. But the Chicago Boys were perfect: they represented no organized group or interest, even though they may have served the interests of particular groups. The economic team was relatively independent of societal pressures, strengthening the autonomy of state actors. For Pinochet, the economic team constituted an excellent cadre of government officials—a party of the government with no outside commitments, one that could serve Pinochet well if he gave them carte blanche to carry out most of their policy objectives.

The appointment of José Piñera as minister of labor in December 1978 marked a new stage in the implementation of neo-liberal eco-

nomics and consolidated its triumph in the bitter struggle with nationalist and statist sectors in the government and the secret police
who sought the reversal of neo-liberalism. With that appointment,
Chile's economic program moved away from its preoccupation with
monetarist and macro-economic policies and moved toward a complete transformation of the state's role in Chilean society. During
three years as minister of labor and minister of mines, Piñera designed ambitious reforms in labor, social security, and mining legislation that were aimed at privatizing many functions that had previously been performed by the state. Pinochet embraced this broad
conception of a free-market society as the cornerstone of the regime's ideology in his famous September 11, 1979, speech on Chile's
"modernizations."[70] Minister of Finance Hernán Büchi, who
worked in the health sector before becoming the manager of the nation's economy, would later skillfully manage macro-economic policies while pressing for an increased reduction of the role of the state
in social policy.

The process of modernization could not be accomplished over-
night, and the neo-liberal economists were in no hurry to see the end
of the military government. They continued to support Pinochet's
leadership, and they opposed setting deadlines for a transition process; they preferred instead an articulation of goals for the regime.
Their position on the deadlines (*plazos*) versus goals (*metas*) debate
brought them closer to the position held by the hardliners, but the
economic team did not make common cause with the *duros*. Indeed,
the Chicago Boys were always concerned that the statist elements
within the regime would reverse their policy gains. Although the
economic team supported the continuation of authoritarian rule,
they also feared that the hardliners of the regime might attempt to
consolidate their own position by criticizing the economic program
that many viewed as favoring the rich and pressing Pinochet to
adopt a more "populist" line. Many civilian *duros*, while not supporting democratic participation, believed that the regime could
best ensure its survival by creating a large civic-military movement
that would draw on populist rhetoric and policies to consolidate itself. Economic liberals feared that Pinochet himself might be
tempted to change his agenda and adopt a more interventionist political and economic strategy, using populist appeals to mobilize
mass support for his own position. They consequently accepted the
steps the *blandos* had taken to liberalize the political system as nec-

essary to stop those forces that had become identified with the hard-liners who were hostile to free-market policies.

General Leigh was caught in the crossfire. His commitment to a return to democratic politics and his ties to moderate labor leaders made him anathema to the hardliners who wanted a more pro-nounced pro-government mobilization and the consolidation of long-term military rule. But Leigh's social policies were viewed with skepticism by the Chicago Boys, who believed that his programs represented a return to the "failed" policies of the past. Although he supported the liberalization of the regime, Leigh was no longer fully committed to radical free-market principles. Thus, the economic team, from a different vantage point and with different objectives, made common cause with elements in the DINA to undermine Leigh's social policies. The Chicago Boys objected to labor reforms and the legalization of unions, because they represented the "failed policies" of the past and raised the specter of parochial interests un-dermining general economic and social policy. Sergio Fernández' ap-pointment to the Ministry of Labor was a defeat of the statist poli-cies that Leigh advocated and an indication of the growing strength that the Chicago Boys had gained in defining public policies beyond the economic and into the social sphere.

Conclusion

During the years when the regime was consolidating its position, government factions in Chile divided along two central issues: reg-ime liberalization and free-market economic and social policies. But a preference for authoritarian politics did not necessarily coincide with a preference for statist economics, nor did advocacy of liberal politics imply support for free-market economics. The major internal actors of the Chilean regime varied in their support on both issues. Some actors, like Leigh, favored the liberalization of the regime while advocating statist policies. Others, like Guzmán after 1978, advocated liberaliza-tion of the regime and free-market economic policies. Still others, such as the DINA and right-wing civilians favored authoritarian policies and statist solutions. And a fourth group, which included monetarists like Sergio de Castro, accepted authoritarianism as a necessary evil in order to help implement free-market strategies. Pinochet and his close ad-visers straddled the fence on these two issues, generally favoring au-thoritarianism and free-market policies. But by allowing all of the players to remain in the arena and by shifting his own views somewhat on both issues, Pinochet gained a certain distance from any particular faction and was able to successfully play one against another. In this way, he reinforced his role as the mediator of conflict within the government and, by implication, his position as the regime's ultimate authority.

It should be noted that Pinochet's option for both authoritarianism and free-market policies helps explain why the Chilean government continued to shun a policy of popular mobilization in support of the regime. Chile remained an exclusionary bureaucratic-authoritarian regime, even though many political advisers wanted Pinochet to create a massive political party in support of his presidency, arguing that it was the only way to break the monopoly that traditional parties held over civilian political loyalties. Pinochet and the Chilean military accepted the argument that structural transformations in the economy and in state-civil society relations would, over time, create a new citizen. Populist mobilization, they believed, would only prolong the patterns of the past. Pinochet's refusal to support a mobilization strategy helped him to maintain military obedience and neutrality, which might have been threatened had the president followed the populist route of Juan Domingo Perón in Argentina or Juan Velasco Alvarado in Peru. Ironically, it was his refusal to seek support from organized popular groups that helped lead to the dictator's electoral downfall in 1988.

Despite the widespread protest movement of the 1983–86 period, the regime managed to stay in power. Pinochet successfully avoided the growing demands for constitutional changes that would permit open elections before the end of his term in 1989. His success was due in large measure to fears by the political right, the military, the business community, and elements of Chile's large middle class that any radicalization of the protest movement might lead to a takeover by parties on the left.

Although the government succeeded in its determination to stick by the constitutional formula elaborated in the 1980 constitution, it failed to win its own contest with Pinochet as standard bearer. Fifteen years of military rule had isolated Pinochet and his advisers from national realities. Chileans may not have been prepared to support a violent overthrow of the regime or militant national protests, but they were more than willing to vote against the "dictator" when given a chance to do so.

The regime, which was committed to observing Chile's legal tradition of fair contests and was convinced that it would be able to win the plebiscite hands down, failed to recognize that most Chileans did not share its view that economic progress had benefited a majority of their countrymen. Nor did the government believe that the politicians and parties that the authorities had vilified for so long would be able to mount an effective campaign to defeat a president who had the vast resources of the state at his disposal. Finally, the regime could not see the degree to which Chileans had been humiliated by a dictatorship that made massive arrests, tortured thousands, and engendered widespread fear.

Chile's transition did not take place through a rupture of the regime nor through a broad pact with the opposition. The transition took place within the framework of the regime's own legality. But the courtesans and advisers, the disciplined military, and the businessmen learned the hard way that political loyalty cannot be imposed; it has to grow from within. Pinochet, whose strength was buttressed by a legalistic edifice, was beaten at his own game by a people who had never fully accepted the legitimacy of his regime.

Notes

1. For the literature on the bureaucratic authoritarian state, see David Collier, ed., *The New Authoritarianism in Latin America* (Princeton, N.J., 1979). Guillermo O'Donnell's pioneering contributions can be found in his *Modernization and Bureaucratic Authoritarianism: Studies in South American Politics* (Berkeley, 1973) and *1966–1973: El Estado Burocrático Autoritario* (Buenos Aires, 1982). For a valuable collection on authoritarianism in Latin America, see James Malloy, ed., *Authoritarianism and Corporatism in Latin America* (Pittsburgh, 1979). For the concept of "exclusionary regime," see Alfred Stepan's insightful *The State and Society: Peru in Comparative Perspective* (Princeton, N.J., 1978).

2. Chile was able to avoid the vexing problem of most military regimes—the sharp discongruity that arises between the military as government and the military as institution, a conflict that often leads to internal military coups. For the basic statement of this problem, see Alfred Stepan, *The Military in Politics: Changing Patterns in Brazil* (Princeton, N.J., 1971). Carlos Huneeus and Jorge Olave contrasted the Chilean military with its counter-

parts in other countries in "La Partecipazione dei Militari nei Nuovi Autoritarismi: Il Cile in una Prospettiva Comparata," *Rivista Italiana di Scienza Politica* 17:1 (April 1987): 57–104.

3. I have argued against the inevitability of the military coup in Arturo Valenzuela, *The Breakdown of Democratic Regimes: Chile* (Baltimore, 1978). The economic determinants of authoritarianism have been extensively discussed in the debate over O'Donnell's "bureaucratic authoritarian thesis." See Collier, *The New Authoritarianism*.

4. One day after the coup, the junta issued Decree Law No. 5, which specified that the domestic "State of Siege" should be understood as a state or time of war. Decree laws are found in Editorial Jurídica de Chile, *100 primeros decretos leyes dictados por la junta de gobierno de la república de Chile* (Santiago, 1973). These observations are also based on interviews with lawyers and individuals closely involved with human rights activities in Chile, including leaders of the ecumenical Comité de Cooperación por la Paz, which functioned in the early days of the military regime, and its successor, the Vicaría de la Solidaridad, which was dependent on the archbishopric of Santiago.

5. The literature on the human rights situation in Chile is voluminous. The most complete record is found in the documents and publications of the Vicaría de la Solidaridad, particularly the *Annual Reports*. The most comprehensive and authoritative single document on the human rights situation in Chile after the advent of military rule is the report issued by the Commission on Human Rights, Organization of American States, *Informe sobre la situación de los derechos humanos en Chile* (Washington, D.C., 1985). My observations on the human rights situation in Chile are based on interviews conducted on research trips to Chile in 1974, 1979, and every year from 1980 to 1986. Particularly helpful were conversations with staff members of human rights organizations in Santiago, including the Vicaría de la Solidaridad, the Chilean Human Rights Commission, and the Fondo de Ayuda Social de las Iglesias Cristianas (FASIC), a protestant organization that championed the defense of groups closely tied to the Communist Party. The OAS Commission on Human Rights estimated that approximately fifteen hundred people were killed as a direct result of the military coup (*Informe*, p. 54). The Vicaría in Chile documented 668 cases of individuals who disappeared after being arrested (*Informe*, p. 77). Most of those who disappeared were leaders of the Socialist and Communist parties and the MIR. In the MIR alone, 123 leaders were never unaccounted for. It is difficult to ascertain how many people were killed after 1973, but I believe these figures are too conservative. A more realistic estimate is three thousand dead, many of them killed in rural areas and small towns, often to settle political and personal scores.

6. Out of 6,931 petitions of habeas corpus filed on behalf of individuals arrested in Chile between September 1973 and December 1974, only 10 were

accepted by the courts. The courts often took weeks to rule on such petitions, thus providing no protection against arbitrary arrest. There are no studies of how the judiciary behaved under the Chilean military government. This section draws on interviews with human rights lawyers and advocates interviewed in Santiago at different times. For a discussion of the judicial system's unwillingness to oversee government actions that resulted in human rights violations, see *Hoy,* no. 482 (October 13–19, 1986). The ecumenical Comité pro Paz was dissolved in 1975 when the Catholic Church withdrew its support at the direct request of Pinochet. It was reconstituted as the Vicaría, an exclusively Catholic organization.

7. General Gustavo Leigh, interview with the author, November 21, 1985.

8. The resolution of the Chamber of Deputies can be found in Andrés Echeverría and Luis Frei, eds., *1970–1973: La lucha por la juricidad en Chile* (Santiago, 1974), pp. 199–211. It was also featured prominently in a widely reproduced speech given by junta President Pinochet on October 11, 1973. See *Realidad y destino de Chile* (Santiago, 1973). It is also the opening document in a booklet published by the government printing office, *Algunos fundamentos de la intervención militar en Chile: Septiembre 1973* (Santiago, 1974), and is reproduced in *Libro blanco del cambio de gobierno en Chile* (Santiago, 1973), the publication the Chilean government used to justify the coup. Decree Law No. 1 is found in *100 primeros decretos de la Junta de Gobierno* (Santiago, 1973). Bando No. 5 is reproduced in *Libro blanco,* pp. 248–49. A similar statement is found in Decree No. 12 of the Ministry of the Interior.

9. *Ercilla,* March 21–27, 1974, p. 9.

10. Decree Law No. 1, issued on the day of the coup, vested all authority in the junta as a collective body; Decree Law No. 9, issued the next day, specified that any references in extant legislation to the president of the Republic would apply to the junta as a whole.

11. The heads of all departments at the Contraloría General de la República, interviews conducted by the author in August 1974, said that nothing had changed in Chile from a juridical point of view, and consequently their work was the same as usual. Laws were no longer being produced by a congress, but by a junta. I was struck by the extent to which functionaries seemed to interpret this change as a formality that did not disturb the underlying legality of the system.

12. See Manuel Antonio Garretón, *El proceso político chileno* (Santiago, 1983), for an articulate and sophisticated statement of the "foundational" characteristics of the Chilean regime. See also his "The Chilean Political Process," in *Military Rule in Chile: Dictatorship and Oppositions,* ed. J. Samuel Valenzuela and Arturo Valenzuela (Baltimore, 1986).

13. See Decree Law No. 77 and Junta de Gobierno, *Declaración de principios del gobierno de Chile* (Santiago, 1974), p. 27. The *Declaration* was writ-

ten by a small group of advisers, although Jaime Guzmán was responsible for the basic draft.

14. See Sergio Carrasco Delgado, *Génesis y vigencia de los textos constitucionales chilenos* (Santiago, 1980), p. 87. For government statements arguing the long-term character of the regime, see Pinochet's speech cited in *El Mercurio* (Santiago), February 24–March 2, 1975, p. 7. General Hernán Béjares had earlier noted that the government would not be able "to accomplish its task in 3, 5, or 10 years." See *El Mercurio Edición Internacional*, February 3–9, 1975, p. 1.

15. For a juridical discussion of the significance of the Decree Law, see Alejandro Silva Bascuñán, "La actual ordenación constitucional," *Revista de Derecho*, Universidad de Concepción, no. 165 (1977): 33–47. Mónica Madariaga, interview with the author, December 4, 1985. I am grateful to José Luis Cea and Mónica Madariaga for some of the information in this section.

16. See Arturo Valenzuela, *Political Brokers in Chile: Local Government in a Centralized Polity* (Durham, N.C., 1977), pp. 220–30.

17. Guzmán had originally joined the government as an adviser to General Leigh but soon realized Pinochet was the rising star. Jaime Guzmán, interview with the author, December 3, 1985, August 5, 1986.

18. See Arturo Fontaine, "Cómo llegaron las fuerzas armadas a la acción del 11 de Septiembre de 1973," *El Mercurio*, September 11, 1974. The account relies too much on the somewhat self-serving accounts of some of the principals, but it is valuable because it is based on interviews conducted only a few months after the coup.

19. For Pinochet's statement about his divine mission, see Patricia Sethi's interview with him in *LASA Forum* 15:2 (Summer 1984): 11–15.

20. This section is based on interviews with top civilian advisers of the regime who played important roles during the early days of the military government, including Federico Willoughby, Jaime Guzmán, and Mónica Madariaga as well as retired high-ranking military officers.

21. It is ironic that General Carlos Prats, who defended the constitution and advocated a professional role for the armed forces, contributed to the politicization of the institution by fostering dialogue among his colleagues in an attempt to maintain the neutrality of the armed forces. See Prats' eloquent statements of concern in his *Memorias: Testimonio de un soldado* (Santiago, 1985), pp. 402–3.

22. Pinochet was not trusted by the generals who led the coup, including Sergio Arellano, Oscar Bonilla, Ernesto Baeza, Washington Carrasco, Sergio Nuño, Manuel Torres, and Arturo Viveros. For Prats' views on Pinochet, see *Memorias*, pp. 486, 510. When Pinochet replaced Prats, he tried to control the mutiny in his ranks by asking the generals to submit signed resignations and threatening that Prats' fate would be "washed with the blood of generals." Viveros, Palacios, and Arellano refused and forced Pinochet to back down. The account of this meeting, revealing Arellano's own views, is found in the

fascinating book by the general's son. See Sergio Arellano Iturriaga, *Más allá del abismo* (Santiago, 1988). For Prats' account, see *Memorias*, p. 496. In his own book, *El día decisivo* (Santiago, 1979), Pinochet argued that he planned the military move against Allende early. Pinochet was charged with developing a plan to ward off an insurrectionary threat as chief of staff of the army. It is clear, however, that this plan was aimed at protecting the state, not overthrowing it, and that Pinochet's attempt to invoke it is an effort to hide his reluctance to join the military conspiracy until the last moment. The plan was approved by General Prats, Pinochet's superior, and other military authorities, and Allende had full knowledge of it although some of the president's ministers were not fully aware of its development. General Prats' *Memorias* supports this interpretation. Allende's knowledge of the contingency plans was confirmed by Joan Garcés, one of Allende's closest advisers, in conversations with the author in May 1989. For an account that documents Pinochet's reluctance to join the conspiracy and his annoyance when Arellano pleaded for his support, see Arellano, *Más allá*, pp. 43–45.

23. See the statements of Nuño, Bonilla, Carrasco, Lutz, Palacios, and Ewing in Genaro Arriagada, *La política militar de Pinochet* (Santiago, 1985), pp. 97–99.

24. The same authority was given to Admiral Merino of the navy in Decree Law No. 26, adopted on the same date, and to Director General César Mendoza through Decree Law No. 80. As junta members, the two men believed they needed broad authority over promotions and retirements to stem any potential subversive activities within the ranks. Decree Law No. 33 was followed in December 1973 by Decree Law No. 220, which gave the commander-in-chief of the army broad and permanent authority in matters of promotion. In effect, Pinochet then controlled the key promotions of colonels to the ranks of general. Eventually, and with some modifications, these emergency measures became permanent tools that gave Pinochet extraordinary control over the careers of high-ranking officers. The best discussion of these laws and their implications can be found in Arriagada, *La política militar*, Chapter 4.

25. These observations are based on interviews by the author with former civilian advisers of Pinochet and with high-ranking military officers, both retired and in active service.

26. See Arriagada, *La política militar*, p. 100. A brief and somewhat superficial account of the promotion process is found in *Qué Pasa*, October 24–30, 1985, pp. 18–19.

27. See Huneeus and Olave, "La Partecipazione dei Militari," pp. 71, 99. It is instructive that the navy and air force gradually withdrew from administrative functions, leaving most of that responsibility to the army.

28. Calculated from information provided in Carlos Huneeus, "El ejército y la política en el Chile de Pinochet: Su magnitud y alcances," *Opciones*, no.

14 (1988). Appointments to regional intendancies and governorships, which routinely went to military officers, have been eliminated from these calculations.

29. The best analysis of military expenditures and purchases is in Augusto Varas, *Los militares en el poder: Régimen y gobierno militar en Chile, 1973–1986* (Santiago, 1987). Some of these figures are from *Hoy*, no. 461 (1986), pp. 28–29. See also *Hoy*, no. 372 (1984), and *Análisis*, no. 129 (1986).

30. Calculated from data in Jorge Marshall, "Gasto público en Chile: 1969–1979," *Colección Estudios CIEPLAN* 5 (July 1981): 69. As Marshall noted, the overall increase in nonmilitary expenditures may be bloated by increases in police expenditures listed under "General Services." Outside of Defense and General Services, public expenditures for personnel declined by 23.6 percent during this period. Expenditures for the purchase of goods also declined for all categories save General Services and Defense. Defense expenditures increased by over 100 percent while nondefense expenditures increased by 2 percent. See Marshall, "Gasto público," p. 79, for the raw data.

31. A list of the ministers who have served the longest time are in Huneeus, "El ejército," pp. 109, 110, 116. The notable exception is General Bruno Siebert, who was minister of public works for over six years.

32. An exception occurred in mid–1977, when the Council of Generals established several working commissions to examine the future of the military government, particularly in light of widespread concern over the operations of the secret police. Those deliberations led to the dissolution of the DINA. Pinochet was able to prevent the council from assuming a more deliberative role by retiring some of the more critical generals. Horacio Toro, interview with the author, August 1989.

33. This applies mostly to the army, less so to navy and Carabineros, and least to the air force. Under Leigh, the air force generals continued to discuss policy issues; these discussions became more frequent as Leigh's struggle with Pinochet intensified.

34. General Gustavo Leigh, interview by the author, November 21, 1985.

35. For the text of Decree Law No. 527, see Eduardo Soto Kloss, *Ordenamiento constitucional* (Santiago, 1980), pp. 145–53. As early as March 1974 *Qué Pasa*, the pro-government magazine, was approvingly calling Pinochet first among equals. *Qué Pasa*, no. 150, March 8, 1974, p. 7.

36. According to advisers who witnessed the scene, Leigh was livid and Merino threw the presidential sash on the floor. For a brief published account, see *Qué Pasa*, no. 167, July 5, 1974, p. 12. For Sergio Diez, a prominent rightist politician and member of the Constitutional Commission, this was the most important step in the consolidation of the regime within the framework of "Chilean traditions." Diez, interview with the author, June 1983.

37. On Pinochet's violations of Decree Law No. 527, see Florencia Varas, *Gustavo Leigh, el general disidente* (Santiago, 1979), pp. 54–55.

38. I interviewed several members of legislative commissions in 1985. For the laws, see Kloss, *Ordenamiento constitucional*, pp. 159–81.

39. Pinochet's attempt to change the rules of unanimity, the junta's resistance, and the 1978 plebiscite are discussed in *Hoy*, March 21–27, 1984, p. 7.

40. Plebiscite results are listed by region in Carrasco, *Génesis y vigencia*, p. 136.

41. See Varas, *Gustavo Leigh*, pp. 153–57, for the text of the memorandum.

42. For Leigh's account, see ibid.

43. I am grateful to Arturo Aylwin, a key figure in the drafting of the new regionalization and municipal government legislation within CONARA, for his help in explaining the process. For a discussion of local politics under the junta, see the excellent dissertation by Alfredo Rehren, "The Impact of Authoritarian Policies at the Local Level: The Case of Chile, 1974–1984" (Ph.D. diss., University of Texas, Austin, 1989).

44. Varas, *Gustavo Leigh*, p. 33.

45. See Carrasco, *Génesis y vigencia*, pp. 89–90.

46. Mónica Madariaga became an opponent of the Pinochet regime after serving in Washington, D.C., as Chilean ambassador to the OAS and realizing that Chile was isolated from the rest of the world and that the military government participated in human rights violations. She also concluded that Pinochet was not interested in a genuine transition to democracy. Madariaga interview.

47. This information is based on interviews with Jaime Guzmán and other advisers to the military government.

48. Prominent advisers holding "nationalist" positions (although they were not necessarily allies of Rodríguez) included Alvaro Puga, Gastón Acuña, and Ricardo Claro.

49. For a description of the formation and organization of the DINA, see "Qué cosa es la DINA," *Chile América*, no. 31–32 (May–June 1977), pp. 172–75. See also John Dinges and Saul Landau, *Assassination on Embassy Row* (New York, 1980), pp. 125–28. These authors argue that the U.S. Central Intelligence Agency had helped structure the DINA and had advised that the intelligence services report directly to Pinochet.

50. The United States prosecutor in the Letelier case noted how the DINA supported Pinochet in his rivalry with other junta members. See Taylor Branch and Eugene M. Propper, *Labyrinth* (New York, 1982), p. 156. General Leigh withdrew his air force officers from the DINA because he was upset that the intelligence organization did not report to the junta as a whole. See Varas, *Gustavo Leigh*, p. 78. It was difficult to tell whether the DINA was operating illegally because several of the articles of Decree Law No. 521 were kept secret, including articles that gave the DINA broad powers to detain individuals. Article 2 of the decree law provided retroactive legal standing for the organization. For a comprehensive indictment of the systematic violation of hu-

man rights in Chile during the first few months of military rule, see Vicaría de la Solidaridad, "Presentación al Presidente de la Corte Suprema, Marzo '76" (Mimeographed, Santiago, 1976).

51. See Organización de los Estados Americanos, Comisión Interamericana de Derechos Humanos, *Informe sobre la situación de derechos humanos en Chile* (Washington, D.C., 1985), p. 77. See also Vicaría de la Solidaridad, *Vicaría de la Solidaridad: Noveno año de labor, 1984* (Santiago, 1984), p. 66. The Vicariate publication, *Dónde Están?* (Santiago, 1979), gives brief biographies of disappeared persons. Volume 2 documents the measures taken against the leadership of the Communist Party in 1976. I interviewed relatives of disappeared persons in 1979 and 1985.

52. These observations are based on interviews with individuals who had direct contact with Bonilla during this period and whose identities cannot be revealed. Fear of the DINA in military circles was stressed by General Leigh and other retired military officers in interviews by the author.

53. For a discussion of the triumph of the hardliners at this time, see Pilar Vergara, *Auge y caída del neoliberalismo en Chile* (Santiago, 1984), p. 108.

54. This section is based on interviews with key advisers to the Pinochet government who played an important role in these events. Many of the details of the internal battles between groups and the actual role of the DINA remain obscure, so the judgments presented here are somewhat speculative. Two prominent former advisers said that at one point they feared for their lives.

55. For reports on the dissolution of the DINA, see *El Mercurio: Edición Internacional*, August 7–13, 1977, p. 1. General Odlanier Mena replaced Contreras and was in turn replaced by General Humberto Gordon, one of Pinochet's closest allies, on July 24, 1980. See *El Mercurio: Edición Internacional*, July 24–30, 1980, p. 1. Although the DINA was dismantled, the CNI continued many of the same activities as its predecessor. For a discussion of relations between the military government and the United States, see Heraldo Muñoz, *Las relaciones exteriores del gobierno militar chileno* (Santiago, 1986), and Heraldo Muñoz and Carlos Portales, *Una amistad esquiva: Las relaciones de Estados Unidos y Chile* (Santiago, 1987).

56. For the Chacarillas speech and Leigh's reaction to it, see *El Mercurio: Edición Internacional*, July 10–16, 1977, pp. 1, 5. Later that year, Pinochet followed up his speech with a detailed letter of instruction on the proposals to the Constitutional Commission. The letter, reproduced in *El Mercurio*, November 12, 1977, called for a new constitutional system that would prevent politicking and demagoguery and that carried a strong anti-parliamentary theme. In August, Leigh made it clear that he was not pleased with a formula that would keep the military in power for such a long time. See *El Mercurio: Edición Internacional*, August 21–27, 1977, p. 1.

57. For a good account of the constitutional drafting process, see Sergio

Carrasco Delgado, *Alessandri: Su pensamiento constitucional, reseña de su vida pública* (Santiago, 1987), p. 120, and Carrasco, *Génesis y vigencia*.

58. For discussion of the constitution, see Carrasco, *Génesis y vigencia,* and the carefully annotated Luz Bulnes Aldunate, *Constitución política de la República de Chile: Concordancias, anotaciones y fuentes* (Santiago, 1981). The commission version of the text is on pp. 220–306. The Constitutional Commission's official title was changed in 1976 to Commission for the Study of the Political Constitution of the State.

59. For a comparison of the constitutional drafts proposed by the Constitutional Commission and the Council of State with the draft approved in the plebiscite, see Bulnes Aldunate, *Constitución política*. The specific differences between the Council of State version and that of the Constitutional Commission are summarized in Carrasco, *Alessandri,* p. 141.

60. Pinochet was influenced in his thinking by former Uruguayan President José María Bordaberry, who had proposed, without success, to the Uruguayan military that the armed forces of that country institute a restricted democracy that was closely supervised by men in uniform. Bordaberry exchanged letters with Pinochet and shared his views with the Chilean general in a lecture trip to Chile. I am grateful to Jaime Guzmán for making available copies of Bordaberry's speeches before the Military Council in Uruguay that were given to Pinochet's adviser.

61. See Luz Bulnes, *Constitución política,* for the text of the constitution. Among those who objected to the sixteen-year term was Enrique Ortúzar, chairman of the commission.

62. See Carrasco, *Génesis y vigencia,* pp. 102–3. Alessandri was afraid that, if he spoke out, the constitution might not be approved, leading to political instability. He objected strongly to constitutional provisions that gave excessive power to the military (i.e., prohibiting presidents from removing military commanders) and to the lengthy transitional formula that would keep Pinochet and the junta in power for such a long term. He was also upset that many suggestions of the Council of State were set aside in favor of the original provisions of the Constitutional Commission and blamed the drafting committee for giving Ortúzar, the commission chairman, too much voice in the deliberations. Alessandri delivered his only public pronouncements on the matter in a speech on November 9, 1983. For the full text, see Carrasco, *Alessandri,* pp. 253–61. His concern over the defeat of the constitution was articulated in a letter to the editor of *La Segunda,* reprinted in Carrasco, *Alessandri,* pp. 144–45.

63. The 1978 plebiscite had been conducted with transparent ballots so that election officials could see which box on the ballot the voter had marked. Not knowing whether opposition to the government would be kept confidential affected election results. These observations are based on interviews with local leaders conducted in small commmunities in the Bío Bío area in August 1983.

64. This account is based on interviews held in Santiago in 1980, 1983, 1984, and 1985. A valuable source was Orlando Sáenz, who was president of the SOFOFA during the UP period. See also "La historia no contada de los Chicago Boys," *Hoy,* no. 374 (September 17–23, 1984), pp. 28–31. The U.S. Senate Select Committee to Study Governmental Operations with Respect to Intelligence Activities (the Church Committee) reported that the Central Intelligence Agency provided 75 percent of the support for the activities of an opposition economic research group—very likely the team described here. See its *Covert Action in Chile* (Washington, D.C., December 18, 1975), p. 30. The best discussion of big business under the junta is Guillermo Campero, *Los gremios empresariales en el período 1970–1983* (Santiago, 1984). Campero argued that business was outclassed by the Chicago Boys because it had no concrete proposals of its own to offer the junta. See pp. 132–33.

65. Hugo Araneda Dörr, interview with the author, August 1974; Fernando Léniz, interview with the author, fall 1985. This section also benefited from lengthy interviews with several knowledgeable persons, including Arturo Fontaine, Cristián Larroulet, Rolf Lüders, Jorge Cauas, Orlando Sáenz, Javier Vial, and José Piñera conducted between 1986 and 1989. A useful account of the rise of the economic team is found in Arturo Fontaine Aldunate, *La historia no contada de los economistas y el presidente Pinochet* (Santiago, 1988).

66. The best study of the economic team that draws exclusively from published sources is Vergara, *Auge y caída*. See also the study by Tomás Moulián and Pilar Vergara, "Estado, ideología y política económica en Chile, 1973–1978," *Estudios CIEPLAN,* no. 3 (June 1980). For the government's position, see the writings of Pablo Barahona in Central Bank publications and Alvaro Bardón. A forthcoming dissertation by Scott Michael (Yale University) describes in detail the rise of the Chicago Boys. See also Juan Gabriel Valdés, *La escuela de Chicago: Operación Chile* (Buenos Aires, 1989). Pressures on the junta during the early years came primarily from small and medium-sized businesses and trade associations that had fueled the more militant strikes against the Popular Unity government. But big business was wary of an alliance with those sectors and contributed to derailing any attempt to create corporativist bases of support and influence on the regime. See Vergara, *Auge y caída,* p. 66. See also Campero, *Los gremios empresariales,* pp. 120–22.

67. Madariaga interview. Miguel Kast, a young economist with ties to the University of Chicago and who became minister of planning, played a key role in the consolidation of the Chicago team. Sergio de Castro was important in convincing Pinochet of the wisdom of the economic team's policies.

68. The link with the University of Chicago began with an AID-sponsored program in the 1950s that sent as many as one hundred fifty Chileans to Chicago to do graduate work. The most successful members of the group returned to staff the economics departments at Catholic University, and some took positions at the University of Chile. The most important figure in the

exchange was Arnold Harberger, a Chicago economist who married a Chilean. Harberger directly recruited Chileans to go to Chicago, with financing from such agencies as the Ministry of Planning and the Ministry of Finance. After the coup, Harberger often interviewed potential candidates in his hotel room, deciding whether candidates should be steered toward general programs in public policy or toward the more technical programs in economics. See *Hoy*, no. 374, p. 29. I confirmed this account in interviews with candidates.

69. Dirección del Presupuesto, "Somos realmente independientes gracias al esfuerzo de todos los chilenos" (Santiago: Dirección del Presupuesto, 1978), p. 389, cited in Vergara, *Auge y caída*.

70. For Pinochet's speech of September 11, 1979, see *El Mercurio*, September 12, 1979, p. 1. Guzmán's handiwork in the speech can be appreciated by examining some of the similarities with the arguments he made in *Revista Realidad* 1:7 (December 1979), reprinted in *El Mercurio* in December 1979. See also his "El camino político," *El Mercurio*, December 26, 1981, pp. C-4, C-5.

Augusto Varas

The Crisis of Legitimacy of
Military Rule in the 1980s

One of the most controversial—and least analyzed—questions in recent years has been what role the armed forces play in democratic transitions.[1] Despite the lack of agreement on this question, it is possible to make some generalizations about the Latin American cases. First, no dictatorship in the region has escaped the need to legitimize itself through elections or plebiscites, either to perpetuate the dictatorship or to arrange for a favorable succession.[2] Second, the armed forces have withdrawn from politics only when the causes that motivated their intervention no longer persist.[3] Third, the factors that lead the armed forces to break with the constitutional order are different from those that lead them to surrender political power to civilians.[4]

The Chilean case, which is exceptional in many respects, contributes in various ways to an understanding of the downfall of dictatorships. In this chapter, I will analyze the characteristics of the legitimation crisis that explain the military regime's defeat in the plebiscite of October 5, 1988. That crisis was aggravated by three systems of tensions and cleavages between (1) the armed forces and government, (2) the armed forces and society, and (3) the armed forces and entrepreneurs.

Legitimation Crisis and Democratic Transition

Since the Second World War, a principal cause of nations making a transition from military dictatorships to democracy has been the impossibility of legitimizing dictatorial governments. Although these governments promise to achieve such long-term objectives as democracy and liberty, they are only transitional regimes. This weakness is the result of public pressure for both democratization and the restoration of popular sovereignty, the breakdown of the messianic self-image of the armed forces, and the need for a solution to problems concerning the administration of justice.[5]

The Chilean military regime is exceptional in that it confronted and solved many of these problems. First, the regime defined itself as transitional but made the end of its rule part of the implementation of a new constitutional order designed to ensure a limited democracy. By defining a long-term solution, the regime attempted to create a new political order. Second, limited liberalization became part of the democratization process. Thus, some civil liberties developed simultaneously with limitations on government power. Third, the messianic ideology of the military was destroyed by civilian supporters of the military government. The neo-liberal economic model supported by these civilians defeated military corporatist schemes early on. Finally, and in contrast to other Latin American cases, the military government itself prosecuted and penalized (although very mildly) a few violations of human rights.[6]

A major reason for the regime's self-imposed constraints lies in the early separation between the government and the military regime and in the emergence of a civilian-military coalition in the government. Beginning in 1975–76, the armed forces were crucial supporters but not the main agents of the regime, leaving a civilian technocracy in their place.[7]

Despite these features, the military government could not legitimize itself. First, the military recognized that ultimate legitimacy could only be gained in Chile through a constitutional order.[8] Second, the self-imposed limitations were not sufficient to legitimize the regime. Third, legitimacy was lost at the level of civil society before the level of government.[9] Fourth, redemocratization was initiated by a civilian-dominated authoritarian coalition that experienced doubts and conflicts about the constitutional norms that guided the transition. These doubts grew as the impending political system required ratification through elections.[10] The executive branch was thus forced to bring about democratization through channels that led to its defeat. The regime failed to attract massive support for its economic and political institutions; as a result, it underwent an identity crisis that led to reliance on a *caudillo* to campaign for the presidency in the 1988 plebiscite.

The regime's structural and political limitations provide an important key for understanding why the military government and its political reform project failed to achieve legitimacy. First, the military regime was not able to structure the desired political system or replace the idea of representative democracy with elitist or technocratic theories.[11] Second, the regime's free-market economic model facilitated an economic boom but failed to benefit the majority of the population through a substitute social welfare program.[12]

The Institutional Illegitimacy of Authoritarianism

The crises of democracies and dictatorships share political and socioeconomic factors that lead those governments to experience a similar loss of legitimacy. But the type of legitimation crisis can be different. The crisis of democratic legitimacy results from the inability of democratic states to solve basic problems and accomplish announced goals.[13] New political and socioeconomic institutions are needed to overcome barriers.[14] In the case of failing dictatorships, the state is ill-equipped to generate political institutions that are capable of attracting civilian loyalty.

One source of the legitimation crisis for the Chilean military regime was lack of support for its governing institutions. The radical measures of economic liberalization and privatization exacerbated tensions between society and a shrunken state apparatus that had previously been actively involved in the economy.[15] This contradiction could only be maintained during the first three years of Chile's military regime, under the exceptional conditions of the "national security" doctrine.[16] Later, the regime failed to achieve sufficient support for a pseudo-constitutional framework that attempted to legitimize a minority government through electoral means. The regime's failure to gather support was demonstrated by the broad civilian demand for constitutional reforms in July 1989.

Distributive Illegitimacy

The illegitimacy of the new institutional arrangements created by the military regime in Chile was aggravated by its structural incapacity to distribute collective goods fairly.[17] Even if a military government can efficiently structure a closed and noncompetitive political system, it still is ineffective in generating a legitimate, nonauthoritarian system for the distribution of goods, services, and political power. In the Chil-

Table 2.1
Reasons for Voting, 1988 Plebiscite

Reasons for "No" vote		*Reasons for "Yes vote*	
Economic situation	72%	Order and tranquility	49%
		Economic situation	38%
Human Rights	57%	Pinochet himself	30%
Disapproval of		Anti-communism or	
Pinochet's government	39%	anti-UP	16%
Return to democracy	21%	Democracy	3%

ean case, the incapacity to distribute collective goods equitably led the military regime to a terminal crisis of legitimacy.[18]

In this context of institutional and distributive illegitimacy, General Augusto Pinochet attempted to strengthen the military regime by affirming his personal leadership.[19] He did so as a means of overcoming the efficacy crisis generated by the economic mismanagement following 1982. This personalistic approach was maintained even during the subsequent economic recovery, but politically Pinochet could not overcome the institutional and distributive sources of illegitimacy. Therefore, the *caudillista* strategy became isolated within the regime, and in the end was supported only by the army.[20]

In comparing the results of a poll conducted in September 1988, just before the October 5 plebiscite, it is significant that there was more consensus in the principal reasons for opposing the military regime than in the diffuse reasons for supporting it (see Table 2.1 for results of the poll).[21] Further, the winning choice concentrated on the two major sources of government illegitimacy: (1) the inability to distribute goods and services and (2) the lack of political space resulting from authoritarian policies. Finally, the importance of economic factors (72 percent) and human rights (57 percent) in the intention to vote "No" contrasts with the reasons for voting "Yes," which prioritized order and tranquility (49 percent) and favorably evaluated the economic situation (38 percent). The low proportion of people who believed that the economic situation favored them confirms both the institutional and the distributive character of the legitimation crisis.

The Armed Forces vis-à-vis
State, Government, and Society

The legitimation crisis of the military regime was exacerbated by the simultaneous and combined effect of three political tensions and cleavages that emerged between (1) the armed forces and government, (2) the armed forces and society, and (3) the government and entrepreneurs.

Military-Government Tensions and Cleavages

This set of tensions produced serious divisions between the armed forces and the government, as well as within the combined executive–high command and the Junta.

ARMED FORCES VERSUS THE GOVERNMENT

The military government first had to resolve the problem of internal hegemony. Even though the composition of the military junta was clear from the start, the junta's institutional future was not as well-planned. This first period was characterized by the progressive clarification of how each of the military institutions expected to fit into government and society. The eventual subordination of the armed forces and the militarized police (*Carabineros*) to the army was due to the army's military power and its historic preeminence over the other branches. Thus, the army high command consolidated itself as the executive power of the nation. This executive–army high command became the guiding force of all military, political, and social processes during the period of military rule.[22]

This solution to the problem of political power ensured hierarchical control, enhanced the strength of the executive branch, and prevented differences over government policies from eroding the basis of government support. The concentration of political activity in the executive branch relieved the armed forces of day-to-day government responsibilities as well as costly inter-branch negotiations. The separation of the military branches from the government gave the executive–army high command uncontested control. The project for sociopolitical and economic reforms was then transferred to neo-liberal civilian sectors without military opposition. As a result, the armed forces as institutions experienced a major political and ideological defeat due to the imposition of a model that was alien to their traditional political thinking.[23]

Therefore, the traditional framework of a military junta composed of the three branches of defense (four in the Chilean case), each responsible for the administration of particular ministries, was not applicable in Chile. The initial plan had been to assign the ministries of finance, education, mining, and foreign relations to the navy; health, employment, and transportation to the air force; economy, defense, interior, and public works to the army; and justice, lands, and agriculture to the Carabineros. By 1976, however, the proportion of ministries directed by men in military uniform had diminished and, more important, their institutional management of each sector of public administration had disappeared. The first cabinet of 1973 was 27 percent civilian; in August 1985, 77 percent of the cabinet was civilian.[24]

By 1975–76, the armed forces' participation in government had given way to their withdrawal as institutions from the direct management of the state.[25] With the executive in charge of the state, the administration used individual military officers according to its needs and not according to those of each defense institution. Even the ministries closest to the concerns of the military—interior, defense, lands, health, and transportation—were directed by civilians or members of other military institutions, who represented the executive branch and not their respective commanders-in-chief (except in the case of the army). In this way, the armed forces remained a pillar of the military regime but did not administer the state or run the government.

This situation was made possible by military tensions in the northern and southern regions of the nation. By 1976, disagreements between Chile and Peru had heightened due to Peruvian opposition to Chilean proposals concerning Bolivia's access to the Pacific Ocean. Furthermore, in 1976–78, tensions developed in the south because of Argentina's opposition to British arbitration over the islands in the Beagle Channel. Both situations captured the attention of the armed forces, especially those that would play a central role in a conflict. The navy, the air force, and the first, fifth, and sixth divisions of the army became heavily involved in preparations for possible conflict. This further distanced the armed forces from the management of the state and contributed to the hegemony of the executive–army high command. Substantial budget increases also facilitated the armed forces' detachment from state functions. Thus, the role of the armed forces was dictated less by institutional interests than by the decisions of the nucleus of the military high command, acting in alliance with a small political and economic coterie.

THE EXECUTIVE VERSUS THE LEGISLATURE

Once the separation between the armed forces and the government had been established, a new political reality emerged within the armed forces. The military junta had assumed a legislative role and had been transformed into a government junta in March 1981. During the late 1970s, the short-lived prosperity resulting from the massive foreign debt prompted the regime to seek its institutionalization through the 1980 plebiscite, backed by civilian supporters on the right. That balloting led to the consolidation and institutionalization of presidential discretionary powers through the 1980 constitution. Even so, the separation of legislative and executive functions gave the military branches greater autonomy from the executive–army high command.

Once the military junta assumed legislative powers, its members acquired new roles and responsibilities as co-managers of the regime but not of government operations. The segregation of the armed forces was partly resolved by involving the institutional high commands in new legislation. This situation coincided with the easing of tensions with Argentina, Bolivia, and Peru, which gave the institutional high command more time to create legislation.

Under these conditions, the executive–army high command felt compelled to ensure the subordination of the armed forces, especially because the new institutional role of the junta as a legislative power could become an effective counterbalance to the executive branch. The executive used the process of promotions and retirements to reward not only ideological and political loyalty but also personal fealty to General Pinochet.[26]

This new form of intra-military relations generated new political dynamics and conflicts. First, the Carabineros became aware of the need to protect their institution from army control. The army's influence with national intelligence agencies, such as the National Information Center (CNI), Plainclothes Police, and the Military Intelligence Service (SIM), had consistently been opposed by the Carabineros. Second, militaristic tendencies within the Carabineros clashed with an army that had assumed police functions in repressive activities. The combination of these two conflicts caused a major crisis, which led to the resignation of the director of the Carabineros in August 1985.

Furthermore, the commander-in-chief of the air force (FACH) confronted the executive high command with dissenting political positions. Thus, the executive–army high command faced the danger of intervening in the air force. In response, air force generals sought to strengthen their institutional identity, distanced themselves from government management, and fortified their corporate position by creating the National Aeronautic Firm (ENAER). They were then able to respond to national political questions with greater flexibility. At the same time, the navy disagreed with the executive concerning the Argentine conflict. Therefore, naval officers entrenched themselves in legislative commissions in order to gain power and confront the high command on issues of institutional interest.

The renewed need to subordinate the armed forces in the 1980s created tensions inside the army high command as well. This led to changes in the army's representation in the military junta, as General César Benavides was replaced by General Santiago Sinclair at the end of 1985. Benavides had been a lukewarm supporter of the opposition's National Accord and a quiet opponent of Pinochet's candidacy.

The institutionalization of the regime coincided with the economic crisis of 1982. This situation provided additional incentives for the commanders of the armed forces to assume stronger roles in the management of the economy. These changes eroded the political unity of the armed forces, as the executive's capacity to enforce political submission within the regime decreased. By 1983, the regime confronted the erosion of its internal bases of political support and the failure of its economic model. The government lost its capacity for initiative at the same time that it faced a more solid and mobilized opposition.

This new situation reproduced some of the conditions that had existed in the military before 1973. There reemerged political divisions within the armed forces despite institutional unity centered on the professional role of national defense; there were disagreements concerning national economic issues and international alignments; and there was an absence of a shared and hegemonic political-military project. The armed forces became confused over their institutional goals, realized their limited political means for launching a fresh project, and hesitated to perpetuate a regime for which they had become little more than the guarantors. During the 1980s, the armed forces entered a new phase in their institutional evolution, reassessing internal operations and redefining relations with the state and society. But these changes were delayed by the *caudillista* approach that Pinochet adopted near the end of 1984. The situation generated by Pinochet's decision was not conducive to open opposition to the army's decisions, but it demonstrated that the army was no longer able to make political choices with the support of the entire armed forces.[27]

During the mid-1980s, a much more diverse and dynamic field of conflict evolved. A hardline-softline polarization developed within the government, the governing junta, and even each branch of the armed forces. Toward the end of the decade, the only factor that bound the armed forces together was their determination to uphold the timetable of an institutional framework that had been imposed on them.

THE ARMY VERSUS OTHER MILITARY INSTITUTIONS

When the army first supported Pinochet's candidacy for the plebiscite, the politicization of that military institution reached its highest level, as Pinochet relied on the army as his only significant organized political force. On the one hand, supportive political groups like National Renovation and, later, UDI were reluctant to cast their lot with what they perceived to be a losing proposition. On the other hand, the more militantly pro-Pinochet National Advance was a smaller and less organized group than the army. Thus, beginning in 1985, Pinochet—in an openly *caudillista* fashion—turned to his own forces, obtaining a political and ideological commitment that involved them in his plebiscite defeat.

The involvement of army personnel in Pinochet's campaign generated a serious controversy. Legally, the armed forces could not be actively involved in politics, even if the candidate was the commander-in-chief of the army. But the army nevertheless understood its relation to the candidate as one of unrestricted loyalty. This sentiment was expressed by such prominent government officials as Admiral Patricio Carvajal in May 1988.[28]

The high level of politicization in the army and its commanders was also clearly exemplified when the intendant of the Fifth Region stated that the military coup of 1973 had been carried out "to get rid of the rats that were destroying our country bit by bit. We will not permit the rats to return to positions [of power] again. We generals prepare battles to win, not to lose them."[29]

Such violations of existing regulations concerning the political involvement of the military forced the defense minister to issue an order prohibiting political activities in the barracks.[30] Opposition forces also supported a policy of nonintervention by the armed forces. Christian Democrat Sergio Molina, coordinator of the Committee for Free Elections, pointed out the legal prohibitions against military involvement in politics.[31] And Andrés Allamand of National Renovation underscored the restrictions in the Administrative Statute of 1960 and the regulatory "Basis of State Administration."[32] There were, furthermore, specific references against politicization in the regulations for institutional discipline within the various armed forces.[33] The episcopate of the Roman Catholic Church finally indicated that "those who must guarantee the fairness of the plebiscite should not take an active part in the support of one of the candidates."[34]

Government supporters responded quickly,[35] backed by the under-secretary of the interior, who argued that the nation had a symbol:

A symbol for what Chile represents, a symbol for the way to lead Chile, a symbol for the way to understand Chile, its problems and its solutions, a symbol that has been key in the past, which is key today and—whatever pain it may cause to some—will be key in the future. This symbol is President Pinochet.[36]

In spite of the affinity between the rightist UDI and officials in the ministries of Defense and Interior, the navy distanced itself from this policy. The institution and its officers did not completely agree with the Pinochet formula. In particular, they objected to Pinochet remaining as army commander-in-chief while running for president.[37]

This tension was finally resolved when the comptroller general, in response to an appeal from Molina and other members of the Committee for Free Elections, issued a verdict that defined strict limits of political action for public administration officials as well as members of the armed forces and police.[38] Despite the army's later moderation in the campaign, the image and professional impartiality of the institution had been tarnished. Thus, the chasm between the armed forces and society deepened before and after the plebiscite.

Cleavages Between the Armed Forces and Society

The legitimation crisis translated into a serious split between the general population and the armed forces and brought the institutional credibility of the armed forces into question. The gulf arose as a consequence of the political role of the armed forces, their marked socio-economic differences from the rest of society, and their participation in repressive activities.[39] Starting in 1973, the armed forces developed a confident view of their role in society. They strived to assume the leadership of state and society, while at the same time depriving the state of various socio-economic activities.

This momentary experience of leadership—together with the threats of an external military confrontation and an internal "war"—created a new socio-cultural reality for the military. The men in uniform, their families, and their social circles found their self-image substantially improved and thereby accepted the less pleasing aspects of their new segregation from the administration of the state, which came under executive–army high command hegemony. But the armed forces also found themselves in a subordinate position to government officials, unable to shape a new social and political order based on military values.

As the armed forces distanced themselves from the management of the state, their initial authoritarian populism and political clientelism gave way to forms of neo-liberal management that led them to a severe crisis. The early policies of the dictatorship favored repression but also underlined the regime's aspiration to create a social order free of significant conflicts and founded on military values and on the ideals of harmony between capital and work.[40] The subsequent distance of the armed forces from government positions prevented the realization of such aspirations. Because they were unable to make a substantive contribution to national reconstruction, the public took a negative view of the armed forces' management and social position.

After 1973, one of the first measures in the area of defense was to reverse the historical tendency toward decreases in military spending. In 1973–74 alone, military spending increased by 40 percent in real terms. The declining economic role of the state and, later, the massive influx of foreign loans gave military spending precedence over socio-economic expenditures. Thus, the changing economic context resolved the historic contradiction between "guns and butter" in favor of guns.[41] The armed forces' new functions of repression and internal security, as well as the war hypothesis that prevailed between 1973 and 1982, justified an increase in military personnel from 110,000 to 165,000. During the same period, the army multiplied the number of its generals from twenty-seven to fifty-two.[42] Decisions concerning the local and international supply of arms, however, were not part of a comprehensive policy but rather a product of decisions of individual branches of the military.[43] In spite of these shortcomings, budget and salary increases enhanced the institutional image of the military as a profession.

The closing of this first phase, which lasted from 1973 to 1976, witnessed a profound segregation of the armed forces and society. The monopoly of power and institutional privileges enlarged the gulf between the armed forces and the rest of the population, particularly during periods of crisis.[44] As an April 1988 poll demonstrated, public opinion identified the armed forces, together with "the rich," as the major beneficiaries of the military government. In response, the majority of the civilian population (81.8 percent of the sample) wanted to cut military spending.[45]

The military role in repressive actions constituted a principal reason for the civilian-military cleavage. The public came to associate the participation of members of the armed forces in national intelligence organizations with massive violations of human rights. One poll reported that 59.3 percent of the population believed that more violations of human rights had occurred during the period of military rule than in the entire history of Chile. This negative assessment translated into a high proportion of the citizenry (71.5 percent) who believed that many human rights problems remained unsolved. According to 69.9 percent of the people polled, those who were found guilty of human rights violations should be severely punished, even if it generated conflicts with the armed forces in the democratic future, as feared by 66.4 percent of the population.[46]

Various regional and national opinion polls indicated that a serious legitimation crisis affected the armed forces because of their involvement with the military regime. In March 1988, 50.5 percent of the public averred that the armed forces should not participate in politics and should return to their barracks. Between July and August 1988, this proportion rose to 67 percent.[47] A growing segment of the population in 1988 (39.4 percent in April, 44.5 percent in May, 43.2 percent in June) also believed that the armed forces could not guarantee a fair plebiscite. They opined that the involvement of the military in the Pinochet candidacy was a mistake (65.7 percent in December 1987; 69 percent in July 1988).

Although a large part of the population viewed the power of the armed forces as enormous, that perception was not matched by the evaluation of the military's proper political role. Of those polled,

43.1 percent saw the armed forces as the institution with the highest concentration of power, compared to 32.9 percent who indicated the government and 9.1 percent who identified the business sector. In answer to the question of who *should* have more power, however, only 2.7 percent ranked the armed forces first, and 3.8 percent ranked that institution second. Most Chileans favored policies that would augment the power of those who would prevent the violation of their socio-economic rights (unions) and their human rights and constitutional guarantees (judges). The low preference for the armed forces, business, and foreign enterprises indicated that the population viewed those institutions negatively and associated them with the deterioration of their rights. These perceptions demonstrated a high level of social delegitimation of the political role of the armed forces. Of those surveyed, 63.8 percent thought that the armed forces should not have as much power as they did.[48]

CONFIDENCE IN THE ARMED FORCES

The distance between the military institutions, the military government, and society translated into a negative public evaluation of the armed forces and the military government, as shown by the population's "level of confidence" in the armed forces and the Carabineros.[49] The general level of confidence in the armed forces was low: 37.7 percent of those surveyed had some confidence, and 35.4 percent had little confidence. By grouping both categories, it can be concluded that 73.1 percent of the population distrusted the armed forces to some extent, compared to 21.7 percent who expressed strong confidence in these institutions. However small it may have been, the one-fifth of the population that fully supported the armed forces is highly significant.

In order to understand the level of confidence in the armed forces, it is important to take into account the various political positions of the population. The majority (74.4 percent) of the left showed no confidence in the armed forces, compared to 56 percent of the right who held great confidence in the armed forces. The political center showed a clear inclination to mistrust military institutions.

Confidence in the armed forces also depended on the people's perception of their personal economic situation.[50] Over a third of the poll respondents, 35.2 percent, believed that their personal economic situation was bad, and 47 percent thought it only slightly better. If we consider both groups together, 82.2 percent of those surveyed believed their personal economic situation was less than

good. This helps to put in perspective the three-fourths of the population who had little or no confidence in the armed forces. Of the
one-fifth who trusted the armed forces, the majority (50.4 percent)
thought that their personal economic situation was good.[51]

CONTRIBUTION OF THE ARMED FORCES

A close analysis of a poll conducted in the southern city of Concepción
in April 1988 shows that the largely negative public views of the military's contributions to regional development were associated with the
respondent's age. Opinions about the contributions of the armed forces
were, on average, negative for the three age groups used in the sample.[52] But there was a tendency for opinion to be more negative among
respondents who were between eighteen and twenty-seven years old.[53]
This is significant, because approximately 57 percent of Chile's population is under twenty-one years of age.

A negative opinion of the role of the armed forces was also associated in the poll with the respondents' views on military service.
Those who thought highly of the military's role in the region believed that military service should be obligatory. Those who judged
the contribution of the armed forces as poor thought that military
service should be voluntary. On this issue, the sample was divided
almost exactly in half.

Views on the role of the armed forces also correlated in the poll
with respondents' socio-economic status and political position. Perceptions of the role of the armed forces depended more on political
position than on socio-economic status. The small group that
showed the greatest confidence in the armed forces consisted of
middle- and upper-class older individuals from the right.

AUTHORITARIANISM AND THE ABILITY TO GOVERN

A poll conducted in Santiago in August 1987 served as the basis for
formulating an index of "perception of the relative ability to govern"
by authoritarian regimes.[54] The index concentrated on the assessment of the power of the armed forces and the perceived capacity of
authoritarian governments, vis-à-vis democratic governments, to
confront problems of social inequality, terrorism, moral crisis, personal security, and public order. Most indicators demonstrated that
most Chileans judged authoritarian governments as less able to govern than civilian governments. The respondents viewed the armed
forces as worse than democratic governments in terms of reducing

social inequalities (58.9 percent), resolving problems of personal security (52.8 percent), dealing with moral crises (50.1 percent), providing public order (44.5 percent), and combating terrorism (43.4 percent).[55]

A closer analysis of the factors affecting this negative perception shows that the most important variables continued to be socio-economic status and political position.[56] Thus, favorable assessments of the regime's relative ability to govern grew as socio-economic level improved, and as political preferences moved from left to right.[57] The levels of perception of the regime's relative ability to govern, which were poor in general, reached almost zero on the left, did not exceed 10 percent in the center, and fluctuated between 20 percent and 40 percent on the right.

THE ARMED FORCES' ABILITY TO GOVERN

Data collected by a comparative Latin American poll provide additional insight into the perception of the armed forces' ability to govern.[58] This poll showed that 76.9 percent of the Chilean population viewed the armed forces as having a poor ability to govern.[59] This proportion is even greater than that found in Brazil in April 1989, when 70 percent of the people opposed the return of the military to government and preferred the consolidation of the democratic system.[60]

Once again, the variables that most influenced this perception in Chile were political position and socio-economic status.[61] Independent of their socio-economic situation, leftists viewed the armed forces as having little ability to govern. Those in the political center who considered themselves in a good economic position departed only slightly from this view. Finally, those who viewed favorably the armed forces' ability to govern had aligned themselves with the right and enjoyed a good socio-economic situation.

These conclusions are reinforced by an analysis of the perception of the armed forces' ability to provide solutions to national problems.[62] In effect, 74.9 percent of those surveyed believed that the armed forces provided little help in solving the nation's problems. Clearly, this perception was strongly associated with political position.[63] Consistently, a positive perception of the armed forces' ability to govern and to solve national problems was expressed principally by those on the right who enjoyed a high socio-economic status.

Tensions between the Armed
Forces and the Entrepreneurs

The third set of tensions that worsened the military government's legitimation crisis related to the ties between entrepreneurs and the armed forces. Considering its narrow social base, the Pinochet administration especially needed the entrepreneurs, but they did little to broaden his support.

ENTREPRENEURS AND DEMOCRACY

Even though the relations between entrepreneurs and the military provided advantages to both groups and were particularly favorable to the private sector, entrepreneurs failed to distribute the benefits they achieved among the majority of the population.[64] This failure became one of the principal factors in the erosion of support for the regime, as demonstrated by the outcome of the plebiscite. The inability of entrepreneurs to distribute benefits widely occurred "in the prevailing sociopolitical context of southern cone countries," where "no single actor has the capacity to impose one socio-political project on the rest."[65] This larger context allows us to understand, first, why democratic competition has certain impassable limits in the region and, second, why modernizing dictatorships cannot achieve a legitimate, stable order. The solution to national problems can only be found through building cooperative coalitions.

In Chile, key notions of equitable distribution of income and political cooperation were absent in organized business activities during the last two decades. Moreover, the importance of these issues was not understood by the entrepreneurs or their associations.[66] Allowing political competition was not a central concern for Chilean entrepreneurs.[67] On the contrary, the political right and its representative business groups consistently supported schemes for limited political competition, or "restricted democracy." Instead of favoring policies that would form long-term coalitions and pacts, business groups emphasized the control of the mass media, an alliance with the armed forces, and a political economy adequate to such narrow interests. The political system derived from these assumptions tended toward authoritarian capitalism.

This nondemocratic orientation helped Pinochet maintain a fragile authoritarian regime. In general, Chilean entrepreneurs were influenced by individual interests and actions that had little or no coordination with other social sectors. Entrepreneurs viewed the achievement of political cooperation as irrelevant or even as prejudicial to their interests, because it would have implied the formalization of a particular regime, institutionality, or order. Because coordination required compromises that limited their freedom of action, entrepreneurs sought other political forms that protected them from the demand for long-term commitments. As a result, entrepreneurs always considered the use of force as an option.[68] Entrepreneurs also clung to the idea of a closed, noncompetitive political system or even the idea of a democracy without parties.[69] Pro-government entrepreneurs favored a strong executive and the expression of public opinion through means other than the ballot box.[70]

MILITARY VERSUS ENTREPRENEURS

The tension between the need for a strong national executive and the desire for full freedom of action was consistently present among Chilean entrepreneurs. The business sector understood that the existence of uncontrolled presidential power could severely limit its own influence. Entrepreneurs were particularly alarmed at the number of government economic positions that were held by active and retired military officers. Military participation in public or private enterprises became one of the reasons why Chilean business elites mistrusted the same strong executive that they so desperately needed.[71]

The results of the 1988 plebiscite exposed the distributive legitimation crisis of the regime, revealing the schism that had developed between the armed forces and entrepreneurial groups. In light of the importance of economic reasons for voting "No," the government reproached businesspeople for failing to distribute the economic benefits they had received as a result of government policies.[72] Entrepreneurs had contributed to the regime's legitimation crisis through their nondemocratic and authoritarian tendencies, their opposition to multiclass alliances, and their failure to reciprocate to those in the middle and working classes who made their success possible. By eroding the regime's capacity for distributing benefits, entrepreneurs had helped precipitate the legitimation crisis of the government long before the 1988 denouement.

Conclusions

In Chile, as the 1980s progressed, the Pinochet regime was unable to obtain the mass electoral support it needed to achieve legitimacy and win the plebiscite. The failure of the Pinochet political formula demonstrated that the regime had no understanding of how it might achieve legitimacy. First, there would have to be relative satisfaction in Chile with the economic recovery of the recent period and entrepreneurial support in the form of a redistribution policy. Second, the regime needed a solution to the human rights issue, or a revised government approach to it, which probably would have eroded the basis of Pinochet's support. Third, Pinochet needed a political agreement among the branches of the armed forces and the Carabineros to support his campaign formula. Fourth, legitimacy required strong citizen backing for Pinochet, the armed forces, and the army that kept him in power. None of these conditions was met, and the regime failed.

The regime's legitimation crisis produced the public's negative view of the armed forces and their political role in Chile. That view became especially critical when members of the armed forces implied that they expected to maintain certain institutional prerogatives in future fiscal, political, and human rights matters. If those prerogatives were to become institutionalized, the military would risk a collision with important sectors of public opinion, which could prolong tensions between civilians and armed forces even after the 1989 presidential elections and the inauguration of the new government on March 11, 1990. The resolution of these tensions presents the new democratic government with a challenge that will be critical to meet for Chile's political future. Similarly, the military needs to relegitimize its institutional functions and tasks in order to capture civilian support and thus bring political stability to the nation.

One of the most important tasks for military relegitimation will be to attract the support of Chile's youth, the center, and the left. Because these segments of the population are the least supportive of the military, the social and political integration of the country depends on an understanding between the armed forces and these civilian groups. The new government and the armed forces will have to provide imaginative solutions in order to bring together important segments of the nation.

Surely, the military was not alone in creating problems, nor is it alone in the need to solve them. Beginning in 1990, the democratically elected government will have to confront not only civil-military issues but also the need to consolidate itself and to provide prosperity. Only a broad political consensus can square this circle.

Notes

1. Representative works include Adam Przeworski, "Some Problems in the Study of the Transition to Democracy," Alfred Stepan, "Paths Toward Redemocratization: Theoretical and Comparative Considerations," and Alain Rouquié, "Demilitarization and the Institutionalization of Military-Dominated Polities in Latin America," in *Transitions from Authoritarian Rule: Comparative Perspectives,* ed. Guillermo O'Donnell, Philippe Schmitter, and Laurence Whitehead (Baltimore, 1986). See also Asha Gupta, "Types of Military Regimes in the Third World" (paper presented at the Fourteenth World Congress of the International Political Science Association, Washington, D.C., August 28–September 1, 1988).

2. Augusto Varas, "Razón y fuerza en la transición del autoritarismo a la democracia," in *Transición a la democracia,* ed. Augusto Varas (Santiago, 1984); Karen Remmer, "Military Rule in South America: State Institutions and Political Outcomes" (paper presented at the Fourteenth World Congress of the International Political Science Association, Washington, D.C., August 28–September 1, 1988).

3. Mario Fernández, "La intervención militar en la política en América Latina," *Revista de Estudios Políticos* (November–December 1985); David Collier, ed., *The New Authoritarianism in Latin America* (Princeton, 1979); Alain Rouquié, *El estado militar en América Latina* (Buenos Aires, 1984); Abraham Lowenthal, ed., *Armies and Politics in Latin America* (New York, 1976); Anton Bebler, "Contemporary Civilian-Dominated Versus Military-Dominated Political Systems in the World" (Mimeograph, Ljubljana, 1987).

4. Augusto Varas, "Las relaciones cívico-militares en un marco democrático: Elementos para un reequilibrio de los vínculos FFAA-Estado-sociedad," *Documento de Trabajo* FLACSO (Santiago, 1988).

5. Guillermo O'Donnell and Philippe C. Schmitter, *Transitions from Authoritarian Rule: Tentative Conclusions About Uncertain Democracies* (Baltimore, 1986), pp. 15, 32, 36.

6. Hugo Frühling, "Justicia y violación de derechos humanos en Chile" (Mimeograph, Santiago, 1988); Luis Maldonado, "Discurso de inauguración del año judicial 1989," *La Epoca,* March 2, 1989; Domingo Namuncura, "Los derechos humanos y las FFAA," *La Epoca,* March 13, 1989; "Reportaje especial: Juicio a los militares," *Hoy,* no. 614, April 24–30, 1989.

7. A detailed analysis of the characteristics of the armed forces-government relationship is in Augusto Varas, *Los militares en el poder: Régimen y gobierno militar en Chile, 1973–1986* (Santiago, 1987).

8. Rouquié, "Demilitarization," pp. 110–11.

9. Przeworski, "Some Problems," pp. 50–51.

10. Stepan, "Paths Toward Redemocratization," pp. 72–75.

11. For a critique of the regime's constitutional positions, see Humberto Nogueira, *Manual del ciudadano: La Constitución de 1980 comentada* (Santiago, 1988); Patricio Aylwin et al., *Una salida político-constitucional para Chile* (Santiago, 1985).

12. Eugenio Ortega and Ernesto Tironi, *Pobreza en Chile* (Santiago, 1988).

13. Juan Linz, *Crisis, Breakdown and Reequilibration* (Baltimore, 1978). An analysis of these tensions in modern-day Argentina is in Carlos H. Waisman, "The Consolidation of Democracy in Argentina: Constraints and Opportunities" (paper presented at the American Political Science Association Convention, Washington, D.C., September 1–4, 1988). For a thoughtful discussion of the effect of poor state performance over political legitimation, see Frederick D. Weill, "The Sources and Structure of Legitimation in Western Democracies: A Consolidated Model Tested with Time-Series Data in Six Countries Since World War II," *American Sociological Review* 54 (October 1989): 682–706.

14. Guillermo O'Donnell, "Tensions in the Bureaucratic Authoritarian State and the Question of Democracy," in Collier, ed., *The New Authoritarianism.*

15. In this I follow the argument of Jürgen Habermas as presented in his *Legitimation Crisis* (Boston, 1973), pp. 36–37. For a discussion of the characteristics of the economic model after 1977, see Arturo Fontaine Aldunate, *Los economistas y Pinochet* (Santiago, 1988).

16. For a synthesis of Chilean military thinking from 1895 to 1976, see Augusto Varas and Felipe Aguero, *El proyecto político militar* (Santiago, 1982).

17. On the "sub-optimal" character of military regimes, see O'Donnell, "Tensions in the Bureaucratic Authoritarian State," p. 310.

18. See Manuel Antonio Garretón, *Dictaduras y democratización.* (Santiago, 1984), for an analysis of this process from the initial stages of the regime to its collapse.

19. The initial stages of this *caudillista* period are described in Ascanio Cavallo, Manuel Salazar, and Oscar Sepúlveda, *La historia oculta del régimen militar* (Santiago, 1988), Chapter 40. Despite economic growth in Chile from 1983 to 1988, real salaries diminished or grew at rates much lower than increases in production. See International Development Bank, *Progreso económico y social en América Latina,* Informe 1988 (Washington, D.C., 1989). See also Arístides Torche, "Distribuir el ingreso para satisfacer necesidades básicas," in *Desarrollo económico en democracia: Proposiciones para una*

sociedad libre y solidaria, ed. Felipe Larraín (Santiago, 1987); and Gonzalo Martner, *El hambre en Chile* (Santiago, 1989). The deterioration of the purchasing power of salaries was publicly recognized by Sergio Onofre Jarpa, president of the National Renovation Party, on the television program "Almorzando en el Trece," July 17, 1989.

20. For an expression of such support, see the declarations of Colonel José Zara, director of the Army Paratroopers and Special Forces School, in *La Epoca,* April 1, 1988.

21. The poll provides an accurate reflection of the motives for voting in the plebiscite. It was conducted after Pinochet was nominated as the only candidate, and its results were very close to the actual vote.

22. The Statute of the Government Junta was published in June 1974. All intelligence organisms were centralized in the DINA under the direction of an army officer in active service. In September 1974, Carabineros and plainclothes police became part of the Ministry of Defense. After a year of government by the armed forces, the institutional hegemony of the executive–high command became established and was able to devote itself to formulating both military and socio-economic policies.

23. See Fontaine, *Los economistas y Pinochet,* pp. 106–8, 125. See also Cavallo et al., *La historia oculta,* pp. 68–69.

24. For a comparative analysis of cabinet ministers during the last decades, see Teresa Rodríguez, "Elites políticas: Los ministros de estado" (paper presented at the First Chilean Congress of Sociology, Santiago, 1984); Carlos Huneeus and Jorge Olave, "Autoritarismo, militares y transición a la democracia: Chile en una Perspectiva Comparada," *Opciones,* no. 11 (1987); Carlos Huneeus, "El ejército y la política en el Chile de Pinochet: Su magnitud y alcance" (Santiago, 1988).

25. The proportion of military ministers in Chile's government was greater than in Argentina and Brazil under military rule. A comparison of three Latin American cases appears in Carlos Huneeus, "Transiciones en Europa del sur y América Latina," (Mimeograph, Santiago, 1984).

26. See Genaro Arriagada, *La política militar de Pinochet* (Santiago, 1985).

27. The attempts by the executive to alienate legislative functions from the military junta in order to pass them on to a "bionic" congress, as stipulated by the March 1984 proposal, were systematically blocked and resisted by the armed forces.

28. Major General Eduardo Ibáñez, Indendant for the Eighth Region, stated "we will be one hundred per cent loyal to our commander-in-chief" in *La Epoca,* April 10, 1988. Commander Hernán Núñez indicated that "we are not passive agents of a process for which we are responsible," in *El Mercurio,* June 3, 1988. See also *El Mercurio,* May 22, 1988.

29. General Eduardo Ibáñez quoted in *La Epoca,* June 25, 1988. The general was called into retirement immediately after the plebiscite defeat, even

though he was the first in line to succeed Sinclair as vice-commander-in-chief of the army.

30. Despite this prohibition, Minister of Defense Admiral (R) Patricio Carvajal stated that "there is no propaganda of any kind at the regiments; only civic instruction." *La Epoca,* April 14, 1988.

31. *La Epoca,* April 14, 1988.

32. *La Epoca,* May 28, 1988.

33. The branches of the military have specific limitations for the political participation of personnel. According to the Disciplinary Regulation for the Army and Air Force, included in the Ministry of Defense Decree No. 1445, of 1951, Article 28: "The military person must not get involved in politics. He cannot belong to associations of a political character and attend meetings of a political nature." In the navy, Defense Decree No. 450, of 1969, states in Article 206 that "to belong to some political group, to carry out propaganda or criticism of a political nature" constitutes a serious violation of disciplinary regulations. Regarding the Carabineros, Decree No. 900 of the Ministry of Interior, dated 1967, states in Article 22, paragraph 6, letter F that "participation in political activities of any type represents a serious violation."

34. *La Epoca,* June 10, 1988.

35. For example, Jaime Guzmán, *La Epoca,* May 18, 1988, and Minister of Interior Sergio Fernández, *El Mercurio,* May 20, 1988.

36. Alberto Cardemil, *La Epoca,* June 25, 1988.

37. See the declarations of Admiral José T. Merino in *El Mercurio,* May 28, 1988.

38. *El Mercurio,* July 22, 1988.

39. The barrier to civilian-military relations is difficult to overcome with 569 people detained and disappeared, more than 30,000 detained, an unestimated number of deaths, relocations, expulsions from Chile and exile, thousands of people tortured, threats, and massive raids of shantytowns. See OEA, Comisión Inter-Americana de Derechos Humanos, *Informe sobre la situación de derechos humanos en Chile* (Washington, D.C., September 27, 1985).

40. The early "populist" ministerial cabinets headed by General Oscar Bonilla, General Nicanor Díaz, and General Fernando Matthei are examples of these policies.

41. Carlos Portales and Augusto Varas, "The Role of Military Expenditure in the Development Process, Chile, 1952–1973 and 1973–1980: Two Contrasting Cases," *Iberoamericana. Nordic Journal of Latin American Studies* 1:1 (1983).

42. Arriagada, *La política militar de Pinochet.*

43. Depite budget increases, those who imported arms did not respond to an apt policy for strengthening the military's dissuasive capacity.

44. On the subject of institutional privileges, see María Angélica de Luigi, "Lo que ganan las Fuerzas Armadas," *El Mercurio,* April 2, 1989. General (R)

Luis Danús indicated that the armed forces earned 25 percent more than the average national income. "Entrevista al general (R) Luis Danús," *La Epoca,* April 24, 1989. See also Unión Nacional de Pensionados, "Comparación de Jubilaciones Civiles y Militares," April 10, 1986, and "La realidad de las pensiones," *El Mercurio,* May 16, 1986.

45. These data are from a project in progress directed by Manuel Antonio Garretón of FLACSO–Chile, titled "Propuestas políticas y demandas sociales: Derechos humanos y Fuerzas Armadas."

46. Ibid.

47. Summary of opinion polls conducted by Manuel Antonio Garretón.

48. The analysis that follows is based on polls conducted by the Facultad Latinoamericana de Ciencias Sociales (FLACSO) in Santiago and Concepción between August 1987 and August 1988. This analysis is based on my "La legitimidad social de las Fuerzas Armadas en política," *Documento de Trabajo* FLACSO (Santiago, 1988).

49. Ibid. This analysis is based on questions asked in opinion polls conducted by FLACSO in Santiago and Concepción. A poll conducted in Santiago between July 29 and August 29, 1988, provides reliable information about this subject. The question asked was: "How much confidence (a lot, some, none) do you have in the armed forces?" However general, this question captures the most diffuse demonstrations of support for the armed forces. More specific elements of this adherence are provided in the discussion on the index of authoritarian governments' ability to govern.

50. Perception of socio-economic situation is a dynamic variable and, therefore, is better than socio-economic status, because it is more closely associated (Eta = 0.35) with confidence in the armed forces. Political position shows an even closer relation (Eta = 0.48) with the dependent variable. Both explain (r^2) the variability of confidence within 28.1 percent.

51. The dependent variable of "level of confidence in the armed forces" is a scale between −1, which corresponds to "no confidence," and 1, which corresponds to "a lot of confidence." This scale makes it possible to obtain averages of this variable in dependent variable categories such as "perception of personal economic situation" and "political self-identification." Thus, the people who saw their economic situation as being bad and who identified themselves politically as being on the left had, on average, almost no confidence in the armed forces (close to the negative limit of the scale, −1). The opposite occurred with those who perceived their economic situation as being good and who placed themselves on the political right. This group had, on average, a lot of confidence in the armed forces (close to the positive limit of the scale, 1). The corresponding tests show independence in the effect of both variables and are statistically significant.

52. The question asked was: "How would you classify the contribution (a lot, little or nothing) of the armed forces to the region?"

53. It is possible to detect this tendency with a simple regression analysis. Even if this analysis shows the independence of age with respect to opinion about the contribution ($r^2 = .014$, fundamentally due to the artificial continuity of the "contribution" variable), there is a statistically significant 12 percent. An analysis of the same data that takes into account the effects of age over other political dimensions can be seen in Angel Flisfisch, Mauricio Culagovski, and Marcelo Charlín, "Edad y política en el Chile autoritario: Un análisis exploratorio y conjeturas para un futuro democrático," *Documento de Trabajo* FLACSO, no. 387 (Santiago, October 1987).

54. This index is based on the following questions: (1) "Who do you think has the most power in Chile?" with choices assigned separately to first and second place; (2) "Who do you think should have the most power in Chile?" with choices assigned separately to first and second place; (3) "Do you think that authoritarian governments are better, the same, or worse than democratic ones for reducing social inequalities?" (4) "Do you think that authoritarian governments are better, the same, or worse than democratic ones for eliminating terrorism?" (5) "Do you think that authoritarian governments are better, the same, or worse than democratic ones for ending the moral crisis?" (6) "Do you think that authoritarian governments are better, the same, or worse than democratic ones for providing more personal security?" and (7) "Do you think that authoritarian governments are better, the same, or worse than democratic ones for assuring public order?"

55. This percentage emerges from the distribution of frequencies of the index of ability to govern, in which 63.8 percent is located at level zero.

56. The variable socio-economic strata is associated more closely (Eta=38 percent) than political position (Eta=19 percent) with the perception of relative ability to govern. The variables of sex and age are not statistically significant.

57. Socio-economic level was determined by four categories constructed on the basis of whether or not the interviewee possessed a car, television, telephone, or domestic servants. The scale of self-determined political position ranged from one (left) to ten (right).

58. This index was elaborated by comparing the present government with those of the left, the right, and Christian Democracy on the basis of the issues: (1) civilian control over the armed forces; (2) ability to command respect for the laws and public order; (3) guarantees for the free expression of opinions; and (4) capacity for fighting crime.

59. This percentage increases to 85.7 percent if one includes the intermediate category on five levels.

60. *La Epoca,* April 1989.

61. Eta=0.39 and 0.26, respectively; $r^2 = 0.183$.

62. Based on the question: "Do you believe that the armed forces are help-

ng a lot, some, or not at all to solve the problems of Chile?"

63. Political position (Eta=0.46) is more closely associated than the socio-economic level (Eta=0.21) with the perception of the ability to solve the nation's political problems.

64. Ortega and Tironi, *Pobreza en Chile*; Torche, "Distribuir el ingreso"; and Martner, *El hambre en Chile*.

65. Angel Flisfisch, *La política como compromiso democrático* (Santiago, 1987), p. 71.

66. Guillermo Campero, "El tema de la democracia en las organizaciones empresariales y los sindicatos de trabajadores," *Opciones*, no. especial (August 1984): 170–76; Guillermo Campero, *Los gremios empresariales en el período 1970–1983: Comportamiento socio-político y orientaciones ideológicas* (Santiago, 1984).

67. An important historical antecedent is discussed by Gonzalo Catalán in "Notas sobre proyectos autoritarios corporativos en Chile," *Escritos de Teoría* 3–4 (December 1978–January 1979): 100–160. See also Carlos Ruiz, "Las tendencias dominantes de la ideología política de la derecha chilena y la democracia: 1970–1980," *Opciones*, no. especial (August 1984): 147–69.

68. This analysis draws on Stephen D. Krasner, ed., *International Regimes* (Ithaca, N.Y., 1983).

69. See Manuel Feliú, *La empresa de la libertad* (Santiago, 1988).

70. See Modesto Collados, *Formas de vida para Chile* (Santiago, 1988).

71. *La Epoca*, April 3, 1988.

72. Commander Hernán Núñez, *La Epoca*, October 11, 1988.

Eduardo Silva

The Political Economy of Chile's Regime Transition: From Radical to "Pragmatic" Neo-liberal Policies

The economic crisis of 1981–83 in Chile severely challenged the military regime's pretensions to project radical neo-liberal economic policies and Pinochet's rule through the rest of the twentieth century. The extreme monetarist approach to an open economy contributed heavily to Chile's worst economic depression since the 1930s. Mass mobilization between 1983 and 1984 called into question the regime's timetable and its conditions for a political transition. Chilean policy-makers grappled with two related problems. They wanted to manage the economic crisis and restore growth within the framework of a modified neo-liberal model. They also needed to defuse political opposition and create favorable electoral conditions for the 1988 plebiscite. Chile's retention of neo-liberalism during those trying times represents an unusual case in South America.

These events raise some questions about the Pinochet regime: First, why did the regime cling so tenaciously to neo-liberalism? Second, what factors underpinned radical neo-liberalism, influenced the shift from the radical to the pragmatic neo-liberal model, and sustained the latter after 1984? And third, what were the consequences of pragmatic neo-liberalism for the politics of the transition?

The Pinochet Regime and Neo-liberalism

The military launched a coup d'état in 1973 to resolve a deep societal crisis in Chile, which the armed forces attributed to the failings of a developmental path that exacerbated class tensions. As a result, the Chilean armed forces sought a developmental route that was different from that taken by Marxism or traditional Chilean pressure group politics. The Chicago Boys and neo-liberalism offered such a model; they offered a transformation of Chile's economy and society that might eradicate Marxism.[1] The military regime retained neo-liberalism despite the 1981–83 crisis, because its renunciation would have meant the abandonment of the armed forces' vision of a new Chile.

The military interpreted its mission as one of restoring both economic growth and political stability. Consequently, the junta—and increasingly Pinochet, as he consolidated his rule—relied on groups that offered a double promise. First, they had to help discipline upper-, middle-, and, especially, lower-class groups whom the military believed were responsible for Chile's profound crisis. Second, their economic plans had to deliver economic growth; they had to recast the Chilean economy and, thus, society in order to establish the foundations for new institutions.[2]

Until 1981, the Chicago Boys served the purposes of the junta and Pinochet quite well. They were not only prepared to discipline labor, but they were also distinct from the traditional peak associations of businessmen and landowners. The Chicago Boys seemed to loathe those associations as much as the military did. The junta deeply mistrusted organized entrepreneurs, believing that entrepreneurs placed their narrow sectoral interests above the general good of the nation. In the junta's analysis, interest group politics shouldered much of the blame for Chile's economic stagnation and inflation, important contributing factors to the rise of the left and, therefore, to the nation's current crisis.[3] The Chicago Boys also offered a coherent blueprint for economic transformation. They wanted to change an import-substituting, regulated, statist economy into an export-oriented, free-market economy. If successful, a market-driven system would ensure economic development, transform society from collectivism to individualism, discipline social actors, and serve the general welfare of the nation.[4]

The core clique within the Chicago Boys, however, offered an added attraction. Although they did not belong to any traditional organized business groups, they controlled many of Chile's major corporations. They were the top executives—or the entrepreneurs closely linked to them—of vast conglomerates that expanded rapidly between 1974 and 1978. With the benefit of superior financial capability, they gained control over the Chilean economy's most dynamic sectors: financial services, forestry, export agriculture, mining, and import/export firms. They also acquired manufacturing firms and, if necessary, poured resources into them to make them competitive with foreign producers.

These conglomerates gave the junta an independent economic base that was capable of sustaining economic growth within a neo-liberal paradigm that focused on foreign finances and international comparative advantage. For example, by 1978, the three conglomerates to whom many top economic policy-makers were linked—commonly known as the Cruzat-Larraín, Banco Hipotecario de Chile (BHC), and Edwards economic groups—controlled 53 percent of the private-sector banking system's total assets and 42 percent of its dollar credit, as well as 71 of the 250 largest Chilean firms, which amounted to 40 percent of those firms' total assets.[5]

From the neo-liberal perspective, the establishment of a sound economy required a combination of orthodox stabilization and economic restructuring. These measures would reduce the role of the state and subject the economy to the rigors of the domestic and world marketplace.[6] The initial stabilization program eliminated most price controls, unified the exchange rate, and used deflationary policies to slash fiscal deficits.[7]

Restructuring policies included a partial dismantling of Chile's mixed economy through considerable privatization, financial system liberalization, and thoroughgoing trade reform.[8] Nevertheless, the public sector retained some controls. The Central Bank regulated the inflow of foreign currency to the nation's capital account. Relatively high real exchange rates (see Table 3.1) and a grudging retention of differential tariffs offered some protection against imports. In December 1977, however, the regime decreed that by mid-1979 Chilean customs tariffs would be reduced from the 10 to 35 percent range reached in August 1977 to 10 percent across the board.[9]

Between 1974 and 1977, the military regime introduced economic policies that were quite radical. But what followed after Pinochet made economic ministries and agencies the exclusive preserve of the Chicago boys was even more extreme. Protected by an authoritarian policy process that isolated them from virtually all social groups, except the top directors of a handful of powerful Chilean conglomerates who agreed with them, the Chicago Boys developed the radical neo-liberal project.[10]

The Chicago Boys set out to create a coherent set of pro-business-cycle policies in the context of free and open markets. Most of these economists were dogmatic, inflexible, and insulated from all opposition.[11] Following the initial economic stabilization and restructuring policies applied until 1978, the radical neo-liberal model strove to perfect a program that, once established, would automatically adjust the Chilean economy to domestic and world business cycles. Ideally, policy-makers would not be required to intervene in the process of adjustment and, least of all, to undertake reflationary measures.

The radical neo-liberal model consisted of three key features. First, it relied on manipulating the exchange rate to control inflation. In 1979, Finance Minister Sergio de Castro fixed the nominal exchange rate at thirty-nine pesos to the dollar. Second, the finance minister developed a fiscally neutral money supply. The quantity of money would automatically adjust to supply and demand according to the level of Chile's international reserves.[12] This radical monetarist approach to managing the balance-of-payments, with its neutral monetary policy based on a dollar standard, lasted for three years (from mid-1979 to mid-1982).

Third, Chile's capital account was liberalized in 1979 and 1980. Restrictions on bank intermediation of foreign funds were eased and then lifted. In conjunction with an international financial system that was flush with liquidity due to petrodollar recycling, capital account liberalization generated plentiful funds at low rates.[13] Loans under Article 14 of the Exchange Law increased by almost 100 percent in 1979. These loans required minimum maturities of twenty-four months in order for foreign lenders to be assured of access to hard currency in the future. In 1980, external credits obtained by Chilean private banks more than tripled.[14] The radical project did not stop there. The Chicago Boys also introduced a series of "social modernizations" that were intended to apply market principles to the organization of social services and administration. The most notorious acts were privatization of retirement benefits and health insurance, decentralization of government administration, and the adoption of a restrictive labor code.[15]

The flood of foreign savings fed an economic "boom" that helped subdue social groups that had been excluded from the policy process. Easy credit allowed entrepreneurs who had been shut out of the policy-making process, especially producers for domestic markets, to overcome the negative effects of a 10 percent flat tariff rate. These

Table 3.1
Key Domestic and International Economic Indicators, 1970–1988

Year	GDP (%)	CPI	Fiscal Deficit % GDP	Interest Rates (30–90 days, annualized)	Real Exchange Rate Index	International Reserves Millions of US$	Copper ¢/lb	Oil $/bb (average)	World Interest Rate US Prime
1970	2.1	32.5	2.9	—	76.6	393.5	64.2	—	—
1971	9.0	20.0	11.2	—	—	162.7	42.3	—	—
1972	−2.9	77.9	13.5	—	—	75.8	48.6	2.8	—
1973	−7.1	352.9	24.6	—	—	167.4	80.8	3.7	—
1974	1.0	504.7	10.5	—	99.9	94.0	93.3	12.3	—
1975	−12.9	374.8	2.6	121.0	136.4	−129.2	55.9	12.8	—
1976	3.5	211.9	2.3	51.4	110.6	107.9	63.6	13.7	—
1977	9.9	92.0	1.8	39.4	92.2	273.3	59.3	13.0	—
1978	8.2	40.1	0.8	35.1	111.4	1,058.0	61.9	13.0	—
1979	8.3	33.4	−1.7	16.6	114.8	2,763.8	89.8	18.6	—
1980	7.8	31.2	−3.1	12.2	100.0	4,073.7	99.2	31.9	15.3
1981	5.5	9.5	−1.7	38.8	87.2	3,775.3	79.0	36.1	18.9
1982	−14.1	20.7	2.3	35.1	98.7	2,577.5	67.0	33.6	14.7
1983	−0.7	23.1	3.8	15.9	116.1	2,022.7	72.2	29.7	10.8
1984	6.3	23.0	4.8	11.4	122.4	2,055.9	62.5	28.7	12.0
1985	2.4	26.4	3.1	11.1	150.0	1,886.7	64.3	26.4	9.9
1986	5.7	17.4	2.2	7.7	164.6	1,778.3	62.3	13.8	8.4
1987	5.7	21.5	0.8	9.4	170.0	1,871.1	80.8	17.8	8.2
1988	7.4	12.7	—	7.2	—	2,133.6	117.9	14.2	9.3

Sources: Column 1: PET, *Serie de indicadores económico sociales, 1960–86* (Santiago, 1987); and Felipe Larraín, in this volume, Table 9.1. Column 2: PET, *Indicadores*; INE, *Compendio Estadístico, 1989* (Santiago, 1989); and José Pablo Arellano, "Crisis y recuperación económica en los 80," *Colección Estudios CIEPLAN*, no. 24 (June 1988). Column 3: Sebastián Edwards, "Economic Policy and the Record of Growth in Chile, 1973–1982," in Gary M. Walton, ed., *The National Economic Policies of Chile*; and Cristián Salinas C., "Evolución del endeudamiento externo en Chile: 1982–1987," *Banco Central de Chile*, Serie de Estudios Económicos, no. 31. Column 4: J.P. Arellano, "Crisis y recuperación"; and INE, *Compendio Estadístico*. Column 5: "Síntesis Estadística," *Colección Estudios CIEPLAN*, no. 18; and J.P. Arellano, "Crisis y recuperación." Column 6: Banco Central de Chile, *Boletín Mensual*, no. 728 (1988). Column 7: PET, *Indicadores económicos*; UN, *Yearbook of International Trade Statistics*; and International Monetary Fund, *International Financial Statistics*. Column 8: UN, *Yearbook of International Trade*; and IMF, JFS. Column 9: IMF, JSF.

entrepreneurs borrowed to expand, diversify, or survive in an atmosphere of prosperity. Plentiful loans also helped producers for international markets to overcome the drawbacks of an increasingly overvalued peso (the result of the fixed exchange rate) which made Chilean exports less competitive in foreign markets. The middle class, as never before, borrowed cheap dollars and consumed goods and services, many of them imported, that had been the preserve of the upper classes. Even some segments of the lower class managed to borrow in order to consume.[16]

By 1980, the authoritarian regime had apparently achieved one of its main goals. After many sacrifices by large-scale producers for domestic markets, medium and small entrepreneurs, professionals, and especially the lower classes, economic transformation and development finally seemed within reach. Many economic indicators turned favorable (see tables 3.1, 3.2, and 3.3), with steady increases in GDP growth, the level of hard-currency reserves, wage indexes, and nonmineral exports. Moreover, inflation, interest rates, and unemployment declined, although the number of jobless was still at least twice that of 1970. Official discourse successfully swept some of the less upbeat data under the carpet: the worsening balance-of-trade figures, the falling levels of domestic savings, and an increasingly overvalued peso, with the attendant problems of a loss of competitiveness for Chilean exports and an imbalance between internal and international prices.[17]

The Shift from Radical to "Pragmatic" Neo-liberalism, 1981–1988

When Chilean policy-makers opened the domestic economy to the extent they did, they also left it vulnerable to the negative effects of extreme fluctuations in the world economy. The economic crisis that engulfed Chile between 1981 and 1983 severely challenged the plan of the triumphant new power elite to project the radical neo-liberal economic model, and Pinochet's authoritarian rule, through the remainder of the twentieth century. The economic crisis, however, neither brought Pinochet's reign to an abrupt end nor induced the regime to abandon the neo-liberal model. It only prompted its modification.

The shift from radical to "pragmatic" neo-liberal policies took place over three distinct periods: automatic adjustment, 1981–82;

Table 3.2
Composition of Chilean Exports, 1970–1987
(in millions of US$)

Year	1970	% of total	1974	% of total	1979	% of total	1980	% of total	1981	% of total	1982	% of total
Traditional												
Mining	952.3	85.6	1,871.1	83.4	2,241.1	59.5	2,902.6	60.2	2,177.5	56.8	2,123.7	57.3
Copper	839.8	75.5	1,716.2	75.6	1,799.6	47.8	2,200.4	45.7	1,737.8	45.3	1,684.6	45.5
Semitraditional	46.8	4.2	144.7	6.5	382.5	10.2	513.1	10.6	443.0	11.5	464.3	12.5
Nontraditional	113.4	10.2	226.5	10.1	1,139.8	30.3	1,402.4	29.1	1,215.9	31.7	1,117.7	30.2
Farm and Sea	—		54.8	2.4	264.5	7.0	339.9	7.0	365.4	9.5	374.9	10.1
Industrial	—		167.7	7.5	862.5	22.9	1,045.7	21.7	850.5	22.2	742.8	20.0
Total Exports	1,112.5		2,242.3		3,763.4		4,818.1		3,836.5		3,705.7	

Table 3.2 continued

Year	1983	% of total	1984	% of total	1985	% of total	1986	% of total	1987	% of total
Traditional										
Mining	2,296.6	59.9	1,982.5	54.2	2,120.7	55.7	2,096.1	49.9	2,603.3	49.8
Copper	1,835.7	47.9	1,586.6	43.4	1,788.7	47.0	1,757.1	41.8	2,234.7	42.8
Semitraditional	505.5	13.2	524.6	14.3	481.6	12.7	568.9	13.5	695.1	13.3
Nontraditional	1,033.4	26.9	1,150.1	31.4	1,201.8	31.6	1,533.8	36.5	1,925.3	36.9
Farm and Sea	327.5	8.5	428.1	11.7	515.1	13.5	683.0	16.3	796.3	15.2
Industrial	705.9	18.4	722.0	19.7	686.7	18.1	850.8	20.2	1,129.0	21.6
Total Exports	3,835.5		3,657.2		3,804.1		4,198.8		5,223.7	

Source: Ricardo Ffrench-Davis, "Origen y destino de las exportaciones chilenas, 1865–80," *Notas Técnicas CIEPLAN*, no. 31 (1981); and Banco Central de Chile, *Boletín Mensual*, selected issues.

Table 3.3
Balance of Payments, 1973–1987
(in millions of US$)

Year	1973	1974	1975	1976	1977	1978	1979	1980
Current Account	-294	-211	-491	148	-551	-1,088	-1,189	-1,971
Exports	1,309	2,151	1,590	2,116	2,185	2,460	3,835	4,705
Imports	-1,288	-1,794	-1,520	-1,473	-2,151	-2,886	-4,190	-5,469
Balance	21	375	70	643	34	-426	-355	-764
Capital Account	354	273	584	-215	459	1,234	1,200	1,921
Errors and Omissions	-60	-62	-93	67	92	-146	-11	50
Balance of Payments	-21	-55	-344	414	118	712	1,047	1,244

Year	1981	1982	1983	1984	1985	1986	1987
Current Account	-4,733	-2,304	-1,117	-2,111	-1,329	-1,137	-808
Exports	3,836	3,705	3,831	3,651	3,804	4,199	5,223
Imports	-6,513	-3,643	-2,845	-3,288	-2,955	-3,099	-3,994
Balance	-2,677	62	988	363	849	1,100	1,229
Capital Account	4,631	2,380	1,049	1,923	1,332	1,049	899
Errors and Omissions	102	-76	68	188	-3	88	-91
Balance of Payments	67	-1,165	-541	17	-99	-228	45

Source: Banco Central de Chile, *Boletín Mensual*, selected issues.

crisis management, 1983–84; and reequilibration, 1985–88. An understanding of these policy changes requires an examination of several key factors. First, at the eye of the storm that swept Chile in the early 1980s stood the regime itself, with Pinochet and the junta at its center. The regime wanted to give up as little as possible of the economic, social, and political transformation on which it had staked its prestige. The rulers strove to retain a policy process that was as independent as possible from societal forces, to preserve the neoliberal economic model in order to continue to discipline social actors through market mechanisms. The government also struggled to keep the political transition within the bounds of the 1980 constitution. It wanted to establish a "protected" democracy to shield the authoritarian regime's economic and social project from participatory, redistributionist politics.[18]

External and domestic factors conditioned the degree to which the military government accomplished those goals. At the international level, perceptions concerning the restoration of international liquidity and the behavior of international financial organizations influenced the course of economic policy changes. At the national level, several key factors contributed to revisions: the economic depression, the collapse of the conglomerates that had supported radical neo-liberalism, criticisms from entrepreneurs who eventually formed an alternative "pragmatic" neo-liberal policy coalition, rising unemployment, and an upsurge of mass mobilization.

Automatic Adjustment, 1981–1982

The first period of policy crisis occurred during the U.S.-induced slowdown in international lending and the ensuing deep world recession of the early 1980s. Foreign savings had underwritten Chile's "boom," and the private sector was highly indebted—in 1981, it held 83.9 percent of Chile's net foreign debt.[19] As a result, a reduced dollar flow to Chile, a fixed exchange rate, and automatic adjustment produced a series of mounting problems beginning in mid-1981. By the end of 1982, international reserves had fallen by almost US$1.5 billion, and after a comfortable $1.2 billion surplus in 1980, the balance of payments revealed an alarming $1.1 billion deficit. Moreover, real annual short-term interest rates shot up from 12 percent in 1980 to 39 percent and 35 percent in 1981–82, and the government's commitment to procyclical policies contributed to a wrenching 14 percent drop in GDP.

Despite mounting criticism from entrepreneurial groups, the Pinochet regime retained as much of the radical model as it could for as long as it could. Throughout this period, the regime steadfastly maintained an unswerving commitment to automatic adjustment. Major policy changes did not occur until mid-1982, when the Chicago Boys reluctantly devalued and established a preferential dollar for debtors. They also reduced wages, but that was a revision they welcomed. The Chicago Boys had initially proposed a wage reduction instead of devaluation, but the junta had checked the plan.[20]

The main reason for the late timing of the devaluation was that policy-makers first thought that the world recession would be mild and that international liquidity would soon be restored. Thus, in 1981, the only measure they took to alleviate the situation was to open the capital account even more, this time to short-term movements.[21] They had little success. By the end of 1981, international reserves had dwindled by almost $300 million, and domestic credit remained ruinously tight at a high of 38 percent per year for short-term loans.

In 1982, the regime conceded that previous international conditions would not be restored. The authorities had to act to stabilize the deteriorating balance-of-payments, especially the huge current account deficit, and to lower skyrocketing interest rates. Adjustment required massive deflation to bring overvalued internal prices into accord with international prices. That meant either currency devaluation (ending the fixed exchange rate), or wage reductions (abrogating the 1979 labor code's 100 percent cost-of-living adjustment clause).[22]

A debate erupted over whether to devalue or to reduce wages. The regime did both. First, it depreciated the peso by 18 percent in July 1982. Shortly thereafter, it eased cost-of-living adjustment rules, which paved the way for wage reductions. The real wage index (1970=100) declined from a high of 102 in 1982 to 91 in 1983 to 87 in 1985. The government also introduced a preferential dollar for debtors, a subsidy that by late 1987 had cost the Central Bank US$3.4 billion.[23] These policy changes represented a retreat from the radical neo-liberal model. But the regime steadfastly refused to initiate reflationary measures to ease pressure on usurious domestic interest rates. Pinochet backed the Chicago Boys in their resolve to apply automatic adjustment.[24] Thus, a crucial component of the radical model remained firmly in place.

Still, within the confines of the radical neo-liberal model, the regime did what it could to ease pressure on interest rates. In April 1982, Pinochet replaced Finance Minister Sergio de Castro with another Chicago Boy, Sergio de la Cuadra. The new minister's plan for lowering interest rates revealed deep tensions between the government and the key conglomerates that had supported radical neo-liberalism. De la Cuadra blamed the conglomerates' voracious credit needs for Chile's exceptionally high interest rates. In their bid for rapid expansion, the conglomerates' banks—among Chile's largest—had placed a disproportionate amount of resources in firms they controlled. For example, in June 1982 BHC's Banco de Chile had loaned 17 percent of its funds to other BHC companies. Banco de Chile, the nation's largest bank, was responsible for 20 percent of the Chilean financial system's credit in 1982. Cruzat-Larraín's Banco de Santiago, Chile's second largest bank and responsible for 12 percent of outstanding credit in the nation, had 44 percent of its loans in related firms.[25] This situation drove up interest rates, because the conglomerates' debtor companies soaked up the lion's share of available credit to stave off bankruptcy. De la Cuadra calculated that pressure on interest rates would abate if he removed from the market the very loans that the conglomerates were struggling to rollover. But that required breaking up the conglomerates.

To disarticulate the combines and to lower interest rates, de la Cuadra authorized the Central Bank to purchase unrecoverable loans from Chilean financial institutions, which they would then buy back over a ten-year period at low interest rates. Because the conglomerates' major nonfinancial holding companies were responsible for such a large proportion of their financial institutions' nonperforming loans, the debt buyout scheme threatened to break the link between the two. Control of the combines' major nonfinancial firms would revert to the Central Bank, because it would be their major creditor. But de la Cuadra's tactic failed, and the conglomerates managed to evade the new rules.[26]

The regime had moved away from the radical neo-liberal model. It had devalued the peso, established a preferential dollar, reduced wages, and attempted to intervene in the financial sector. It had introduced cost-cutting measures for business to stave off the political consequences of economic collapse. But the government refused to resort to countercyclical measures—increased monetary emissions and fiscal deficits—which the private sector called for to spur economic recovery.[27] Had the regime acceded, it would have moved away not only from the radical model but also from neo-liberalism in general, which stressed orthodox stabilization and deflation.

Crisis Management, 1983–1984

Between 1983 and 1984, the government introduced its most significant shifts from radical neo-liberalism as it confronted the political consequences of the economic crisis. As mass protests gathered momentum in Chile, even Pinochet's highly authoritarian regime needed a limited base of social consent to maintain order. Policymakers initiated reflationary measures to reduce interest rates and spur economic recovery. They also abandoned their commitment to sectorally neutral general policies, bowing to some of the demands of business and landowning peak associations, which had formed an alternative capitalist coalition to the conglomerates that had supported radical neo-liberalism.

In 1983, the full measure of the disastrous economic performance in 1982 caught up with Chile. Business failures reached unprecedented numbers, and unemployment, which stood at 25 percent in December 1982, had climbed to 30 percent by the end of 1983.[28] Moreover, the year started out with an economic bombshell. As 1982 drew to a close, it seemed that the entire banking system was in danger of collapse. The conglomerates could not roll over their loans indefinitely, and domestic interest rates had to be reduced for there to be any hope of economic recovery. To avoid a total breakdown of Chile's financial system, "Superminister" Rolf Lüders (who was both minister of finance and minister of economy) resorted to drastic measures to break up the erstwhile key supporters of radical neo-liberalism—the major conglomerates. In January 1983, Lüders placed the conglomerates' major financial institutions in receivership, with government-appointed intervenors, and dissolved others. With that, the state, paradoxically, took effective possession of approximately 80 percent of the once private financial system and gained indirect control of firms that were deeply indebted to them.[29]

In the midst of this economic wreckage, and faced with a government bent on riding out a deepening economic depression, leaders of the private sector clamored for pragmatic reflationary and sectorally specific measures to get the economy moving again. They wanted high real exchange rates, debt relief, increased monetary emissions, lower interest rates, public works projects, tax reform to reduce business costs, and protection from imports. At this stage, however, these demands constituted more of a manifesto than a coherent economic program.[30] An alternative capitalist coalition capable of replacing the conglomerates that had backed radical neo-liberalism had not yet emerged.

As long as entrepreneurial opposition remained relatively inchoate, the government did not give big business much. In March 1983, a new minister of finance, Carlos Cáceres, introduced an emergency economic plan that fell far short of expectations. Cáceres claimed that IMF conditionality measures left him without resources to do what the private sector wanted.[31] But between May and July 1983, mass mobilization and the maturation of a "pragmatic" capitalist policy coalition induced the regime to make greater concessions.

The collapse of the Chilean economy ignited a protest movement that shook the regime to its core. For three years, the opposition staged a monthly "national day of protest." After being initiated by organized labor, middle-class groups and resurgent political parties quickly joined in and took charge. The regime did what it could to repress the tumult with force. Although the mass demonstrations could not topple the government, they did challenge the limited character of the political transition—its timetable, Pinochet's candidacy, the perpetual state of emergency, the restricted status of political parties, exiles, and the political exclusion of Marxists. Tensions within the regime, between hardliners and softliners, erupted over these points as well.[32] Moreover, the protest movement linked the repudiation of authoritarianism with a rejection of economic transformation along neo-liberal lines. A vast majority of Chileans raised their voices against an economic model that had imposed such unpredictability, unfairness, and hardship on them.

Most capitalists, although they feared opposition political parties, had also had enough of the radical neo-liberal model. Spurred by the alarming political consequences of Chile's seemingly bottomless economic crisis, the sectoral peak associations of large-scale landowners, industrialists, merchants, mineowners, and construction entrepreneurs strove to turn their 1982 manifesto into a coherent alternative economic program to radical neo-liberalism. By mid-1983, under the aegis of the Confederation of Production and Commerce

(CPC), their umbrella organization, they had achieved their goal and had sent their proposal, *Recuperación económica: Análisis y proposiciones*, to the government.[33]

In drafting *Recuperación económica*, the CPC and its member associations also forged an enduring pragmatic capitalist policy coalition. In the short term, it stressed countercyclical measures to overcome the recession. In the longer term, the pragmatic capitalist coalition demanded greater flexibility in meeting the needs of individual economic sectors. All of the participants supported reflationary measures, such as fiscal deficits at around 4 percent of GDP, and 30 percent inflation, as well as high real exchange rates, credit and protective policies tailored to the requirement of specific economic sectors, and lower taxes. They also strongly supported the construction sector in its bid for public works and housing projects. Industrialists and landowners demanded export incentives and more protection from foreign competition. But the pragmatic coalition's program stopped short of requests for differentiated tariffs, because landowners, mineowners, merchants, and construction entrepreneurs opposed industrialists on that issue.[34]

From mid-1983 to mid-1984, the pragmatic capitalist coalition took advantage of political and social unrest to persuade the government, which had previously excluded them from policy-making, to accept their policy recommendations. Whether as a group through the auspices of the CPC or by individual peak associations, the pragmatic coalition doggedly pressed for policy changes along the lines hammered out in *Recuperación económica*.[35]

Pinochet's regime faced a daunting task. It had to defuse the political opposition to keep the controlled transition on track, and it had to get the market economy back on its feet in order to project its continuance past the constitutional transition period. The regime gambled that a combination of repression, cosmetic negotiation with the opposition, and economic recovery would achieve those ends. With respect to economic recovery, Pinochet and his advisers were finally ready to listen to the private sector. Political stability required mildly reflationary policies, which would reduce unemployment, recapture the solid allegiance of business, and blunt the opposition's attack.

Pinochet reshuffled the cabinet several times in 1983 and 1984 to show his increasing commitment to economic reactivation. He also introduced changes in the policy process that drew private-sector peak associations more directly into the decision-making process. In 1984, Minister of Economy Modesto Collados, former president of the CPC's Construction Chamber, introduced a "Triennial Plan." All of the CPC's member associations helped draft it and, not surprisingly, it reflected many of the concerns put forward by the pragmatic capitalist coalition. The fiscal deficit shot up to 3.8 percent of GDP in 1983 and to 4.8 percent of GDP in 1984; real annual short-term interest rates came tumbling down from 35 percent in 1982 to 11.4 percent in 1984; public works projects that had previously been elaborated by the Chilean Construction Chamber emerged; the real exchange rate rose by another five percentage points in 1984; the private sector and the government reached a compromise on debt relief; and, beginning in 1983, agriculture and industry received protection from unfair international competition.[36]

Until 1983, the sharp decline in international lending and the rise in interest rates contributed to the unraveling of the radical neoliberal model. But at first, the Chicago Boys introduced few changes because the Pinochet regime's authoritarian policy process continued to isolate them from inchoate opposition. Between 1983 and 1984, however, two factors persuaded even the highly centralized Pinochet regime to make adjustments in the radical model. First, economic contraction precipitated the collapse of the Chilean financial system, which culminated in the final break between the government and the conglomerates that had supported radical neo-liberalism. Second, mobilization by the masses and opposition by a full-fledged alternative capitalist policy coalition erupted nearly simultaneously. Under these circumstances, the regime negotiated key policy changes with the new capitalist coalition, which laid the foundations for pragmatic neo-liberalism. The aim of that new policy package was to end the economic crisis and prepare the ground for renewed economic growth, to spend the fury of the protest movement, to disarm the opposition, and to get the transition to regime institutionalization back on track.

The change from dogmatic, orthodox neo-liberalism to a more flexible, "pragmatic" neo-liberalism brought some tangible benefits. By 1985, the economy had begun to recover, the private sector's confidence in it was beginning to return, and the national days of protest had ceased to be a threat. Pinochet's regime had weathered the storm. But a number of problems remained. The banking system's virtual insolvency and its privatization presented grave diffi-

culties. Equally worrisome was the situation of the leading productive companies that those banks controlled. The end of the IMF's
temporary approval for higher fiscal deficits in 1984 was an added
complication.

Reequilibration, 1985–1988

During the third period of policy adjustment, the diminution of
pressure from below and the return of business confidence allowed
Pinochet's new minister of finance, Hernán Büchi, to reequilibrate
the neo-liberal model. On the one hand, Büchi retreated from some
of the more overtly reflationary policies of 1983 and 1984. These had
actually been a departure from neo-liberalism, since they were
Keynesian in inspiration. From 1985 on, Büchi emphasized stringent
management of the fiscal deficit, balance-of-payments, and inflation.[37] On the other hand, Büchi retained a number of policy
changes that had been advocated by the pragmatic capitalist coalition. His successful balancing of prudent macroeconomic management and entrepreneurial needs earned Büchi a prominent role in
the political transition, as he became the military regime's presidential candidate in 1989.

Between 1985 and 1988, the economic model remained neo-liberal in that it emphasized orthodox stabilization and was still
committed to economic restructuring in the pursuit of open, competitive free markets. In this context, pragmatism essentially
meant greater flexibility in the management of economic problems than the Chicago Boys' orthodoxy had allowed in the past.
For example, the government stressed the maintenance of economic development based on Chile's comparative advantages,
but it did not ignore production for domestic markets as policy-
makers had during the 1975–81 period.

Two measures adopted in the 1983–84 period—policies that were
in keeping with neo-liberalism—ensured the balance between the
creation of an open economy and the maintenance of protection for
domestic market producers. One policy was a commitment to high
real exchange rates, which rose another 28 percentage points between 1984 and 1987. High real exchange rates were very useful.
They encouraged exports and discouraged imports and kept both exporters and producers for domestic markets contented. From a macroeconomic point of view, they generated trade surpluses, which

helped Büchi to prudently manage the nation's balance of payments and its foreign debt obligations. Other protective policies involved the use of slightly higher across-the-board customs tariffs (which eventually settled at 15 percent), coupled with surcharges and other measures based on degrees of unfair international competition in specific products.

The policy instruments used to combat unfair competition further illustrate the flexibility of the pragmatic approach and its greater willingness to consider the specific sectoral needs of Chilean entrepreneurs. For example, landowners benefited from price protection for traditional agricultural cultivations, which previously had been hard-hit by the Chicago Boys' policies. By the same token, industrialists profited from tariff surcharges on subsidized imports (especially on textiles and footwear).[38]

Policy measures adopted between 1985 and 1988 to promote nontraditional industrial exports provided yet another example of the greater flexibility of pragmatic neo-liberalism in the pursuit of an export-oriented development strategy. These new laws reimbursed industrialists for duties on imported ingredients for manufactured goods destined for export. They also exempted from the value-added tax the suppliers of locally manufactured component parts for exported products.[39]

Greater flexibility in the consideration of entrepreneurial needs by economic sector extended beyond the consolidation of an export-oriented economic model. The regime also maintained its commitment to public works in the form of subsidies for low income housing and aided landowners who produced traditional crops with special credits.[40] Furthermore, unlike the pre-crisis period, the new policy-makers were not adverse to market regulation, especially in the financial sector (for example, the authorities drafted much more restrictive bank regulations).[41]

Along with the return to fiscal austerity, extensive privatization between 1985 and 1988 dispelled any lingering doubts about the Pinochet regime's commitment to neo-liberalism. As a result of the 1981–83 banking crisis, the state had wound up in control of substantial financial and nonfinancial assets and had the option to retain them and to reestablish a more mixed economy. Instead, Pinochet reaffirmed his devotion to the ideal of transforming Chile into a market economy and society.[42] The authorities privatized virtually all of the companies that the government indirectly controlled as a result of the economic crisis. They also spun-off many assets that the state had historically controlled in steel and iron works, coal mines, nitrate and sugar refineries, explosives manufacturing, public utilities (telephones and power), and pharmaceuticals.[43]

Moreover, debt/equity swaps in the privatization of both firms owned directly by the state and of companies that the state controlled indirectly as a result of the financial crisis had three important consequences. The debt/equity swaps were discounted debt notes—equity in Chilean companies—sold in world markets to foreign investors.[44] The swaps helped to amortize the foreign debt, bolster the balance-of-payments with an influx of hard currency (US$1.839 billion to the end of 1988), and intertwine foreign investors with local capitalists in joint purchases of companies privatized by the regime.[45]

What variations in external and domestic conditions allowed the Pinochet regime to sustain the modified version of the neo-liberal project between 1985 and 1988? At the international level, the Latin American debt crisis precluded a reversion to the radical model. And although IMF conditionality after 1984 forced Chilean authorities to return to more deflationary policies, other more favorable external conditions staved off economic decline. Lower oil prices (from $36 per barrel in 1981 to $24 in 1986 and $14 in 1988), declining world interest rates (from 18 percent in 1981 to 8 percent in 1986 and 9 percent in 1988), and higher copper prices (81 cents per pound in 1987 and 118 cents in 1988) helped Chile to meet IMF-imposed fiscal deficit targets and to enjoy economic growth. By the same token, privatization and debt/equity swaps reduced the fiscal deficit and guaranteed an influx of badly needed hard currency.

At the domestic level, the lack of voluntary foreign loans consolidated the shift in dominant capitalist economic policy coalitions begun in 1983. Because of the conglomerates' heavy reliance on external funding, the debt crisis irrevocably destroyed those that had been radical neo-liberalism's core capitalist support group. The crisis also turned more traditional capitalists—organized in the sectoral peak associations of large-scale landowners (SNA) and businessmen in industry (SOFOFA), commerce (CNC), mining (SONAMI), and construction (CCHC)—against the Chicago Boys' extremism; the traditional capitalists had only tolerated it because high levels of international liquidity had allowed them to prosper. By 1983, the debt crisis had induced them to form an alternative pragmatic policy coalition under the leadership of the Confederation of Production and Commerce.

The conglomerates that had supported radical neo-liberalism had ruthlessly discriminated against peak associations, especially producers for domestic markets, and backed the dogmatic, inflexible policies that benefited them. They had dominated the financial intermediation of foreign loans—most of their companies were in internationally competitive areas—and they possessed the economic wherewithal to modernize manufacturing industries while their competitors went under.

By contrast, flexibility predominated in the pragmatic neo-liberal policy coalition organized by the Confederation of Production and Commerce. That meant less zeal in the application of orthodox stabilization and a sensitivity to sectoral needs within the confines of a free-market economy. Because producers for international markets within SOFOFA and the SNA, along with the CNC and SONAMI, dominated the new capitalist coalition, a commitment to economic development based on comparative advantage also prevailed. Exporters had the advantage, because the debt crisis limited the amount of foreign savings on which Chile could draw. The exporters offered hard currency to a nation that was obligated to maintain surpluses in its balance-of-trade in order to meet its foreign obligations and to finance internal growth. By 1987, semi-traditional and non-traditional products, mainly from the private sector, had jumped to 50.2 percent of total exports from only 16.6 percent in 1974.

But the pragmatic coalition of organized business did not exclude producers for domestic markets in industry (SOFOFA) and agriculture (SNA) as the radical coalition had. Chile also had to substitute imports, such as wheat, sugar, oleaginous and dairy products, consumer durables, and household appliances, in order to simultaneously trim import bills and spur economic growth. At a time of high unemployment, their expansion also offered jobs, which contributed to political and social stability.

Between 1985 and 1988, in the context of continued scarce foreign savings, the pragmatic policy coalition—that is, capitalists organized in the major producer associations—consolidated most of the gains it had obtained from the Pinochet regime during the previous period, including high real exchange rates, comparatively low interest rates, inflation control without sacrificing economic growth, low across-the-board tariffs with protection from unfair foreign competition and export promotion for industry, low taxes, and market-determined wages. Moreover, the reprivatization of banks and industries that the state had involuntarily controlled since early 1983 strengthened the pragmatic coalition's economic base. Most of those firms were acquired by surviving older conglomerates that were more in tune with the pragmatic coalition's priorities; those combines were dominated by their productive, rather than financial, components.[46]

Changes in the policy process, which began between 1983 and 1984 and were extended from 1985 to 1988, also bolstered the pragmatic neo-liberal capitalist coalition and its policy preferences. The Pinochet regime created three major mechanisms that enabled the peak associations of the CPC to participate in economic policy-making—that is, in the drafting of decrees, ordinances, and legislation—that affected their sectors: the Ministry of Economy's National Commissions for Commerce and Industry, the junta's legislative commissions, and the Economic and Social Council (ESC). Organized capital's expanded presence in the policy process made past inflexible neo-liberal approaches all but impossible to sustain.[47]

Pragmatic neo-liberalism also helped to blunt the protest movement. Renewed economic growth and the appearance of political liberalization dampened the zest of the middle classes for mobilization.[48] Their deeply ingrained class fear of shantytown dwellers (linked to Socialist and Communist parties), who had competed for control of the movement in 1984, further contributed to middle-class demobilization. And last, but not least, the regime successfully lured the opposition's centrist political parties away from confrontational tactics with the promise of political liberalization within the constitutional timetable. Moreover, the opposition came to accept many of the pragmatic neo-liberal model's elements, such as prudent fiscal and balance-of-payments management and the open economy.

These, then, were the key international and domestic factors that sustained pragmatic neo-liberalism between 1985 and 1988. Moreover, from 1985 forward, modified neo-liberalism and favorable international conditions produced sustained economic growth, which the military regime needed for a successful political transition.

Pragmatic Neo-liberalism and the Politics of the Transition

Both the style and results of pragmatic neo-liberalism had important consequences for the character of the transition process. The old adage that nothing succeeds like success contains a powerful kernel of truth in the Chilean case. For the Pinochet regime, defusing the opposition and recovering economic growth were two sides of the same coin—to get the transition and institutionalization process that had been established by the 1980 constitution back on course. With regard to economic policy, the regime's goal was to promote a strong private sector in a healthy market economy. Ideally from the regime's point of view, sustained economic growth would help Pinochet win the plebiscite, without recourse to fraud. If the worst were to happen, Pinochet would lose the plebiscite but capitalists would be strong enough on their own to defend the market economy from social democrats.

From a macroeconomic perspective, without considering its inequitable distributive effects, the Chilean economy did quite well.[49] In the context of relatively favorable international conditions, it experienced sustained GDP growth, relatively low interest rates, small fiscal deficits, trade surpluses, low inflation compared to most Latin American economies, tightening labor markets (unemployment dropped from 23 percent in 1984 to 14 percent in 1988), and even progress in the wage index, from 87 in 1985 to 94.5 in 1988 (see Table 3.1 and Table 3.3). These positive conditions influenced the opposition's moderate stance on economic policy during the campaign for the plebiscite. As early as January 1983, for example, the opposition repeatedly committed itself to prudent fiscal, balance-of-payments, and foreign-debt management. The opposition concentrated on political democratization rather than economic change. As the 1980s wore on, the experiences of Argentina, Brazil, and Peru further dampened arguments against economic policy reversals.[50] Moreover, booming semi-traditional and nontraditional foreign sales, which provided over 50 percent of Chile's export earnings in 1987, led Pinochet's foes, who had until recently supported import-substitution industrialization, to endorse the military regime's export-oriented growth strategy.[51]

Throughout the campaign for the 1988 and 1989 elections, the opposition emphasized distributional issues within the limits of the

Table 3.4
Privatized State Enterprises, 1986–1988

Company	Percent Privatized	10 Major Shareholders (proportion of percent privatized)	Foreign Control (proportion of percent privatized)	Foreign Control as a % of 10 major Shareholders
Industrial				
CAP	100.0	44.3	39.2	88.5
ENAEX	66.6	100.0	34.4	34.4
IANSA	87.3	55.0	50.1	92.5
LAB.CHILE	67.2	37.2	18.0	48.4
SOQUIMICH	100.0	62.5	39.5	63.2
Communications				
CTC	64.8	70.0	63.4	90.6
ENTEL	51.1	70.8	33.7	47.5
TELEX–CHILE	100.0	100.0	0.0	0.0
ECOM	100.0	n.d.	0.0	0.0
Utilities				
CHILMETRO	100.0	58.4	25.9	44.4
CHILGENER	100.0	71.7	61.1	85.2
CHILQUINTA	100.0	72.5	30.7	42.2
EMEC	100.0	100.0	0.0	0.0
EMEL	100.0	n.d.	0.0	0.0
EMELAT	100.0	48.0	0.0	0.0
ENDESA	31.6	47.8	25.6	53.6
PILMAIQUEN	100.0	100.0	95.5	95.5
PULLINQUE	100.0	100.0	0.0	0.0
Mining				
SCHWAGER	44.0	51.1	32.3	63.1

Source: Patricio Rozas and Gustavo Marín, *El "mapa de la extrema riqueza" 10 años después.*

neo-liberal model.[52] But the success of pragmatic neo-liberalism also persuaded the opposition to revise its stance on one of the few economic policy issues it had taken a stronger position on: state participation in the economy. Between 1983 and 1988, Pinochet's adversaries retreated from more traditional mixed-economy approaches that emphasized the desirability of state investment in public enterprises as a model for development.[53] By 1988, the opposition still praised a mixed economy but redefined state action as merely industrial policy (targeting growth industries, supplying tax incentives for investment, allocating special credits, and so on); it no longer mentioned state enterprise.[54]

Three factors in addition to the success of market-driven growth strengthened the private sector and convinced the opposition that it had to appease powerful capitalists and postpone the demands of weakened labor groups. First, the degree and style of privatization induced Pinochet's foes to retreat from their earlier, more traditional interpretations of mixed economies. The extent of privatization hampered the opposition's initial intent, because it would have to invest significant resources in new plant and equipment or it would have to expropriate, with compensation, the state-owned firms that the regime had privatized from 1986 to 1988. (Table 3.4 shows the extent of privatization of state-owned enterprises, as well as foreign participation, in privatized companies during the period).

Far-reaching privatization gave capitalists control over an enlarged economic base.[55] A challenge to their right to that property would have involved the opposition in a costly, and divisive, political battle at a time when it had to maintain unity and husband political resources.[56] Moreover, if the opposition had not unconditionally guaranteed property rights, then production would have undoubtedly declined after the plebiscite, which might have had negative electoral consequences for the opposition at a later date.

Second, debt/equity swaps in privatization reinforced the favorable position of capitalists. They tied the maintenance of a favorable balance-of-payments position—and, thus, economic stability—to foreign investment in Chile. Anything less than a commitment to a market economy might easily have deterred those foreign investors.[57]

Third, pragmatic neo-liberalism's institutional changes—broader capitalist participation in the policy-making process—had implications for the opposition's moderate economic policy stance. The inclusion of sectoral peak associations in economic policy-making had two political consequences. First, it recaptured their unconditional loyalty to the Pinochet regime. The unity between the regime and *all* business and landowning groups deprived the essentially middle- and lower-class drive against Pinochet of any significant capitalist support (for example, producers for domestic markets among manufacturers and landowners), which was necessary to build a movement with sufficient force to extract larger concessions from the regime. Second, it gave the private sector practice in pressure-group politics.

In the final analysis, sustained economic growth, favorable macroeconomic indicators, privatization, and changes in the policy process all strengthened the Chilean private sector economically and

politically during the transition. These business elites had wrung
concessions from both the opposition and the regime. And, although
the regime lost the plebiscite, the economic successes of pragmatic
neo-liberalism placed Chilean capitalists in a relatively strong position, *ceteris paribus*, to defend thereafter the gains they had won in
authoritarian Chile. As if the institutional legacies of authoritarianism were not daunting enough, progressive democratic administrations will face this additional constraint in their efforts to build a
more equitable society.

[handwritten annotation]: constraints:
1 — legal & instit legacies of author
2 — strength of capitalists

Notes

1. For the military's political project see Manuel Antonio Garretón, *The Chilean Political Process* (Boston, 1989); and Augusto Varas and Felipe Agüero, *El proyecto político militar* (Santiago, 1984).

2. For the relationship between economic growth and political stability, see Charles Lindblom, *Politics and Markets* (New York, 1977).

3. Pilar Vergara, *Auge y caída del neoliberalismo en Chile* (Santiago, 1984); and Arturo Fontaine, *Los economistas y el Presidente Pinochet* (Santiago, 1989). Also see Arturo Valenzuela's chapter in this volume.

4. See Alejandro Foxley, *Latin American Experiments in Neo-conserva-tive Economics* (Berkeley, 1983); Sebastián Edwards and Alejandra Cox-Edwards, *Monetarism and Liberalization: The Chilean Experiment* (Cambridge, 1987); Joseph Ramos, *Neo-conservative Economics in the Southern Cone of Latin America 1973–1983*, (Baltimore, 1986); Gary M. Walton, ed., *The National Economic Policies of Chile* (Greenwich, Conn., 1985).

5. Fernando Dahse, *El mapa de la extrema riqueza*, pp. 147–56.

6. Alejandro Foxley developed this definition in his *Latin American Exper-iments*.

7. See Vergara, *Auge y caída*; Fontaine, *Los economistas*; and Laurence Whitehead, "Inflation and Stabilization in Chile 1970–77," in *Inflation and Stabilization in Latin America*, ed. Rosemary Thorp and Laurence White-head (New York, 1979).

8. For privatization, see Corporación de Fomento de la Producción, *Pri-vatización de empresas y activos, 1973–1978* (Santiago, n.d.); for bank liber-alization, see Ricardo Ffrench-Davis and José Pablo Arellano, "Apertura fi-nanciera externa: La experiencia chilena en 1973–1980," *Colección Estudios CIEPLAN*, no. 5 (July 1981); for trade reform, see Ricardo Ffrench-Davis, "Im-port Liberalization: The Chilean Experience," in *Military Rule in Chile: Dic-*

Eduardo Silva   123

tatorship and Oppositions, ed. J. Samuel and Arturo Valenzuela, (Baltimore, 1986), pp. 51–84.

9. Vittorio Corbo, "Chilean Economic Policy and International Economic Relations since 1970," in Walton, ed., *The National Economic Policies of Chile*, p. 114.

10. For the relationship between the Chicago Boys and the conglomerates, see Dahse, *El mapa de la extrema riqueza;* and Eduardo Silva, "Capitalist Coalitions and Economic Policymaking in Authoritarian Chile, 1973–1988" (Ph.D. diss., University of California, San Diego, 1991).

11. Manuel Valdés (CPC, SNA), Tássilo Reisenegger (SOFOFA) and Juan Villarzú (budget director in 1974), interviews with the author, Santiago, 1988–89. Domestic market producers in agriculture and industry protested tariff reform, but to no avail. See Guillermo Campero, *Los gremios empresariales en el período 1970–1983: Comportamiento sociopolítico y orientaciones ideológicas* (Santiago, 1984).

12. Edwards and Cox-Edwards, *Monetarism and Liberalization*, pp. 45–48.

13. For the impact of international variables, see Stephany Griffith-Jones and Osvaldo Sunkel, *Las crisis de la deuda y del desarrollo en América Latina: El fin de una ilusión* (Buenos Aires, 1987); and Jonathan Hartlyn and Samuel A. Morley, eds., *Latin American Political Economy: Financial Crisis and Political Change* (Boulder, Colo., 1986).

14. Edwards and Cox-Edwards, *Monetarism and Liberalization*, pp. 55–56.

15. For reforms in retirement benefits, health insurance, and the restrictive labor code, see José Pablo Arellano, "Sistemas alternativos de seguridad social: Un análisis de la experiencia chilena," *Colección Estudios CIEPLAN*, no. 4 (November 1980); Dagmar Raczynski, "Reformas al sector salud: Diálogos y debates," *Colección Estudios CIEPLAN*, no. 10 (June 1983); Jaime Ruiz-Tagle, *El sindicalismo chileno después del plan laboral* (Santiago, 1985).

16. Foxley, *Latin American Experiments;* Alejandra Mizala, "Liberalización financiera y quiebra de empresas industriales: Chile, 1977–82," *Notas Técnicas CIEPLAN*, no. 67 (January 1985).

17. For wages, unemployment, domestic savings, and investment, see Table 9.2 and Table 9.3 in Felipe Larraín's contribution to this volume.

18. For the 1980 constitution, see Manuel Antonio Garretón, *El proceso político chileno*, (Santiago, 1983), esp. chapters 6 and 7. Alejandro Foxley, interview with the author, Santiago, 1988.

19. Ricardo Ffrench-Davis, "El Problema de la deuda externa y la apertura financiera en Chile," *Colección Estudios CIEPLAN*, no. 11 (December 1982): 121–22.

20. Fontaine, *Los economistas y el presidente Pinochet;* Ascanio Cavallo, Manuel Salazar, and Oscar Sepúlveda, *La historia oculta del régimen militar* (Santiago, 1988), Chapter 35; and Campero, *Los gremios empresariales*.

21. Corbo, "Chilean Economic Policy," pp. 120–21.

22. Sebastián Edwards, "Economic Policy and the Record of Economic Growth in Chile, 1973–1983," in Walton, ed. *The National Economic Policies of Chile*, pp. 35–39.

23. José Pablo Arellano, "Crisis y recuperación económica en los años 80," *Colección Estudios CIEPLAN*, no. 24 (June 1988): 81. With respect to the sequencing of these measures, at first the regime only devalued the currency. But the Confederation of Production and Commerce, which had been working on a set of demands (including wage reductions, preferential dollar and reflationary policies), met with Pinochet two days after the devaluation. Shortly afterward, the regime decreed the additional measures. Confederation of Production and Commerce, Minutes of the Executive Committee Meeting No. 562, June 16, 1982.

24. For the Chicago Boys' and Pinochet's positions, see *El Mercurio*, June 19, July 8, 1982.

25. These were the conglomerates' two flagship banks. They also controlled other financial institutions that were, by and large, among the most important in Chile at the time. The percentage of funds controlled by competitors usually paled in comparison. For more details, see Arellano, "De la liberalización a la intervención," p. 24.

26. Sergio de la Cuadra and Salvador Valdés, "Myths and Facts About Instability in Financial Liberalization in Chile: 1974–1983," in *Financial Risk and Regulation in Commodity-Exporting Economies*, ed. Philip L. Brock (San Francisco, forthcoming).

27. Campero, *Los gremios empresariales*, p. 275.

28. For these and other employment and wage figures, see Table 9.2 in Felipe Larraín's contribution to this volume. The unemployment figure corresponds to open unemployment plus government emergency work programs.

29. Ascanio Cavallo et al., *La historia oculta del régimen militar*, Chapter 37; José Pablo Arellano, "De la liberalización a la intervención," pp. 18–25; *Qué Pasa*, no. 615, January 20, 1983.

30. *La Tercera de la Hora*, July 22, August 1, December 6, 1982; *Ercilla*, nos. 2453 and 2470, August 4, December 1, 1982; *Estrategia*, August 2, 1982; *El Mercurio*, August 15, 1982.

31. Campero, *Los gremios empresariales*.

32. Garretón, *El proceso político*, and *Reconstruir la política*.

33. Confederación de la Producción y Comercio, *Recuperación económica: Análisis y proposiciones* (Santiago, July 4,1983).

34. Confederación de la Producción y Comercio, Minutes of the Executive Committee Meeting No. 577, November 9, 1982; *La Tercera de la Hora*, June 20, June 27, November 9, 1982.

35. *Recuperación económica* was a synthesis of proposals (which appeared in an appendix) put forth by the CPC's individual peak associations. Once the

regime acceded to changes, those original documents—which contained the central document's main points in addition to more sectorally specific petitions—became the individual peak associations' negotiating platforms. See SONAMI, "Memorandum: Documento de la Junta Ampliada de SONAMI," April 5, 1983; Cámara Chilena de la Construcción, "Programa de reactivación económica dentro de un sistema de economía social de mercado" (Santiago, June 3, 1983); SNA, "Planteamientos de la SNA al gobierno," in *El Campesino*, no. 8 (August 1983); SOFOFA, "Memorandum económico: Plan alternativo de emergencia y medidas complementarias" (Santiago, June 1983), which later became "Una política de desarrollo industrial," *Revista Industria* 87:1 (February 1984): 5–23. Many of the proposals put forward in these documents became policy in the government's Plan Trienal, which appeared in August 1984.

36. For the business sources for Plan Trienal participation, see Sociedad de Fomento Fabríl, *Memoria, 1983–84* (pamphlet). It is also interesting to compare the SOFOFA's "Una política de desarrollo industrial" with the "Programa Trienal, 1984–1986," *Revista Industria* 87:4 (August 1984). For Sociedad Nacional de Agricultura proposals to the Plan Trienal, see *El Campesino*, nos. 6 and 7 (1984). Cámara Chilena de la Construcción data are from Pablo Araya, Director of Planning, interview with the author, Santiago, May 1989. For the first surcharges on industrial imports, see Sociedad de Fomento Fabríl, *Informativo SFF*, no. 1 (1983). For protection for agriculture, see *El Campesino*, nos. 8 and 12 (1984).

37. For an interesting review of these policies, see Laurence Whitehead, "The Adjustment Process in Chile: A Comparative Perspective," in *Latin American Debt and the Adjustment Crisis*, ed. Rosemary Thorp and Laurence Whitehead (Pittsburgh, 1987), pp. 117–61.

38. Sociedad de Fomento Fabríl, *Informativo SFF*, no. 1 (1983); *El Campesino*, nos. 8 and 12 (1984). For a review of sectoral policies in agriculture, see Ministerio de Agricultura, *El sector agrícola chileno: Políticas y resultados*, 4th ed. (Santiago, 1989).

39. Ministerio de Economía, *Medidas de fomento a las exportaciones chilenas ponen el mundo en sus manos* (Santiago, 1988).

40. Pablo Araya and Claudio Gaete (CChC) interviews with the author, Santiago, 1989; and SNA, "Memoria de actividades de la SNA," *El Campesino*, no. 12 (1984); *El Campesino*, nos. 1 and 2 (February 1985). Also see various editions of Ministerio de Agricultura, *El sector agrícola chileno: Políticas y resultados* (Santiago, 1985–87).

41. *Qué Pasa*, no. 797, July 17, 1986; no. 803, August 28, 1986; no. 805, September 11, 1986; no. 806, September 18, 1986.

42. See Whitehead, "The Adjustment Process in Chile."

43. Patricio Rozas and Gustavo Marín, *1988: El "Mapa de la extrema riqueza" 10 años después* (Santiago, 1989).

44. See Ricardo Ffrench-Davis, "Conversión de pagarés de la deuda externa en Chile," *Colección Estudios CIEPLAN*, no. 22 (December 1987).

45. Debt/equity swap statistics are from SOFOFA, "Síntesis Económica," *Revista Industria*, 92:2 (March 1989). For firms privatized and a breakdown of ownership, see Rozas and Marín, 1988.

46. For the composition of the new dominant conglomerates, see Patricio Rozas and Gustavo Marín, *Estado autoritario, deuda externa y grupos económicos* (Santiago, 1988).

47. Interviews by the author in Santiago with Jaime Alé (Sociedad de Fomento Fabríl), 1988; Gustavo Ramdohr (president of ASEXMA), 1988; Lee Ward (director, Comisión de Comercio Exterior, Ministerio de Economía), 1989; Jaime Palma (secretary, Comisión de Comercio Interior, Ministerio de Economía), 1989; Beltrán Urenda, (president, Consejo Económico y Social), May 1989. See also República de Chile, *Consejo Económico y Social*, issues from the Constituent Session, May 23–24, 1984, to the 49th Ordinary Session, March 14–16, 1989; Augusto Lecaros Z., "Representación de los intereses de la sociedad en el estado y Consejos Económicos y Sociales" (M.A. thesis, Pontificia Universidad Católica de Chile, Instituto de Ciencia Política, 1987).

48. For the course of the protest movement and the middle class, see Garretón, *Reconstruir la política*, and his chapter in this volume.

49. For the distributive effects of the neo-liberal model, see Alejandro Foxley, Eduardo Aninat, and José Pablo Arellano, *Distributive Effects of Government Programmes: The Chilean Case* (New York, 1979); and René Cortázar, "Distributive Results in Chile, 1973–1982," Walton, ed., *The National Economic Policies of Chile*.

50. For the opposition's conservative approach to fiscal and balance-of-payments management as early as January 1983, see *Qué Pasa*, no. 612, December 30, 1982; those themes were reiterated until the plebiscite was held. See *La Epoca*, October 2, 1988. By mid-1988, the opposition had also abandoned the idea of following the Argentine or Peruvian foreign debt management strategy. See *El Mercurio*, August 14, 1988. Also see Ernesto Tironi, *Es posible reducir la pobreza en Chile* (Santiago, 1989), esp. pp. 44–51.

51. For the opposition's endorsement of export-oriented growth, see "Documento político," *Estrategia*, editorial, February 1, 1988; and an interview with Edgardo Boeninger in *Estrategia*, 17 October, 1988. The point was also made by Alejandro Foxley in an interview with the author, Santiago, 1988.

52. Tironi, "Democracia y mejoramiento de remuneraciones"; García, "Crecimiento equitativo: Políticas de empleo e ingresos"; Sergio Molina, "El compromiso de Chile: Construir un orden social justo," in Centro de Estudios del Desarrollo, *Materiales para Discusión*, nos., 178, 191, 200 (July, September, and November, 1987).

53. Acción Democrática pledged itself to the more traditional interpreta-

tion of mixed economy in September 1983 and 1985. See *Qué Pasa*, no. 647, September 1, 1983; and *Hoy*, no. 424, September 2, 1985. Also see Joseph Ramos, "Democracia y propiedad," Centro de Estudios del Desarrollo, *Materiales para Discusión*, no. 76 (March 1985); and Ernesto Tironi, "Una economía mixta de concertación: Alternativa para Chile?" Centro de Estudios del Desarrollo, *Materiales para Discusión*, no. 45 (November 1984).

54. *Estrategia*, October 17, 1988; and *La Epoca*, December 26, 1988. Also see Tironi, *Es posible reducir la pobreza en Chile*, esp. chapters 2 and 5; Felipe Larraín, "Desarrollo económico para Chile en democracia," in *Desarrollo económico en democracia*, ed. Felipe Larraín (Santiago, 1987), pp. 19–80.

55. For example, opposition economist Andrés Sanfuentes declared that government privatizations sought to tie the future democratic government's hands. See *La Epoca*, November 6, 1988.

56. The opposition constantly denounced the regime's headlong rush to privatize public enterprises. It conceded, however, that what the state had spun off before the plebiscite would remain in private hands, although privatizations after the plebiscite might be called into question. See *El Mercurio*, December 9, December 16, December 20, 1988.

57. Tironi, "Democracia y mejoramiento de remuneraciones," p. 6. For the opposition's unambiguous commitment to a market economy, see *La Epoca*, October 2, December 26, 1988. Of course, that dedication was there earlier as well, but in a more social democratic form. See Alejandro Foxley, *Para una democracia estable* (Santiago, 1985).

Guillermo Campero

Entrepreneurs under
the Military Regime

The social and political behavior of entrepreneurs in Chile experienced important changes under military rule. Even though entrepreneurs gave their support to the regime of General Augusto Pinochet,
it is clear that important conflicts existed both between them and
their government and among themselves. The conflicts were most
intense during the first decade of the military government, from
1973 to 1982. Subsequently, they tended to diminish, giving way to
entrepreneurial behavior that was more compatible with government goals. Especially from 1983 to 1989, entrepreneuers developed
an aggressive economic, social, and political discourse that strived
to compete with the social and political discourse that had predominated in Chile since the 1940s. Before Pinochet came to power, the
state workers and political parties had been privileged as agents of
progress and development and had manifested distrust toward the
private sector in general and entrepreneurs in particular. Under military rule, entrepreneurs attempted to change these views by playing
a more active role, not only as economic but also as ideological and
political actors. They wanted to change their historically defensive
attitude and assume an ideologically active presence in society, ultimately hoping to become protagonists in the process of national
growth and development.

But the entrepreneurs faced two important problems. First, the
neo-liberal discourse on which their effort was based encountered
resistance in many social sectors, particularly among workers and
the young, who closely associated neo-liberal ideology with Pinochet's dictatorship and its social and political consequences. In
addition, many social groups associated the entrepreneurs with the
consequences of military rule and viewed them as the major bene-

ficiaries of the regime. Second, the discourse faced opposition from some entrepreneurs themselves. Although such internal conflicts were not readily apparent during the years of military rule, clear differences existed within the business community between neo-liberals and corporatists.

The role that entrepreneurs may play in the future will depend largely on their ability to overcome both difficulties. They will have to build the social and political trust necessary to improve their legitimacy among other social actors. The entrepreneurial leadership will also have to turn neo-liberal ideology into the consensual ideology of the business community, thus achieving greater representativeness. Should entrepreneurs be successful in both respects, they are likely to emerge as a significant group capable of rallying their constituents behind a common ideology and strategy and negotiating with the future democratic government as a unified bloc. They could also become a solid representative of the groups that hope to maintain the regime's social and economic model in a democratic future.

Entrepreneurs in Chile have a strong chance of becoming the representatives of those groups that wish to preserve important aspects of the regime's socio-economic model, especially if the political right fails to assume the leadership for continuing the model through a strong right or center-right movement such as National Renovation. If entrepreneurs lack broad support for the role they wish to play and if their internal tensions are not resolved, then they are unlikely to become significant social and political actors. Instead, they might become divided between groups that will negotiate their individual corporate interests with the new democratic government, or groups that might seek an authoritarian solution if they believe their interests to be seriously threatened.

Chile's Private Entrepreneurs

Entrepreneurs are frequently thought of as large capitalists. In Chile, however, the majority of private entrepreneurs own small or medium-sized businesses. Of approximately 276,000 entrepreneurs, about 240,000 own small businesses; only 36,000 own medium or large businesses. Approximately 60 percent of the first group are merchants or suppliers of services, 28 percent are in transportation, 7 percent are industrialists, and 5 percent are in agriculture or mining. In the second group, 30 percent are merchants, 30 percent are in industry, 20 percent are in services (including banking and finance), and 20 percent are in agriculture and mining. Their economic assets and lifestyle mainly correspond to the middle class, not the bourgeoisie. It is important to consider this social and cultural characteristic when analyzing the social and political behavior of Chile's entrepreneurs.[1]

Chilean entrepreneurs are organized in two major confederations, which are known as *gremios empresariales* (entrepreneurial organizations): the Council of Small and Medium-Sized Business (CPME) and the Confederation of Production and Commerce (CPC). The CPC primarily represents the large entrepreneurs, but it also includes some medium-sized businesses. The quantitative representation of both the CPME and the CPC is limited to no more than 20 percent of their social bases, but they are more powerful than this figure would suggest. Actually, both organizations act as official representatives for their constituencies, and, especially in crisis situations, they rally most entrepreneurs behind the organizations' strategies.

The CPME is a weaker organization than the CPC, not only because it has much less economic strength but also because of the diversity and dispersion of the entrepreneurs it hopes to represent. In addition, the CPME's constituent groups are comparatively new and have less tradition than those affiliated with the CPC. Nevertheless, the CPME gathers together the fundamental social bases of the entrepreneurial sector. This is the sector that played a key role in the fall of the Popular Unity government in 1973. Despite its capacity to mobilize, however, the CPME did not provide political and ideological leadership. Between 1972 and 1973, CPC organizations such as the Society for Industrial Development (SOFOFA) and the National Agricultural Society (SNA) played the critical ideological and strategic role.

Despite the heterogeneity of Chilean entrepreneurs, they agree on at least four ideological points: (1) the defense of private property as a natural and inviolable right, (2) free enterprise, (3) a negative view of political parties and their influence over the economy, and (4) the idea that democracy must be protected from its "enemies," especially the Communists. In Chile, entrepreneurs believe that this protection demands military tutelage over democracy.

Although there is consensus on these points, there are also important ideological differences.[2] Owners of small and medium-sized enterprises define themselves as "working people," emphasizing that their skills and accomplishments are the result of personal effort. This self-definition is frequently used to distinguish such entrepreneurs from the large entrepreneurs and the intellectual or professional middle class. Owners of small and medium-sized enterprises view large entrepreneurs as having too much influence in politics because of their economic power and perceive them more as investors than as producers because of the connections of large entrepreneurs with the world of high finance. Owners of small and medium-sized enterprises view the professional and intellectual members of the middle class with suspicion as well; they believe that these groups have enjoyed greater prestige in Chilean society and have occupied more important social and political positions.

The large entrepreneurs, for their part, view themselves as part of the liberal capitalist tradition. They dismiss the concept of "national enterprise" as state protectionism for low-productive activities in the internal market, and they favor international competition. Although the large entrepreneurs agree that politicians have had excessive influence, they do not believe that entrepreneurial *gremios* should seek to replace competitive politics in favor of corporatism. Instead, they advocate the privatization of economic activities and envision a central role for market forces. Socially, these entrepreneurs are relatively more cosmopolitan and relate comfortably with intellectuals and politicians. They are also less prejudiced about matters of social mobility.[3]

During the early years of military rule, the corporatists and neoliberals were in constant conflict. The corporatists were found among owners of small and medium-sized enterprises, particularly those oriented to the internal market. This ideological position is especially strong among merchant, transportation, and agricultural and mining organizations. The liberal capitalists were generally owners of large or medium to large enterprises. Each group hoped that the Pinochet regime would respond to its own orientation.

Entrepreneurs and the Military Government, 1973–1982

Entrepreneurs and their organizations had no unified economic and social project at the beginning of military rule in Chile. The unity they had displayed during the 1972–73 period was basically a defensive attitude with respect to the "threat" of Salvador Allende's regime. During the first two years of military rule, entrepreneurs strongly supported the regime's "National Reconstruction" effort, which the entrepreneurs adopted in the form of a crusade that called for the unity of all business groups.[4] But conflicts emerged even that early between leaders of the 1972 mobilization against the Allende government and the leaders of the CPC. The leaders of the mobilization sought to maintain and strengthen the organization and power of the *gremios,* but the CPC supported the demobilization of any power structures that could impede the "national unity" efforts of the military government. Despite these differences, entrepreneurs displayed unity during the National Reconstruction period.[5]

After 1975, the implementation of the neo-liberal economic model exacerbated the conflicts that had begun in 1973.[6] Not only was the power of the *gremios* threatened, but the very economic survival of small and medium-sized enterprises was also at stake because of the regime's general economic policy as well as its new orientation toward international markets. The neo-liberal economic policies and the lack of support for the *gremios* presented the small and medium-sized entrepreneurs with two difficult trials. They had assumed that the military government would apply a completely different political and economic scheme. Politically, the entrepreneurs had hoped that their *gremios* would be recognized and acquire institutionalized influence over social and political matters. Economically, they had hoped for state protection and development policies that would privilege and support them. When it became apparent that neither expectation would be fulfilled, these entrepreneurs reacted with frustration and shock. They considered themselves the true "social force" that made military intervention possible, and they expected the new government to be "their" government. They also viewed the large entrepreneurs as the beneficiaries of the new economic model, which added to the antagonism already directed toward that traditionally upper-class group.[7]

Between 1975 and 1980, conflicts occurred between the two entrepreneurial sectors and between entrepreneurs and the government, but there was no open and public confrontation.[8] There are three reasons why a confrontation was avoided. First, despite a negative impact on small and medium-sized enterprises, government discourse that affirmed the necessity to accept drastic economic measures for the sake of "future prosperity" was still effective.[9] Second, the economic "boom" that began in 1978 created an artificial, yet significant, climate of prosperity. Third, economic criticisms not-withstanding, entrepreneurs and their organizations continued to give strong political support to the military government.

In spite of these factors, which weakened the visibility and the criticisms by those entrepreneurial groups that were affected most by the economic model, business groups in general were able to bring important problems before the government. There was, for example, the need to define the "strategic character" of some economic activities, such as food production, as part of a broader national security policy. Entrepreneurs argued that Chile should develop self-sufficiency in food production in order to protect itself from the instability of international commerce. Also, the national industry crisis was increasing Chile's foreign dependence. Entrepreneurs argued that the economic model was destroying the country's industrial base and dismantling a development effort that had been initiated some forty years earlier.[10] Business groups were also concerned about the "dualistic" character of the effects of the economic model. Entrepreneurs argued that the insertion of economic activities into a free-market model created a dichotomy between "successful" and "unsuccessful" areas of the economy. This led, they argued, to uneven development, unemployment, exclusion, and dangerous social tensions.[11]

Frequent clashes took place between the entrepreneurial sectors and the government over these three points, but the disagreements did not degenerate into generalized and open conflicts. The most active groups in the disputes were truckowners, merchants, small and medium-sized landowners, and some industrialists. The entrepreneurs and their organizations even entertained the idea of submitting a new "Demand of Chile," referring to the letter presented to the Allende administration in 1972 that had served as the economic, social, and political basis for their struggle against the Popular Unity government.

The plebiscite for approving the 1980 constitution partially placated these economic criticisms. The majority of the entrepreneurial organizations supported the military regime's constitutional project. This support was unrestricted among the large entrepreneurs. Small and medium-sized entrepreneurs supported the regime politically, but maintained their economic discrepancies.[12]

The triumph of the government's constitutional project weakened the ability of the most critical entrepreneurs to express their opposition to the economic model. This lasted until mid–1981, when the first serious sign of the crisis of the economic model occurred—the bankruptcy of the Viña del Mar Sugar Refinery Company (CRAV-CRAVAL). From then on, the entrepreneurial protests reappeared and acquired more force than they had during the 1975–80 period.

The Entrepreneurial Revolt, 1981–1983

The onset of the economic crisis activated the protests of the entrepreneurs that were most affected by the economic model.[13] Contrary to the previous period, the crisis had now touched even the most successful entrepreneurial groups. Until 1980, the Ross group, for example, was ranked among the nation's top twenty private business groups. When the group declared bankruptcy during the economic crash, it was a blow to the heart of the economic system.[14] This event caused a resurgence of criticisms about the economic model that had been in place since 1975. The model's credibility was seriously questioned, diminishing the exhilaration over the economic "boom."

The international recession of the early 1980s seriously affected the Chilean economy. Chile's dependence on foreign credit, the lack of productive investment, and the breakdown of its industrial and agricultural base made the nation particularly vulnerable to the effects of the recession. All of these elements made up the foundation for the "entrepreneurial revolt" headed by the organizations of the small and medium-sized entrepreneurs, joined occasionally by the large industrial and agricultural entrepreneurs. The government reacted by declaring that the internal and foreign crises were temporary and did not require policy changes, much less alterations of the economic model. The adjustments would be, for the most part, "automatic." The CPC agreed with this interpretation, especially during 1981. Although criticisms of that position later arose, especially from the SNA and the Association of Metallurgic Industries (ASIMET), the associations of large entrepreneurs linked with the CPC never truly disassociated themselves from the the government's view of the crisis.

The organizations of the small and medium-sized entrepreneurs, reacted strongly. They argued that the crisis was not transitory but that it revealed the economic model's structural deficiencies. They also reactivated the organizations that had given them strength in the struggle against the Popular Unity government. At the end of 1981, they proposed the reconstitution of a confederation that was similar to the 1972 National Command for Entrepreneurial Action. Their goal was to achieve organizational forms that would allow them to confront the crisis and pressure the government and the large entrepreneurs who supported its policies. The confederation was to include both professionals and labor unions.

Even though the confederation did not fully materialize, the initiative could claim some success. For example, agriculturalists, truckowners, and merchants carried out a number of joint activities beginning in 1982.[15] These activities went beyond the 1981 declarations. Entrepreneurs began to suspend payments on their debts, auction their property, organize truckowner and merchant strikes in provincial cities, and plan for a national strike. The pressure on the government was intense. In February 1982, *El Mercurio* editorialized that "although taking the form of an economic critique, this really is a political debate. . . . The intensity of this debate indicates that there will be [important] political consequences."

The actions of these entrepreneurs were prompted by their indebtedness to state and private banks, but their demands were also aimed at the replacement of the civilians who directed the nation's economic policy.[16] These demands were highly political, since the Chicago Boys represented more than just an economic team and were in reality an important component of the military regime's political program.

The situation deteriorated until October 1982, when entrepreneurial organizations that were critical of government policies took more decisive actions. They began with the *Declaración de Valdivia* (the Valdivia Proclamation) of October 23, 1982. Although the proclamation originated in the southern city of Valdivia, it was an expression of national entrepreneurial discontent that had been accumulating since 1981. The proclamation declared:

We view with profound alarm the destruction of the entire agricultural and industrial productive apparatus. . . . The liquidation of assets . . . is generating social chaos in the form of unemployment for thousands of Chileans. This process ultimately leads to the disappearance of an entire entrepreneurial class, with all the political and social consequences it signifies for the country's future. . . . The long-term interests of the Republic require the preservation of the national patrimony, the survival of the productive sector, and the survival of labor-generating activities. . . . We hold economic policy makers responsible for the breakdown of the national productive apparatus and for the transfer of resources from the productive sector to the financial system.[17]

The proclamation was supported by nearly all organizations that represented small and medium-sized entrepreneurs, especially those in the south. Indebted entrepreneurs began to disrupt the auctions of agricultural and industrial properties, and they organized street demonstrations in Lanco, Valdivia, Osorno, and Temuco. Many of the demonstrations resulted in violent confrontations with the police and representatives of the creditor banks.

The Valdivia Proclamation was followed by the *Declaración de Rancagua* on November 22, 1982. The new proclamation reaffirmed the position taken in the Valdivia Proclamation, scheduled a National Assembly of Entrepreneurs in Temuco for December 3, and invited opposition labor unions such as the National Union Command (CNS) and the Workers' Democratic Union (UDT) to participate. In the meantime, protest activities and mobilizations continued. The primary objectives of the Temuco convention were to strengthen organizations through the incorporation of labor unions and to prepare a broader proposal calling for a "political opening" to ensure citizen participation in economic decisions. Some leaders even proposed the creation of a parliament that would place checks on government power.

Large entrepreneurs affiliated with the CPC had remained aloof during this process. They were trying to establish direct negotiations with the military government and were against direct mobilization. The CPC responded to the invitation to join the Temuco convention by stating that its members would support the entrepreneurial confederation "only if their intentions were purely business-related" but not if their intentions were political.[18] They were afraid of the political consequences resulting from the Temuco convention.

The government reacted harshly to the call for business people to gather in Temuco, suspecting that economic criticism could turn into political criticism. Exasperated by the entrepreneurs' mobilizations, protests, and invitations to labor unions, the government interpreted these activities as opposition to the regime. Consequently, the government ordered police to block the entrance to the facilities of the Society for Agricultural Development (SOFO) in Temuco, the site of the convention. Two days later, organizer Carlos Podlech, leader of the National Association of Wheat Producers (ANPT), and CNS leader Manuel Bustos were expelled from the country.

The government's response demonstrated the magnitude of the threat presented by entrepreneurial discontent. That threat had to be eliminated, even at the cost of a break with the sector of entrepreneurs that had been key to installing the military regime in 1973. During the following months and until May 1983, entrepreneurs made various attempts at protesting and mobilizing. They even proposed a general work stoppage. The government responded harshly and threatened to use force against those entrepreneurial leaders who "waged politics." At the same time, it offered partial solutions to the problem of indebtedness in an attempt to weaken the entrepreneurial mobilization. This strategy effectively diffused entrepreneurial cohesion due to both fear and accommodation to government offers. Also influential was the failure of the critical entrepreneurial group to obtain the support of the CPC, even though the crisis had deeply affected industrialists affiliated with the SOFOFA and some members of the SNA.

The government's methods of economic and political pressure for some and cooptation for others, as well as the withdrawal (if not the opposition) of the large entrepreneurs, slowly diluted the mobilization. The costs of confronting both obstacles became too high for the organizations of small and medium-sized entrepreneurs. Their defeat transferred the initiative of entrepreneurial action to the organizations of large entrepreneurs in the CPC.

In 1981, the CPC had proposed to the government a plan for handling the economic crisis. The purpose of the plan was to work with the government in order to avoid confrontations. The defeat of the more critical entrepreneurs reinforced the approach taken by the large entrepreneurs. Thus, the historical relationship of dominance of this sector over the organizations of the small and medium-sized enterprises was reestablished.

Various factors pushed the large entrepreneurs even closer to the government. In particular, the emergence of intense opposition activity in May 1983, led by the copper workers' union and joined by many other social sectors, put the military regime in a serious political predicament. Large entrepreneurs viewed opposition activity as a threat of destabilization and thus closed ranks with the government.

Entrepreneurial Activity from
1983 to the Plebiscite

The years between 1983 and 1988 can be seen as two periods. The first, from 1983 to 1985, marked a time when the organizations of large entrepreneurs took the initiative for confronting both the economic crisis and the political situation that resulted from the "protests" of 1983. This initiative consisted of an emphasis on "economic reactivation" developed in conjunction with the government and involved support for a political opening administered by the regime according to the terms of the 1980 constitution. The second period, from 1986 to 1988, marked the emergence of an entrepreneurial ideology that attempted to turn the entrepreneur into a central figure in Chilean society. The development of this ideology was facilitated by the reactivation of the economy and the consolidation of the position of entrepreneurs in the larger spectrum of business activity. By 1988, entrepreneurs were no longer defensive actors; they aggressively competed for a place in society.

The Negotiated Reactivation, 1983–1986

The organizations that represented the large entrepreneurs had agreed with the government that the 1981 economic crisis was a temporary problem. As the crisis worsened, critics of this position began speaking out within the organizations. Because of these discrepancies and the mobilizations of small and medium-sized entrepreneurs, large entrepreneurs admitted that the crisis was serious and needed a reassessment. But they feared that their recognition of the problem could damage the military regime and lead to political instability.

The change in attitude was prompted by two important events. The first was the election on July 29, 1982, of Jorge Fontaine as president of the CPC and of Ernesto Ayala as president of the SOFOFA. Fontaine had led the CPC during the final years of the Popular Unity goverment and was regarded as an appropriate figure for dealing with "periods of crisis." Ayala represented the entrepreneurial "old guard" that had been closely linked to the administration of Jorge Alessandri. Although both leaders were decidedly government supporters, they differed from their predecessors in that they had stronger and more independent personalities. Previous leaders had been more accommodating to the military government and had not given much emphasis to the autonomy that entrepreneurs affiliated with the CPC and the SOFOFA now required in order to confront the economic crisis. Naturally, this autonomy did not involve opposition to the government but was seen as necessary for strengthening entrepreneurial organizations and making their views heard by the government. Fontaine and Ayala advanced the view that the entrepreneurial sector had more clarity than the government about the means needed to overcome the economic crisis. The government was perceived as married to the excessive dogmatism of the Chicago Boys and their theory of "automatic adjustment." For their part, Fontaine and Ayala believed that more pragmatism was needed to save the economic model.

The second event was the public declaration by the CPC on December 4, 1982, and again on January 6, 1983, that acknowledged the seriousness of the crisis. They also announced the need for an "Entrepreneurial Program" that represented their position.[19] Nevertheless, there were serious internal differences among the various sectors of the CPC, particularly because each sector tried to protect its own narrow interests. As a result, the development of a comprehensive Entrepreneurial Program was delayed. Only in June of 1983 did a document entitled "Towards Financial Normalization" appear. In July, after numerous debates, entrepreneurs agreed on a document entitled "Economic Recovery: Analysis and Proposals," which revealed that the entrepreneurs differed with the government on matters of economic policy. Between 1983 and 1984, the entrepreneurs and the government confronted each other, although without questioning what both called "the foundations of the model." But the government was unwilling to make substantial modifications in its economic program, and none of the entrepreneurs' proposals was accepted.[20]

Even though the business sector represented by the CPC failed to implement its overall Entrepreneurial Program and had to negotiate its proposals in piecemeal fashion during the 1983–85 period, it was still able to gain some influence. Even before the presentation of its program, for example, had industrialist Manuel Martín appointed minister of economy in February 1983. Subsequently, the entrepreneurial sector succeeded in having the construction entrepreneur Modesto Collados named minister of housing, and, later, minister of economy. In 1985, the new minister of economy was another entrepreneur, Manuel Délano, who had headed the Chamber of Commerce. In 1984, Jorge Prado, a leader of the SNA, became minister of agriculture; and in 1986, Samuel Lira, former president of the National Society of Mining, became minister of mining.

The government maintained an ambiguous line in matters of economic policy during this period. At times, it favored the orthodox line of the Chicago Boys, who had a significant presence in the Ministry of Finance. At other times, the regime favored the more pragmatic position of the entrepreneurs. This ambiguity was resolved in 1985 when Hernán Büchi became minister of finance, as he struck a balance between the views of the Chicago Boys and the entrepreneurs.

Also during this period, the government sought to achieve a balance between the large entrepreneurs and the protagonists of the "entrepreneurial revolt" of 1982. Even though the small and medium-sized entrepreneurs had been defeated, they were still important to the government. The appointment of Sergio Onofre Jarpa as minister of the interior in 1983 was intended not only to open negotiations with the opposition, but also to mollify the small and medium-sized entrepreneurs (above all the truckowners) who trusted Jarpa. Jarpa had been president of the Democratic Confederation (CODE), which had united the political parties opposed to Allende from 1972 to 1973. From that position, Jarpa had established close relations with entrepreneurial organizations and was accepted as a reliable leader by the representatives of the merchants, truckowners, and small and medium-sized landowners. Also, the appointment of a new finance minister in April 1984 sent an encouraging signal to owners of small entriprises, as Minister Luis Escobar was in favor of providing them with greater state protection.

The process of "negotiated reactivation" was fairly complex. Precisely because of its policy of balancing the different tendencies in the business community, the government kept changing its methods of confronting the crisis. CPC-affiliated entrepreneurs repeatedly reminded the government of the need for a coherent economic policy based on a long-term plan. By mid-1984, the government had formulated a three-year plan (1984-86), which incorporated many of the entrepreneurs' proposals. This plan included agricultural and mining investments, a policy of job expansion, and an increase in import tariffs in order to protect national industry (from 20 to 35 percent).

Nevertheless, entrepreneurs continued to insist on the need to broaden the scope of the economic measures. In particular, they called for agricultural policies designed to help the most depressed areas of agricultural production and the development of government purchasing programs. They encouraged the devaluation of the peso in order to establish an exchange rate that would favor exports. They also urged the government to find a solution to the problem of entrepreneurial indebtedness and to regularize the banking system, in which the government had intervened in 1983.[21] Negotiations between the entrepreneurs and the government were long and at times difficult. One of the most conflict-ridden areas of the negotiations was tariff policy. The government had agreed to raise tariffs from 20 to 35 percent, but the majority of entrepreneurs favored differential tariffs oscillating between zero and 35 percent. The entrepreneurs favored a flexible tariff policy because some constituents benefited from low tariffs and others from higher ones. The controversy on this point was serious enough to involve discrepancies within the government itself.

The level of conflict that characterized the negotiation process was exacerbated by disagreements among entrepreneurs. The defense of narrow sectoral and corporate interests hindered the achievement of consensus with the government. It also hampered the unity that leaders like CPC President Fontaine attempted to provide to entrepreneurs. Toward the end of 1984, General Pinochet asked the entrepreneurs to reach a "minimum consensus" in order to overcome a crisis that threatened the stability of the government. The consensus was reached in 1985, when Büchi was appointed minister of finance.

Büchi welcomed the calls for the devaluation of the peso. He reduced tariffs, first to 30 percent and later to 20 percent (as a compromise solution to the demand for differential tariffs), and set in motion the process of reprivatization of the intervened-in banks. In agriculture, he applied a three-year plan, fixed prices, developed government purchasing programs, and rescheduled debts. These measures contributed to the relative success of the government's policy, which combined with the first signs of economic reactivation and eased the tensions between the government and the entrepreneurs. On February 28, 1985, the CPC, the SNA, and the Chilean Construction Council (CCHC) made a joint public declaration that government policy was moving in the right direction by contributing to the consolidation of the private sector.

Only a few business groups—including members of ASIMET, the small merchants, and the transportation sector—maintained a critical position toward the government. They believed that the economic reactivation did not favor national industry and that small and medium-sized firms continued to operate under depressed conditions. In June 1985, these sectors attempted to reconstitute a new confederation in order to advance their views. Some participated in the protests of the opposition and joined the Civic Assembly in 1986.[22] Nevertheless, the inability of these groups to achieve substantial results pushed them closer to the policies of the large entrepreneurs.

Taking advantage of the legitimacy and prestige achieved by their agreements with the government, the leaders of the CPC and SOFOFA sought to strengthen the political and ideological aspects of entrepreneurial leadership. These leaders considered the economic reactivation of 1985 as a product of the pragmatic policy that they had proposed to the government. Consequently, they disseminated the image of entrepreneurs as being responsible for solving the economic crisis.

Entrepreneurial strategy then turned to the development of a socially oriented discourse. The entrepreneurs concentrated on the employment problem and insisted on the "social" aspects, if not the advantages, of the free-market economy. Private enterprise was presented as the engine of development and as the locus for the achievement of "social harmony." At the same time, the private sector was depicted as the bearer of the country's modernization and was assigned a principal role in inserting Chile into the world economy through exports. The entrepreneurs were summoned by their interest organizations to disseminate and defend "the success of private enterprise." As Fernando Aguero, vice-president of SOFOFA, put it in a speech to the organization on January 24, 1985, "Entrepreneurs must constantly appear before the general public, the universities, and all centers of influence, to proclaim the truth about private enterprise. . . . in this way there will be more people sharing our ideas."

It is in the context of these ideological developments that entrepreneurs in August 1985 invited opposition union leaders of the CDT and CNT to discuss a "social partnership" between workers and entrepreneurs. The invitation was received positively and meetings took place with the participation of Manuel Bustos, leader of the CNT, and Eduardo Ríos, president of the CDT. Even though specific agreements were not reached, the entrepreneurs were able to convey an image of political pluralism to the public. Likewise, the annual National Meeting of Entrepreneurs (ENADE) in 1985 concentrated on social themes (employment, social harmony) and, for the first time, approached political themes, including the transition to democracy. Entrepreneurs endorsed the timetable established in the 1980 constitution and called on their peers to consider that the "social harmony necessary for a peaceful transition" could only be achieved by increases in salary and employment levels.[23]

The process of "negotiated reactivation" put the CPC in a position to provide solid entrepreneurial leadership. Nineteen-eighty-five was a year of intense political struggles involving the massive mobilization of students and shantytown dwellers. In September, the "National Accord" was formed, in which some political leaders of the democratic right joined for the first time with leaders of the center and center-left to achieve the consensus necessary to facilitate the transition to democracy. Entrepreneurs, for their part, attempted to play an active role in defending the existing economic and social order. They strengthened their leadership and developed a socially oriented discourse. The three years following 1985 were marked by this strategy.

The Battle of Ideas, 1986–1989:
Entrepreneurs as Central Actors?

In *La empresa de la libertad*, CPC president Manuel Feliú quoted Spanish entrepreneur Alfredo de Molinas: "we will be unable to raise the GNP if we fail to share the principles of free enterprise with the rest of the population. Development will continue to be weak and ephemeral. . . . It is not enough to be the motors of development; it is also necessary to win the battle of ideas."[24] This quotation illustrates the perspective with which the entrepreneurs approached the social and political processes of the period from 1986 to 1989. Business leaders had attempted to change the image of entrepreneurs from one that emphasized personal economic gain and corporate competitiveness to one that promoted them as the instigators of social and economic development as well as active advocates of social harmony. Their aim was to preserve the social and economic model imposed by the military regime.

We can argue over whether this strategy was only a means to present the entrepreneurs as supporters of the government or if reflected true convictions, but it is most likely that both elements were present. What is clear during the last period of the military government is that entrepreneurs assumed ideological positions that were designed to attract public support. Although they were critical of the Chicago Boys, entrepreneurs drew from the economists' positions ideas that appeared to be supported by "modern science." Likewise, the preeminence of neo-liberal currents worldwide and the crisis of socialist views also influenced entrepreneurs and prompted them to compete more aggressively in the "battle of ideas."

The new entrepreneurial discourse promoted the diffusion of an optimistic outlook regarding the economic development of the country, wherein entrepreneurs argued that the current economic model was the "only one capable" of overcoming underdevelopment. It presented entrepreneurs and private enterprise as the "motor" of this economic model and, therefore, of development and modernization. It advanced "economic freedom" as the basis of political freedom and presented entrepreneurs and private enterprise as central actors in the production and distribution of goods, the main basis of social harmony. The new discourse advanced the idea of the freedom to undertake economic activity as the foundation of modernization and progress, while the state served as the creator and preserver of favorable conditions for this liberty and as the protector of the weakest economic and social sectors. It defended the search for profit and wealth as a legitimate social objective, which permitted the development of the enterprising spirit that is essential for modernization and progress. And it presented entrepreneurs as being genuinely interested in democracy; enterprise develops best under a democratic system, provided that the system is modern and assures the freedom to engage in entrepreneurial activity. Most of these concepts have always formed part of entrepreneurial discourse in many countries. What was new in the Chilean case was that, for the first time, entrepreneurs developed these ideas for use in public discourse.

The strategy for the development of ideological cohesion was in place by 1986. Invitations were extended to opposition parties to discuss their economic and social programs, and entrepreneurial leaders publicly responded to the programmatic proposals of the political parties. Entrepreneurs made a concerted effort to disseminate their ideological views in the press and through their own communications media. The press understood that there had been a change in entrepreneurial strategy and reported frequently on the entrepreneurs' ideological positions.

The most important development of the period was the entrepreneurial emphasis on massive gatherings, which served as vehicles for promoting entrepreneurial ideology. This policy of dissemination gained importance after Manuel Feliú was elected president of the CPC.[25] Feliú was an appropriate leader for the organization because of his early participation in the development of an ideological agenda and his political and organizational skills.

During 1986, the CPC brought Alfredo de Molinas, a Spanish entrepreneur and vice-president of the Spanish Confederation of Business Organizations (CEOE), to Chile. He was introduced as a qualified representative of the same ideological views espoused by the Chilean entrepreneurs. De Molinas became the mentor of leaders like Feliú and held various "indoctrination" sessions with the nation's business leaders. His public conferences were widely covered by the press.

In August 1986, the First Meeting of Northern Entrepreneurs was held, bringing together a large number of entrepreneurs from northern Chile. The congress concentrated on both ideological and corporate themes. During the same month, the CPC convened the leaders of all its affiliated branches in Viña del Mar in order to elaborate a "long-term proposal" regarding its strategy of ideological and political diffusion.[26] Also in August, the New Entrepreneurs Congress took place. The congress was directed toward young people, and was intended to promote "a spirit of enterprise" among them. Organizers of the meeting invited Carl Dieter Osterman, president of the Young German Entrepreneurs; Juan Rosell, president of the Young Business Initiative of Spain; and Iván Bardina, a young Chilean entrepreneur and founder of an important computer firm in California's Silicon Valley. At the meeting, Manuel Feliú stated: "We will never allow that creating enterprises, making profits, getting ahead, and living better as a result of our labor be a motive of shame and insult in our society. . . . Only by encouraging entrepreneurial activity can we have an active and developed society."[27]

These events culminated in the November 1986 meeting of ENADE, which brought a large number of business leaders together under the slogan, "the entrepreneur—motor of development."[28] In describing the objectives of this meeting to the press, the president of the CPC stated:

this is the first time that the private sector will attempt to define the place of entrepreneurs in society. We are focusing on the future, not on narrow economic themes as has been the case in the past. . . . We are seeking to present a comprehensive economic, social, and political program. . . . We must prepare ourselves for a future in which entrepreneurs will play a critical role in Chilean development.[29]

The "ideological campaign" of 1986 had the important effect of motivating the entrepreneurs to address social issues and to take a more active role in society and politics. Also, because of the ENADE meeting, entrepreneurs knew that they had to develop a profile of social concern for the 1988 plebiscite if they were to avoid the image of being mere beneficiaries of the military regime. This was a crucial realization.

As a consequence, the entrepreneurs concentrated on two main activities. The first was ideological and concerned the advancement of liberal discourse. The second was political and involved the defense of a military regime that largely accounted for the entrepreneurs' own unity. The combination of these two aspects characterized entrepreneurial behavior during the 1987–88 period.

The Entrepreneurs during the 1987–1988 Plebiscite Campaign

The CPC provided the leadership for entrepreneurs during the plebiscite campaign. It was one of the most decisive civilian supporters of the government, but there were still several entrepreneurial groups that did not support the CPC strategy. These groups included members of metallurgical organizations, truckowners, and small merchants, who continued to maintain that the reactivation had not benefited their constituencies and that the government had an inadequate social policy. These groups insisted that the return to democracy should be accelerated. Some truckowners and merchants continued to participate in the Civic Assembly, and they later supported the Broad Social Agreement (ACUSO). They had little effect in the campaign, however, because they could not publicly announce their support of the opposition. Although they were critical of government policy, they were unwilling to be perceived as part of the opposition.

Another small group of entrepreneurs formed "Entrepreneurs for Democracy" in August 1988. This organization represented small entrepreneurs, many of whom had previously supported the Popular Unity government and who founded firms as a means of subsistence after 1973, and executives of corporations who belonged to opposition parties. The Entrepreneurs for Democracy achieved political visibility as an opposition sector, but they did not carry much weight in the business world. And finally, the Social Union of Christian Entrepreneurs (USEC) incorporated Catholic entrepreneurs and executives who had links to the Church. This group remained neutral and did not follow the leadership of the CPC. Like Entrepreneurs for Democracy, this group was limited in size and in the influence it had on entrepreneurs in general. These small organizations offered little competition and the entrepreneurial leadership of the CPC was not truly challenged.

The CPC followed two complementary policies. One was ideological and was expressed through the strategy of the "battle of ideas." The other was political and was manifest through a policy of explicit government support. The CPC ideology was developed through the CPC and an ad hoc organization called "Entrepreneurs for Development" (created in June 1988), which was composed of leaders of the CPC, the SOFOFA, and the Council of Small and Medium-Sized Enterprises. The organization's political policy was developed through Civic Committees and was led by former CPC President Jorge Fontaine. The Civic Committees were formed in August 1987; and although they declared themselves "independent," they admitted to being "groups identified with the principles of [the military] government."[30] Both campaign approaches, but particularly the ideological one, had as their central theme the "progress and modernization" that, according to the entrepreneurs, the country had reached because of the military regime and its economic and social model.

The entrepreneurs emphasized the regime's economic and social accomplishments and muted its authoritarian character and repressive practices. They did not wish to be associated with the dictatorial aspects of the government but rather with its modernization and perceived success. Moreover, they tried to present entrepreneurs and private enterprise as the principal representatives of the modern state. They proposed an advance toward a "liberal order" and what they called a "free society" founded on the capacity to engage in entrepreneurial activity and become integrated into the modern world. In this respect, Pinochet's candidacy became a serious problem for many entrepreneurs, because he was associated with both dictatorship and modernization. Nevertheless, the entrepreneurs accepted Pinochet's candidacy for fear that any other candidate would fail to maintain the social and economic model.

In addition to "modernization," the ideological campaign also concentrated on the "social role of the entrepreneur." The ENADE meeting in 1987, for instance, emphasized "the human factor in business." This slogan underscored the entrepreneurial desire to better the image of business in society by emphasizing improvements in labor relations within the firm and in the distribution of benefits. Entrepreneurs reaffirmed the ideological view advanced in 1986, which made progress and social harmony key concepts in defining their relation to society. As CPC President Manuel Feliú stated at ENADE'87, "we must strive for the values, principles, and above all the benefits of free enterprise to be shared by the majority of our compatriots. . . . We must contribute to solving the problems of the poor . . . share benefits . . . and restrain excessive consumption."[31]

CPC leaders presented these views frequently in 1987 and 1988. They made constant mention of social problems and promoted measures to increase employment and raise salaries. They called on entrepreneurs to play a dominant role in the nation's social and political life, to defend their ideology, and to not give up the leadership position they had already achieved. The CPC organized meetings with university students and young entrepreneurs, promoted the creation of new enterprises, and proposed an entrepreneurial plan to hire apprentices.

The CPC's actions provided the basis for the creation of "Entrepreneurs for Development," an entity that directed the "battle of ideas" after June 1988. This organization produced a document called "Commitment to Freedom," which became the entrepreneurs' declaration of ideological principles. The "Commitment to Freedom" called for: freedom of enterprise, a free market, free competition, and free trade. The declaration also proclaimed the entrepreneurs' support for a subsidiary state founded on the law and supported the principles of solidarity and work for the common good.

This widely distributed document informed all public declarations by CPC entrepreneurs. According to its promoters, the Entrepreneurs for Development would concentrate on events in 1988 but would also promote and disseminate entrepreneurial views beyond the plebiscite. This organization, which eventually included representation in the provinces, led entrepreneurial action for the remainder of the campaign.

The Civic Committees provided direct political support to Pinochet's candidacy. As opposed to Entrepreneurs for Development, which concentrated on ideological messages more than on support for a candidate, these Civic Committees fully participated in the political campaign. The committees carried out social solidarity actions, especially in the poorest urban areas. One initiative was the creation of a "Solidarity Foundation" that was designed to bring groups of entrepreneurs into closer contact with the poor.

Until shortly before the plebiscite, both the Entrepreneurs for Development and the Civic Committees maintained a campaign line that emphasized progress and the promise of the future. When polls showed that the opposition could win, they changed this line and began to use elements of a "Campaign of Terror," pointing to the dangers the country would face if the "Yes" option for Pinochet were defeated. This demonstrated that entrepreneurs, despite their modernizing and future-oriented discourse, were still haunted by old fears. By the time the plebiscite was held, entrepreneurs were torn between their ideological optimism and their fear of the social powers represented by the opposition.

Entrepreneurs in the Post-Plebiscite Period

On October 5, 1988, the opposition won the plebiscite by a wide margin. The stock market experienced drops of 11 percent and 16 percent in value by October 6, but it quickly returned to normal. Predictions of economic chaos resulting from an opposition victory had not been realized. Leading entrepreneurs recognized the results of the plebiscite and issued calls for calm and unity.[32]

Entrepreneurs were initially fearful and uncertain. Many thought that the government would win the plebiscite despite public opinion polls. Also, many entrepreneurs feared retaliation from the opposition because of their close association with the government. Nevertheless, the political tranquility that followed the plebiscite and the continuation of military rule until March 1990 contributed to the entrepreneurs' changing attitude.

At this point, three tendencies developed among the entrepreneurs. The first can be called a "corporate retreat" of an individualistic type, as many entrepreneurs concentrated on their particular corporate interests in case the political situation deteriorated. These entrepreneurs postponed investment decisions and explored opportunities in other countries. They halted all of their public activity, and some dismissed opposition union leaders from their companies in order to prevent future conflicts.[33]

The second tendency involved the re-emergence of the critical entrepreneurial sectors that had been overshadowed by the CPC leadership during the previous three years. During the last months of 1988 and the early months of 1989, these groups reformulated their views and strengthened their organizations. The Association of Exporters of Nontraditional Manufactured Goods (ASEXMA), headed by ASIMET past president Gustavo Randohr, combined the defense of national industry with an interest in issues of social and economic equity. Other groups included representatives (especially truckowners and merchants) of the heavily indebted small and medium-sized enterprises. Although these groups experienced a significant revival, they were still far from overcoming the disarticulation they suffered in 1983.

The third and most important of these tendencies involved the reactivation of the "battle of ideas." This tendency persisted in the effort to make entrepreneurs strong social actors, capable of overcoming the plebiscite defeat and preparing for the defense of entrepreneurial interests in the 1989 elections. With this tendency, the entrepreneurs demonstrated a capacity for rapid reactivation under the leadership of CPC President Manuel Feliú after October 1988. This powerful entrepreneurial sector poised itself to play an active role in the presidential and parliamentary campaign. As Feliú stated, "If the right or center right is politically incapable of effectively defending free society, we the entrepreneurs should assume this role."[34]

The strategy of the CPC centered on four principal lines: (1) strengthening efforts of ideological dissemination among entrepreneurial organizations as well as public opinion; (2) opening discussions with labor unions; (3) emphasizing the social role of the entrepreneur, especially with respect to labor relations; and (4) challenging the opposition political parties to define their views concerning the role of private enterprise, the market economy, and the current economic model.

The CPC took political initiatives that were designed to win concessions prior to the 1989 elections and to achieve the maximum organizational and ideological strength to confront the future. As opposed to the entrepreneurial behavior displayed in 1970, when they initially sought accommodation with the Allende government, entrepreneurs now planned on playing the role of strong interlocutors with a well-defined project. Because Pinochet was no longer a decisive factor, as he was before the plebiscite, it became easier for entrepreneurs to emphasize the modernizing aspects of the military government. Without Pinochet, the "liberal order" and the "free society" had better chances of success.

Soon after the plebiscite was held, the CPC moved to strengthen Entrepreneurs for Development, the principal instrument of the "battle of ideas." This organization coined the slogan, "A free society, the great enterprise of all Chileans," and ENADE '88 convened under the theme "a commitment to freedom and development." At the ENADE meeting, Manuel Feliú called on entrepreneurs to become involved in the political and social process. As he put it, "we must prepare for the year before the elections by assuming a leading role in the battle of ideas. The task of the entrepreneurs . . . will be to examine the proposals of the parties and make our opinions known."[35]

In November 1988, the CPC invited the labor federations CUT and CDT to engage in a dialogue with entrepreneurs concerning a new social arrangement. Only the CDT attended, but the event gave business leaders an opportunity to demonstrate that they were actively interested in dialogue with the workers. Entrepreneurs also engaged in a press campaign to demand that the opposition parties define their positions on the role of private enterprise. They also expressed their concern on matters of salary, employment, and labor relations. It is clear from these actions that entrepreneurs viewed the development of a greater social sensitivity as the key to winning the "battle of ideas." They knew that their legitimacy was weak and that they could not convincingly defend the existing social and economic system unless they showed that they could help improve the quality of life of most Chileans. Because of this, they were well-disposed to offer economic and labor improvements. Entrepreneurs were aware that, insofar as entrepreneurs had failed to improve on their social image, the government and its supporters blamed them for the plebiscite defeat. They responded to this charge by emphasizing their accomplishments since 1986, but they realized that they needed to do much more.

Leaders like Manuel Feliú and others understood this for some time and were keen on changing society's image of the entrepreneur. They relied on two important assets: (1) the economic success that they believed the economic model had achieved and (2) the ideological discourse that united them, at least symbolically. Despite defeat in the plebiscite, entrepreneurial leaders believed that these assets would allow them to become central actors in the social and political process. Their goal was to rally entrepreneurs behind a cultural, as opposed to a narrowly defined economic, revolution. They met some obstacles in the corporatism and short-term interests of some entrepreneurs, but the position gained strength among their leadership. This new development will undoubtedly make entrepreneurs significant actors in the national political process.

Conclusion

Large entrepreneurs have acquired an ideological presence that is more consistent and aggressive than ever before.[36] They have moved from a defensive posture that concentrated on narrow corporate and short-term political interests to one that supports decisive intervention in larger political, economic, and social matters. Today, entrepreneurs offer an ideology that is designed to compete with the developmentalist and socialist ideologies of previous years. Entrepreneurs no longer view themselves as subordinated to a "social ethic" that questioned their financial motives and viewed their activity as detrimental to the common good. They now believe that the pursuit of profit and wealth *is* the engine of progress and that all of society benefits from this pursuit. This ideological confidence provides entrepreneurs with a high level of organizational consistency and strength.

Entrepreneurial organizations now have leaders who enjoy high public visibility and who are convinced that entrepreneurs have won and must play a significant role in society. They have been able to strengthen their organizations and provide them with a strategy. Their goal has been not only to play a part in the 1989 elections, but also to have an active role in the defense of their ideology and their sectoral interests thereafter. They view themselves as actors who should gain hegemony in society. And they are keen to convince the public, politicians, workers,[37] and the youth of the benefits of the "liberal order," of which they feel they are the principal protagonists. Entrepreneurs are ready to play this role independently of the political parties of the right, especially if those parties prove to be weak or unable to perform it themselves.

Because Pinochet was a liability, entrepreneurs benefited somewhat from his loss of political stature. Their credibility had been compromised by association with the dictator, but they can now advance the themes of "modernization and progress" more freely.

Large entrepreneurs are likely to emerge as powerful interlocutors with the new democratic government. Their power is based on the existence of an important private sector, national or foreign, that is not dependent on the state and that enjoys sufficient autonomy to question state policies. This is why entrepreneurs supported the privatization of large public enterprises and sought a solution to entrepreneurial indebtedness before the end of 1989.

Entrepreneurs are also trying to reach an agreement with the unions in order to achieve "labor peace." They are not attempting to establish agreements at the national level but at the company level. Another entrepreneurial objective is to increase their presence at universities and professional institutes. Their "battle of ideas" targets those groups that are likely to become the intellectual and technical leaders of Chilean society.

Nevertheless, in pursuing their strategy to achieve a relevant role in society, entrepreneurs also face some obstacles. First, entrepreneurs suffer from low esteem in public opinion polls. Even though they succeeded in promoting a more modern image of themselves, they are still not perceived as a group that is genuinely interested in the social welfare of their country. Furthermore, the entrepreneurs' effort to distance themselves from the repressive aspects of the military regime has not been very successful. Especially among young people, entrepreneurs continue to be perceived as "allies of Pinochet."

Second, although large entrepreneurs have attracted an important segment of the small and medium-sized businesspeople to their ideological position, there is still a strong anti neo-liberal current among that group. Owners of small and medium-sized enterprises continue to believe that they are among the groups most harmed by the economic model.[38] Furthermore, a nationalist ideology that favors state action is still strong among the smaller entrepreneurs. They reject the extreme liberalization of the market, the unregulated subjection of Chile to international economic forces, and the stripping away of the strategic and developmental role of the state. Not only does a corporatist ideology remain strong in this group, but its members also resent the repression of their organizations and the lack of support they received from the large entrepreneurs during trying times. Chile's smaller entrepreneurs may seek to establish a corporatist link to the new democratic regime in order to recover some of their power.

If small and medium-sized entrepreneurs do not endorse the strategy of the large entrepreneurs, then the CPC will probably lose significant social strength. Politically, this strength can be decisive when dealing with a democratic government, as was the case during the Popular Unity period. It is possible that these smaller entrepreneurs will negotiate their interests in a pragmatic manner with the democratic government, an approach that is not shared by the more ideological groups affiliated with the CPC.

Third, although the entrepreneurial sector linked to the CPC has achieved a significant social and political presence, it still requires strong political support. The National Renovation party (RN), the Independent Democratic Union (UDI), and the Free Democratic Center (CDL) constitute the possible bases of such political support, but only the first of these conglomerates has any electoral clout. RN contains both neo-liberal currents and other tendencies that are contrary to this line, as can be seen in the following of such leaders as Sergio Onofre Jarpa and entrepreneur Roberto Fantuzzi. Before joining National Renovation, Fantuzzi and others formed the National Labor Front, a group that was highly critical of neo-liberal positions. As a result, the political party backing for the ideology and strategy of the large entrepreneurs is still weak.

The leadership of the CPC must confront three challenges: (1) the improvement of the negative image of entrepreneurs in large segments of the public, especially on matters of social justice; (2) the consolidation of an "ideological hegemony" representing the entire spectrum of entrepreneurs; and (3) the strengthening of a political party counterpart that is sympathetic to their discourse and strategy. If the CPC's is successful in these areas, then entrepreneurs are likely to remain powerful actors in Chile. They have already begun to address these problems through (1) the establishment of a dialogue with political and union leaders; (2) a search for some basic guarantees before the 1989 presidential and parliamentary elections; (3) the promotion of an image of social concern; and (4) support for a policy of privatization that may ensure their autonomy from the state.

The emergence of entrepreneurs as powerful actors who are identified with "modernization and progress" will also depend on their ability to change their image as a group that flees to the barracks as soon as it feels threatened. To discard the authoritarian option, the new ideas that entrepreneurs have developed must overcome some of their old fears, especially with regards to the social forces represented in the opposition to military rule. This will not be easy. Pinochet's twilight role as the guardian of the entrepreneurial class has left many entrepreneurs fearful. They know that they must compete politically and socially in order to achieve their goals, and, although competition is at the heart of their liberal philosophy, the challenge makes them nervous.

Notes

1. These figures are based on statistics provided by Javier Martínez and Arturo León, "Clases y clasificaciones sociales" (Santiago, CED–SUR, 1987). Some estimates make the figure as high as 600,000 entrepreneurs, but it is difficult to confirm this figure on the basis of official statistics. This number probably includes artisans and holders of saving accounts.

2. Guillermo Campero, *Los gremios empresariales en el período 1970– 1983* (Santiago, 1984), chapters 2 and 3 and the conclusion.

3. On the views of the large Chilean entrepreneurs, see Manuel Feliú, *La empresa de la libertad* (Santiago, 1988), Chapter 2.

4. Entrepreneurs held a congress on December 1–3, 1973, when they outlined a system of entrepreneurial participation in the social and economic administration of the nation. The proposal was presented to the government that same month.

5. During these first two years, the government had an ambiguous policy concerning entrepreneurs: it did not reject their proposals but did not support them either. General Gustavo Leigh supported entrepreneurial aspirations, but others, like the Chicago Boys, were opposed. The Chicago Boys argued that a formal link to the entrepreneurial organizations would limit government independence in matters of restructuring and adjustment. This argument was eventually accepted, and the government began to reject the entrepreneurial proposals.

6. Tomás Moulián and Pilar Vergara, *Estado, ideología y políticas económicas en Chile, 1973–79* (Santiago, 1980).

7. The leader of the small merchants, Rafael Cumsille, evaluated the results of the economic policy as follows: "there is an economic group that has neither party nor religion and is only concerned with their interests . . . we did not fight so that this small group would benefit . . . the economic policy

harms the middle and lower classes." CPC leader Jorge Fontaine responded that Cumsille's statements were "demagogic." *El Mercurio*, November 21, 1974.

8. Campero, *Los gremios empresariales*, chapters 2, 3, and 5.

9. In 1975, the industrial GNP fell by 25 percent with respect to 1974, principally affecting the textile, machine-tool, and electronic industries.

10. Spokespersons for ASIMET declared in December 1977 that "the vulnerability of Chilean industry . . . is putting the existence of the entire industrial base at risk. This . . . brings dependence and increases the gap which separates us from the industrialized countries." *Ercilla*, December 21, 1977.

11. The leader of the truckowners, León Vilarín, stated in September 1978 that "if it is true that this system, in the long run, as they say, can be good, there will be very few survivors who will get to witness the success. . . . People's patience is being tried and this is dangerous. . . . This is not what citizens asked for on September 11 [1973]. . . . If you ask me to define the regime, I consider that we are living under an economic dictatorship administered by a group of civilians with support from the armed forces." *Hoy*, September 13–19, 1978. Two years later, another leader of the truckowners stated: "The economic policy has created two classes in this country: the rich and the poor. In addition, it has weakened the middle class. . . . We had thought that this government would make an effort to rescue the classes in most need from poverty." *El Mercurio*, April 10, 1980. See also *Hoy*, April 16–22, 1980.

12. Spokespersons for the organization of small landowners, the Confederation of Agricultural Producers (CPA), stated that "we do not approve of the errors committed by some sectors of the government. . . . We support the armed forces but we are not in agreement with its economic policies as they relate to agriculture." *El Mercurio*, August 21, 1980.

13. For an examination of the crisis of the economic model, see CIEPLAN, *El modelo económico chileno: Trayectoria de una crítica* (Santiago, 1982).

14. The bankruptcy of CRAV-CRAVAL dragged down with it five hundred small and medium-sized farmers who had their crops contracted to this company. It also affected twenty-four banks that had loaned US$357 million to the enterprise. The general stock index fell by 7 percent.

15. Examples of these actions are provided by the National Association of Wheat Producers (ANPT), which sent provincial delegations to hold talks with the government. Meetings of the small landowners affiliated with the CPA, and those of Valdivia, took place in February and March 1982 to discuss the impact of economic policy on agriculture. The truckowners called for a plebiscite to decide on matters of economic policy on March 13. Other meetings involved merchants and farmers who formed committees to deal with problems of indebtedness (Valdivia, March 1982). A National Transportation Congress took place in March 1982.

16. The organization of small landowners within the CPA formally asked for the dismissal of the economic team on July 24, 1982. *El Mercurio*, June 24, 1982.

17. *El Mercurio*, October 24, 1982.

18. *El Mercurio*, December 1, 1982.

19. The drop of the GNP to 14.3 percent at the end of 1982 was an important factor that led to the recognition of the magnitude of the crisis.

20. On August 15, 1983, Finance Minister Carlos Cáceres responded to the CPC that the government would only treat some of the entrepreneurial proposals on an individual basis.

21. The state intervened in various banks and financial associations on January 13, 1983, effectively placing the financial sector in government hands.

22. The Civic Assembly included several union leaders and had an active participation in the "protests" that continued in 1986. See Manuel Antonio Garretón in this volume.

23. CPC President Jorge Fontaine addressed these subjects at ENADE'85 on November 12, 1985.

24. See Feliú, *La empresa de la libertad*.

25. Feliú was elected president of the CPC on July 21, 1986. He had previously been President of the National Mining Society (SONAMI).

26. Manuel Feliú outlined the objectives of the meeting as follows: "to establish a structure that will help disseminate the advantages of the free enterprise system. . . . We work for the long run so that future governments will know what we think." *El Mercurio*, July 19, 1986.

27. *El Mercurio*, August 20, 1986.

28. This meeting was significant in that for the first time it also counted on the auspices of the Council of Small and Medium-Sized Enterprises (CPME). The CPME had been in conflict with the government and with the CPC between 1975 and 1982. This underscored the stature achieved by the CPC and the subordination of the small and medium-sized entrepreneurs.

29. *El Mercurio*, November 5, 1986.

30. Jorge Fontaine in *El Mercurio*, August 6, 1987.

31. *El Mercurio*, November 23, November 25, 1987.

32. Statement issued by the CPC on October 7, 1988.

33. Roberto Fantuzzi of ASIMET called on entrepreneurs to change this conduct. He stated that "entrepreneurs who voted yes and who wish to win the elections [in 1989] should not behave in this way, nor provoke chaos." *La Epoca*, October 16, 1988. Manuel Feliú added at ENADE'88: "The entrepreneur should not play the grotesque role of the ostriches. . . . he should confront reality and the political future." *El Mercurio*, December 1, 1988.

34. *El Mercurio*, December 1, 1988.

35. Ibid.

36. On the subject of entrepreneurial ideology, see CEPAL, "Chile, transformaciones económicas y grupos sociales (1973–86)," *Working Paper* (Santiago, November 1988), esp. Chapter 1.

37. The SOFOFA started a campaign of ideological diffusion targeting the workers of affiliated enterprises in January 1989. The proposals and methodology of this campaign are discussed in a SOFOFA document of restricted circulation titled "Relaciones de trabajo en las empresas," December 14, 1988.

38. A detailed study of opinions of the small and medium-sized entrepreneurs is by the Centro de Estudios Públicos (CEP), "Estudio social y de opinión pública entre pequeños y medianos empresarios de Santiago," *Working Document*, no. 95 (Santiago, December 1987).

Part II: The Regime's Opponents

María Elena Valenzuela

The Evolving Roles of
Women under Military Rule

The military government's attempts to produce global transformations in Chilean society caused political and economic crises that deeply affected women. Government policies and discourse furthered the oppression of women by utilizing patriarchal forms of domination. In response, many women formed groups, organized, and occupied new spaces, replacing their previous forms of political participation. Through actions that redefined political spaces and widened the form and content of politics, women mobilized to survive and to promote gender-specific demands and political activity. The authoritarian government was thus confronted with resistance from women, whose new organizations and activities became the means for changing their condition of subordination and for redemocratizing all of society.

The period of political opening that began in 1983 was an important time in Chile for both women's mobilization and the reconstitution of political parties. Tensions appeared because of the pressure that political parties applied on women's organizations. Women's groups resisted the potential loss of autonomy, but at the same time they saw the need for channels of expression and social representation. Since that time, different formulas for relations between women's organizations and political parties have evolved. Although the women's movement did not achieve unity during the period after 1983, the women's issue became a legitimate concern, and each social and political institution had to articulate its distinct position concerning women. As a result, women were able to form Women for Democracy which, in conjunction with the Coalition for Democracy, the broad coalition of opposition political parties, paved the way for Chile's return to democracy.

I will examine the effects that military government discourse and policies had on women and the role the women's movement played in the process of social and political transformation, especially after 1983. My general hypothesis suggests that the growing contradiction between traditional legal, cultural, and social definitions of women and the new role women began to play under the military regime became the principal dynamic element of the period. Once the traditional political organizations re-emerged, however, women's activity lost its relative importance in the face of those organizations' tendency to reconstitute preexisting structures of discrimination.

The Military Government and Women

Policies developed by the military regime toward women were based on a traditional conception of women's roles in society. The government promoted women's return to family life and discouraged their participation in the work force and in government, focusing instead on their roles as mothers. This attempt to return to the past occurred amid conditions that opened opportunities and even pushed women to assume new roles. Thus, female participation in the labor market increased from 25 percent in the 1970s to 30 percent in the 1980s.

Since the University of Chile was founded in 1842, women have come a long way in education. Today, women make up 40 percent of the university's student body. And although the enrollment of men exceeds enrollment of women by 2.6 percent at the primary level, women's participation in secondary schools exceeds men's by 5 percent.[1] At the same time, the percentage of women in the work force with a university education increased from 2.6 percent in 1960 to 15 percent in 1982; the participation of men with the same educational level increased from 2.3 to 7.9 percent during the same period. But in spite of this women receive incomes that equal only 49 percent of what men with the same educational level earn. Similarly, women with eight or fewer years of formal education earn only 59 percent of what men with the same educational background earn.

In spite of women's changing roles in Chilean society, the Pinochet government was reluctant to address them. This was evident in the maintenance until 1989 of the *potestad marital*, which gave a husband rights over his wife and her property. According to the marriage law, a husband owed protection to his wife in exchange for her obedience. The government also promoted keeping women out of the labor force. Women who were employed outside the home were treated as a secondary force and as such were discriminated against in favor of men. Government programs for unemployment aid established barriers to women's income, and the labor legislation developed by the government eliminated some protective clauses for working mothers. Moreover, the modernization in some sectors of the economy did not improve the situation of working women. Discrepancies in salaries continued; and, even though the proportion of domestic workers decreased, it still represented 25 percent of the female work force. Between 1960 and 1985, women had median incomes of between 68 and 38 percent of those received by men with identical educational backgrounds. The labor market also continued to be highly segmented, with high levels of work-force polarization between male and female jobs, which stayed relatively constant between 1960 and 1982, the date of the last census in Chile. Moreover, the modern sectors of agriculture and fishing, which are oriented toward the export market and which employ significant numbers of women, provided unstable and irregular work.[2]

In the political arena, the government gave women the role of educating children for the fatherland, thus ensuring the ideological continuity of the regime. The government also assigned women a leading role in maintaining social order but excluded them from the exercise of power. Women's participation in high-level public positions was limited. During the sixteen years of military government, only two women occupied the office of minister of state, and there were never more than two women in undersecretarial posts at the same time. Moreover, women could not be members of the legislative power, which was reserved for the commanders-in-chief of the armed forces. This was an important reversal; in the previous democratic parliament, there had been fifteen women among the senators and deputies.

Since 1973, however, the military regime actively sought the political support of women, considering them natural allies of the government. This alliance was based on their supposedly shared values and ideals, the product of a dualist conception of social relations, in which the principal opposition is that posed between God, represented by virtue, and the human being, represented by sin and flesh. According to this perspective, the human being can approach or distance himself from God to the extent that he controls his instincts and subordinates them to the spirit. When instincts are not controlled by human will, they oppose the will of God. In women, this dualism is expressed in their sexuality-maternity. Through procreation, women redeem the earthly character of their sexual impulses, converting them into the values of dedication, spirit of sacrifice, and selflessness toward their children, all of which bring women closer to God. But men only approach God when they force their earthly instincts to yield by dedicating their lives to a greater end, such as service to God or the fatherland.[3] Stemming from this interpretation were constant references to the divine mission of the armed forces in their defense of patriotic values and in their image as saviors. The alliance that the regime sought to establish between mothers and soldiers, therefore, was based on their shared capacity to defend and transmit superior values.

In this context, the opposite of spiritual was political. The regime defined politics as a greedy, manipulative activity in which people seek earthly power. The armed forces, therefore, distanced themselves symbolically from politics. They assumed control of the state to promote the "common good" and to unify the interests of the nation. Politics were symbolically associated with the masculine-instinctive, and women were "rewarded" for the apolitical character to which their sex entitled them by inviting them to join with the armed forces as the pillars of the new society.[4]

The government strongly encouraged women to organize. Considering the interests of women as being linked to motherhood or the prolongation of their maternal roles, the government promoted "volunteer armies." It restructured pre-existing women's groups, created new organizations through the branches of the armed forces, and developed a parallel institutional structure to the legal political-administrative structure, one controlled by the wives of national, regional, and local authorities.

The diverse organizations that gathered around this official volunteerism were shaped as much by the characteristics of their participants as by the nature of the work they developed. There were organizations with social content and others with a stronger link to government activities. Among the latter was CEMA-Chile, which administered approximately ten thousand mothers' centers throughout the nation. The volunteer members of this organization were primarily the wives of army officials, organized according to military parameters and the military ranks of their husbands. The

Women's National Secretariat channeled civilian female support for the regime in order to promote government programs aimed at the poorest sectors; it trained nearly three million women between 1975 and 1983.

The political role of these organizations was not obvious, but it was effective. Through these groups the regime established a standard for women's legitimate action that reinforced traditional female identities and social spaces.[5] Most regime actions were designed not to improve the living conditions of poor women but to promote their adaptation to these conditions. Women were taught to be good wives, mothers, and homemakers through training programs that enabled them to improve their domestic performance.

The activities of volunteers were fundamental in the implementation of the dictatorial scheme. On the one hand, volunteer organizations fulfilled the clientelistic function of working with the masses, which the armed forces were unwilling and unable to do because it would have brought a discussion of social issues into the barracks. Monolithic control of the armed forces implied keeping military personnel away from direct contact with civil society. Volunteers' institutions were established as channels of communication between the authorities and their bases of support. On the other hand, "volunteerism" served to counteract the negative effects of the free-market economy and helped to palliate the harsh consequences of the neo-liberal economic model for the poorest social sectors.[6] Through training courses and social assistance programs, CEMA-Chile not only helped the members of the mothers' centers to overcome the effects of the economic crisis within their families, but it also reinforced the regime's economic model by diminishing the potential for conflict caused by reversing the redistributive tendencies of the previous democratic period.

The Emergence of Women's Demands

Women mobilized politically only twice during the democratic period before 1973. They were active during the suffrage movement in the first half of the century, and they came together during the Popular Unity period in the early 1970s through *Poder Femenino*, a movement that opposed Allende and demanded protection for women's traditional roles. A period of intense activity in support of women's right to vote during the late 1940s resulted in women casting ballots for president for the first time in 1952.[7] Thereafter began what the late Julieta Kirkwood called "the feminist silence."[8]

Although the period from 1950 to 1973 witnessed important democratic changes—broader access to education and health, higher standards of living, moderate but sustained economic development, and increased political participation of new social groups—the problem of gender inequality was not sufficiently addressed. Paradoxically, the end of more than twenty years of "feminist silence" came during the military dictatorship. The organizational activity of women under the regime was both a response to economic and political crises and a manifestation of opposition to authoritarianism.

New Roles

As part of its attempt to depoliticize Chilean society, the military government repressed and sought to impede the development of social organizations. The prohibition of partisan politics caused traditionally private arenas to become politicized and attract public interest, thus becoming arenas of conflict between the dictatorship and democracy. This unintended politicization of the private sphere created a favorable climate for conflicts derived from gender inequalities, an issue that had been displaced by partisan politics during the democratic period. The dividing line between public and private became blurred, and the private arena, considered by some to be the exclusive domain of women, increasingly became a principal area of confrontation.

The women's movement found expression in different forms. Women organized for the defense of human rights and developed ingenious survival strategies to endure the economic crisis and the effects of regime policies on the poor. Women mobilized specifically as women for the end of the dictatorship and began to redefine their relationship to politics. This led them to question authoritarian relations in all areas of society, which later led to a reconceptualization of democracy.[9] While not all women's groups assumed gender demands as an immediate priority, their actions played an important role in the reappraisal of women's contribution to politics.

A virtual explosion of women's organizations occurred in the context of the progressive decomposition and atomization of the social fabric, which allowed greater autonomy for women. Both official and opposition groups were determined to construct their own spaces, directed by and composed of women, outside the traditional tutelage of the parties and other organizations with historically male leadership. This led to serious tensions between newer and traditional types of organizations.

Because political parties had no channels for expression during the first decade of military rule, they tended to function through social organizations. Once the parties began to reconstruct their own spaces for action after 1983, they tried to control and coopt the social organizations—including the women's groups—that had developed autonomously. This tension, which was especially clear in the opposition, also appeared among government parties. For instance, a group of conservative women identified the regime's attempt to depoliticize women as one of the causes for its defeat in the 1988 plebiscite. The experience of the women's movement during this authoritarian period highlighted the existence of women's issues. The movement also encouraged the development of social and political practices that responded to women's concerns, while seeking to avoid patterns of subordination.

WOMEN AND HUMAN RIGHTS

Ironically, the traditional separation between public and private spheres helped women to assume leading roles in the period immediately following the coup. The regime, which claimed to be defending the most traditional of institutions—the family—had to confront the denunciations of women who mobilized to defend their homes from repression. These denunciations broke the repressive logic of the state, because they were presented, despite their strong political character, as an emotional defense of the family, not as a threat to military rule.

Organizations predominantly composed of women, such as the Families of the Detained and Disappeared and the Families of Political Prisoners, were the first to develop public activities denouncing and opposing the regime after the coup.[10] Other predominantly female groups followed, but human rights organizations still did not identify themselves according to gender. Instead, they stayed within the limits of the traditional definition of women's roles in politics by focusing on giving assistance to the victims of repression. The close links of these groups to the proscribed political parties, out of whose ranks most of the victims of the repression came, led the organizations to give higher priority to partisan activities. This eventually meant less autonomy for the human rights groups and further inhibited their identity as women's organizations.

The regime's approach to dealing with the economic crisis showed no sensitivity to women who faced the problem of survival. In the midst of a growing pauperization, women increasingly assumed the role of head of household, contributing to the feminization of poverty.

The structural economic transformations the government had introduced since 1973 led to high levels of unemployment.[11] By 1983, unemployment had risen to 30 percent of the work force at the national level and to 80 percent in the poorer sectors of Santiago.[12] These high rates of unemployment caused a strong regression in the distribution of income and a fall in the population's living standards.[13] According to a study by Francisco Javier Labbé, the share of total income earned by the poorest Chileans (40 percent of the population) decreased from 12 percent in the 1970–73 period to 9.3 percent in 1984. At the same time, the richest people in Chilean society (20 percent of the population), who had captured 50.5 percent of total income in 1970–73, increased their share to 60.9 percent in 1984.[14]

The fall in family incomes due to the prolonged unemployment of the male heads of household led many women to join the labor market. Earlier studies have demonstrated the high sensitivity of the female work force to fluctuations in the economy.[15] Relatively stable in the 1960s, the female work force grew by 4.5 percent between 1970 and 1985.[16]

Between 1970 and 1982, the proportion of female heads of household among all women in the work force increased by 4 percent.[17] Even when the 1982 census showed that only 22 percent of homes were run by women, this percentage easily reached 40 percent in the poorest areas. As recent studies have shown, these changes brought conflict into marital relations and forced women to take on an extra workload.[18] A study by Lucía Pardo showed that women working at home spent fifty-six hours a week in domestic labor, that is, 16 percent more than legal fulltime work.[19] Moreover, women who worked fulltime outside the home spent an additional thirty-three hours a week on domestic tasks. Therefore, they worked eighty-one hours a week, or 69 percent above the legal level.

The deteriorating economic situation led large contingents of poor urban women to initiate several collective strategies that were designed to satisfy the basic needs of their families. Low-income women formed more than a thousand economic organizations in Santiago alone, including subsistence and craft workshops, soup kitchens, and "collective shopping" programs. These groups consisted mostly of housewives who were trying to feed and support their families under a government that had forsaken its role as benefactor.

The economic crisis had serious repercussions on the personal lives of these women. In the poorest homes, the incorporation of women into the labor force often signified taking daughters out of school to do domestic chores while sons continued their studies. At the same time, the number of homes with female heads of household increased, partly because of the migration of men in search of work and because of the difficulty unemployed men had in adjusting to the new balance of power in the home.[20]

Even though the new economic organizations created by women had survival as a principal objective, they rapidly became promising centers for political organization and the development of gender identity. Women's groups maintained an important degree of autonomy, and most of them did not establish direct relations with political parties. The new roles assumed by women also had important effects in the development of a women's social movement. They called attention to areas of conflict that had previously been ignored, questioning "class contradictions" as the only focus of social struggle. In response, the most orthodox sectors of the Chilean left maintained that women's issues would be resolved with the coming of socialism. For leftist groups, a recognition of gender demands implied that they were admitting differences—even disagreements—within the working class, which could detract from the principal battle against the dictatorship. Thus, the orthodox left opposed gender-specific demands, insisted on the necessity of keeping the family united, and directed all efforts toward the larger struggle.

These poorer women's organizations did not propose the end of gender discrimination, as in the feminist movement based in the middle class. Nevertheless, changes in these women's lives caused by the economic crisis—such as the acquisition of new tasks and responsibilities—resulted in changing attitudes. These women developed a greater sense of personal worth and of gender identity. As María de la Luz Silva concluded:

women's experience of leaving their homes, making contact with other women who were suffering the same problems, and discovering their own unsuspected capacities and abilities had an important impact on their lives. For example, women had a greater sense of self-worth, questioned their gender roles, reevaluated the marital relationship, and assumed their identities as women and as social actors.[21]

This perspective also emerges from a study by Claudia Serrano, who interviewed women who had joined the labor market in the midst of the economic crisis. She discovered that these women continued to work outside the home after the crisis and that there was a shift in marital relations toward more equality. Working-class women showed an increased sense of self-worth, indicated that they had earned self-respect, and saw that it was possible to combine their motherly duties with personal development. Serrano concluded: "we observe in none of the cases a return to the initial position: women in the home, men at work."[22]

WOMEN AND POLITICS: OPPOSITION GROUPS

Under military rule, the organizations of civil society became a substitute political arena that contributed to the politicization of the private and social spheres. This facilitated the emergence of specific demands over and above ideological alignments. Thus, these organizations acquired greater freedom to promote demands that had previously been subsumed by other national priorities. Furthermore, the influence of the international women's movement clearly contributed to the generation of gender identity in the struggle for democracy.[23]

As a result, the concept of "politics" expanded to include the daily universe that had been invaded by the dictatorship. The dividing line between the public and the private became much more hazy as the repressive policies of the regime affected domestic unity and as its economic policies pushed women to join the work force. This breakdown of the distinction between public space as male space and private space (or home) as female space allowed gender issues to become more visible and political. Gender demands assumed an anti-authoritarian character, which was both anti-militarist and anti-patriarchal.

Even though the first mobilizations and organizations of women started in the 1970s, it was not until the period of political opening in

1983 that—in the midst of the recession—the consolidation of a social movement of women occurred. In 1976, a Women's Department
was created within the Coordinadora Nacional Sindical (CNS), which
tried to coordinate the work of the few female union leaders. The
Women's Department sought to organize female workers and the
wives of male workers and encouraged their participation in union
activity.[24] Although women played a marginal and secondary role in
union organization, the creation of the Women's Department was
most significant. It advanced gender-specific demands in a sector
where the existence of sexual discrimination remained unrecog-
nized for fear of breaking the mythic solidarity of the working class.

In 1977, middle-class professional women formed a group that became the Circle for the Study of Women. They discussed the situation of women and built the foundation for the local feminist movement. Most of the women had been politically active in leftist
political parties, where they had played peripheral roles. Because of
their experience, they recognized the authoritarian framework that
characterized society. They rethought their own past and future relationship to politics and sought more active roles.

It was not until the period of political opening, however, that the
mobilization of women took on a wider significance. Women mobilized more for the anti-dictatorial struggle than for gender demands, but the majority of the women evolved through these activities to incorporate a feminist perspective. Many groups were
organized during this period, including the Shantytown Women's
Movement (MOMUPO), which represented the urban popular sectors;
the Committee for the Defense of the Rights of the People (CODEM)
and Women of Chile (MUDECHI), which defined their principal objectives in terms of the anti-dictatorial struggle; and the Feminist
Movement, which consisted primarily of middle-class women who
promoted the establishment of new power relations in order to end
discrimination. After the Feminist Movement was created in 1983,
feminism spread rapidly to the "popular" (lower-class) sectors, destroying the myth that feminist concerns only reflected the interests of middle-class women. Shantytown groups with a clear feminist bent were begun—such as the Women's Liberation Front, the
"Domitilas," and the "Siemprevivas"—even though women in most
of these popular organizations defined themselves in terms of their
domestic roles and were primarily interested in the struggle for survival.

Given the diversity of women's organizations and their shared confrontational nature, the Movement for the Emancipation of Women 1983 (MEMCH-83), was created as an umbrella group, taking its name from the suffragist movement that had led the struggle between 1935 and 1953. MEMCH-83 originally gathered together twenty-four women's groups, and it organized several demonstrations repudiating the regime.[25] The objective of the movement was to promote and coordinate opposition activities among women's groups. Even though these organizations did not actually mobilize a majority of women, they gave important visibility to women's demands.

The women's organizations asserted their independence and autonomy from the political parties, but it was not long before opposition politics engulfed these groups. As political parties reconstituted and redefined themselves after 1983, the parties sought to regain their social bases by coopting the social movements and pressuring them to cede their autonomy. These tensions were aggravated by the formation of two competing coalitions in the opposition—the centrist Democratic Alliance and the more leftist Popular Democratic Movement—which rapidly permeated several of the women's organizations. Women for Life emerged at the end of 1983 in reaction to this political disunity and tried to recover the traditional sense of women's contribution to politics.[26] The sixteen women who formed the group participated as individuals but represented the range of opposition platforms. Women for Life became the reference point for political organizations on women's issues as well as the most important arena for convening and discussing the social mobilization of women.[27]

MOMUPO maintained its independence from the political parties and continued to work with women who lived in the shantytowns. Later the organization took on a feminist identity and combined class and gender dimensions in its work. MUDECHI maintained strong links with the parties of the Popular Democratic Movement and refused to call itself a feminist organization; its goal was to channel the women's struggle against the regime. CODEM, linked with other sectors of the left, also refused to consider itself feminist organization, but later it did assume a gender identity in the struggle against the government. In 1984, the tension resulting from the choices made by the women's groups—some had tried to assert their independence, while others had aligned with one of the political blocs—led to the withdrawal of some organizations from MEMCH-83. As the political spectrum became more clearly defined and as the parties began to act openly and freely, the different social organizations were heavily pressured to choose sides in the anti-dictatorial struggle.[28]

What happened inside MEMCH-83 demonstrates the consequences of increasing partisanship among women's organizations and how they developed their conceptions of politics and the role of women. While the most orthodox sectors of the left argued that gender demands distracted people from the principal objective of ousting the dictatorship, feminist groups refused to prioritize objectives. These groups indicated that women's oppression was a departure point for women's political participation. This is what feminist scholar Julieta Kirkwood identified as the difference between feminists and politicians. She showed that while some women got involved in politics because of their gender-related views, other women joined a political cause as a first priority, assuming that their gender-specific needs and demands would be addressed later.[29]

In spite of the obvious differences among the women's groups, they maintained ties and a common identity due to the widely shared need for change in the social position of women. Despite divisive pressure from political parties, women were able to work together on a variety of occasions. This cooperation culminated in the elaboration of the Women's Bill, which the Civilian Assembly incorporated in the Demand of Chile in May 1986.

The difficult relations between social movements and political parties after a decade of political exclusion led the women's organizations to consider maintaining their independence. They feared being coopted as they had been after winning the right to vote in the 1940s. At first, this led some women to remain loyal to both their parties and feminism, thereby producing a "double militancy." Because of the lack of other institutional channels for representation and participation, however, this double militancy was reoriented as women tried to incorporate feminism into the dominant party structures. This was how organizations such as the Movement of Women for Socialism (1984) were created, in which women combined their political allegiance as political militants with a feminist approach. Later, the Federation of Socialist Women (FMS) was formed, which tried to incorporate feminist views into the formal structure of the Núñez (later Arrate) Socialist Party.[30]

In their approach to politics, feminist groups argued that it was necessary to redefine the concept of democracy, since in their view democracy had never existed for women.[31] As Kirkwood stated, the struggle for democracy should include the struggle for women's liberation or the patriarchal structures would not be eliminated.[32] This argument implied that there was an authoritarian pattern behind both political and personal relations and that both structures, therefore, had to be democratized. It was in this context that the Feminist Movement coined its slogan, "Democracy in the Nation and in the House," seeking not only more equality for women but also a simultaneous transformation of political and day-to-day relations. Without ignoring the problem of class inequality, feminist demands identified expressions of inequality in a broader context, focusing on those social institutions that reproduced discrimination: the family, the educational system, the political parties of all ideologies, the state apparatus, and the legal system.[33] The silence of the opposition with respect to gender demands led twelve women's organizations—including MOMUPO and CODEM—to formulate the "Women's Demands for Democracy" three months before the 1988 plebiscite, which asked for the full incorporation of women's concerns in a democracy.[34]

THE RIGHT

Just as the women's issue divided the opposition into sectors that promoted gender demands as part of the democratic platform and sectors that encouraged women's traditional political participation (subordinating gender interests to an ideological project), the women's issue was also a point of conflict on the right. While the more traditional sectors measured a woman's contribution to society through her domestic roles, the modern sectors demanded greater female participation in politics and called for a response to women's demands in the world outside the home.

The differences within the political right on the women's issue reflected the opposing interests of two sectors. The traditional position, led by Lucía Hiriart de Pinochet and her "army of volunteers," called for the rights of women within the family. The modern liberal sectors of mostly professional women also called for women's rights within the family, but they were concerned with the discrimination against women outside the home as well.

The growing contradiction between traditional female roles and changes in both occupational structure and educational levels opened new perspectives, roles, and needs to women. Because of these changes, middle-class women sensed their exclusion from the public sphere more acutely than poor women did. The Feminist Movement, which was linked to the opposition, had a weak and atomized counterpart on the right, where women's demands were expressed more through individual personalities than collective actions.

The struggle among government supporters over the role of women in society became most evident through two actions. First, the government refused to ratify the United Nations convention for the elimination of discrimination against women, after the Chilean envoy had already signed the agreement. It was only on December 5, 1989, just nine days before the presidential and parliamentary elections, that the government ratified the agreement. Second, it resisted changes in the legal situation of women as stated in the Civil Code of 1855, which had long gone unchanged.[35] In 1975, the government appointed a special commission to plan changes in family legislation that were presented to the executive in 1979. The recommendations pitted modern against conservative sectors within the regime. The conservatives, represented by organizations such as CEMA-Chile and the National Secretariat of Women, championed the "true" rights of women. With the help of Lucía Hiriart de Pinochet, they blocked changes in the law and any discussion on the subject until 1986. A new project presented that year failed, despite strong pressure from women of the right who represented professional sectors. As Alicia Romo, a close collaborator of the regime, said, "the condition of the married woman in civil law is both subordinated and discriminated against; she is limited by the law in her capacities and potential. She is not a whole person since she depends on her husband in a legal condition similar to that of slavery."[36] A reform project that was considered unsatisfactory by a variety of groups was finally approved in 1989.

The gender demands raised by the more modern sectors of the right were not recognized in a significant way by their parties. The discourse of the government and right-wing parties was directed principally to homemakers, whose interests were defined as those of the family. For instance, during the campaign for the plebiscite, the government presented a study through the Economic and Social Council that would grant retirement to homemakers. Meanwhile,

Admiral José Toribio Merino proposed new legislation against abortion—raising the penalties against those who practiced and assisted in abortions—as a way of defending the integrity of the family. The legislation failed to address women's roles in the public sphere, in the universities, in politics, in the workplace, and in solving the problems that faced them in those sectors of society.

As a consequence, the government received the support of only 46 percent of women in the plebiscite, which was 6.5 percent higher than the support of men but which was still below the government's expectations. The government had focused its campaign on women, conscious of their weight in the electorate (nearly 52 percent of the voters in the plebiscite were women) and aware that approximately 30 percent of the registered voters were homemakers, a sector usually thought of as the most conservative.

In a poll taken two months before the plebiscite, women showed radically different preferences according to their activities. Changes in the educational level and occupational structure affected women in different ways, depending on the nature of their position. Housewives, who lived in a more isolated and precarious position, exhibited different behaviors and expectations from women in the work force. This is demonstrated in Table 5.1, in which the intended voting choice of women who work outside the home was similar to that of the corresponding male population.

The regime's defeat in the plebiscite, along with the need to adjust to a new political era, led the women of the modernized right, who had been promoting new roles for women, to take a more active political role. Shortly after the plebiscite, they formed the International Institute for the Development of Women's Political Leadership (IDLPM). Its purpose was to "create consciousness among women, promote women, and assist in the organization and participation that each woman wants to have in diverse political situations, institutions, or parties."[37] Through its very objectives, the IDLPM implicitly criticized the government's treatment of women's issues, especially the official National Secretariat of Women, which emphasized "stressing the importance of women and helping their improvement as mothers, wives and homemakers." Although Lucía Hiriart de Pinochet called on women ten months before the plebiscite to form a great Women's Movement to "support men's decisions and slowly reenter politics," the new IDLPM complained that "the woman has been absent from [politics] and this has been bad for

Table 5.1
Women's Intended Votes, July 1988

	Work/home	Work/force	Student	Retired
YES	45.3	32.8	27.7	48.4
NO	32.1	46.0	59.0	31.7
Don't know/ no answer/ undecided	22.6	21.2	13.3	19.9
Total	100.0	100.0	100.0	100.0

Source: Centro de Estudios de la Realidad Contemporánea, national poll.

her, for her family and for the country."[38] With the nation's return to partisan political activity, women of the political right decided to join political parties of similar persuasion. They constituted approximately 50 percent of the members of the main rightist political parties, yet none of the sixteen senators elected by the political right in December 1989 and only three of the forty-eight deputies in the lower chamber were women.

Political Parties and the Women's Issue

Although there has not been a return to past perceptions of women's role in society, the recent attempts to restore traditional political roles—particularly in popular movements (parties, unions, and base organizations)—have adversely affected the women's cause. But the active mobilization of women's organizations and their capacity for protest against the regime made these groups increasingly legitimate in the context of the anti-dictatorial struggle. The parties of the left, the center, and the right became interested in women's issues, which they incorporated into their platforms after 1983. Both recently created parties and the older parties that survived the political recess and government repression made explicit references to women's issues.

Furthermore, the voting pattern of women in the plebiscite greatly encouraged groups that supported the political participation of women. Women saw themselves as an important political force. They became conscious of their contribution to the electoral struggle and were less willing to continue performing secondary tasks at the margins of power. The plebiscite also demonstrated that, as im-

Table 5.2
Women's Political Participation According to Perceived Roles

Women's Roles	Legitimate Participation	Illegitimate Participation
Traditional	Volunteerism (a)	Human rights (b)
Nontraditional	Modern Right (c)	Feminism (d)

a) This group defends traditional maternal roles and participation in politics as an extension of domestic roles. The activities of female volunteers who supported the military government correspond to this type.

b) This group encourages greater participation of women in politics, but gender demands are not made. Opposition groups that advocated active struggle against the Pinochet government, are closely linked to the parties, and do not incorporate gender demands correspond to this type. They include the diverse groups that promote human rights.

c) This group calls for changes in the situation of women while maintaining the traditional standards for women's participation in politics. This type comprises the modern sectors of the right, which accepted the limits imposed on politics by the military government but not the depoliticization of women or discrimination against them.

d) This group demands new forms of political participation and changes in gender relations. The various feminist currents belong to this type, both those who have become part of opposition parties and those who have chosen to maintain their organizations as independent pressure groups.

portant as women's electoral participation was, this alone did not signify access to power for women. Party and union structures, the main channels for social expression, were still unwilling to share power with women.

The process of integrating women's concerns into party platforms and activities can be understood from two central points of view (see Table 5.2). The first relates to the perceived legitimacy of women's participation in public political affairs. The second refers to whether this participation occurs through traditional or nontraditional female roles.

In general, women's issues were incorporated throughout the political spectrum through a masculine conception of politics, which implied including some women's demands without giving women power.[39] Women were expected to participate in politics as wives and mothers and as supporters of men's actions. It was as if women were expected to extend their domestic roles into the realm of politics and become, as Elsa Chaney put it, *supermadres* administering oversized homes.[40]

Women confronted the global crisis of Chilean society specifically as women in their female-discriminated-subordinate roles.[41] Even though this crisis opened the possibility of entering the public arena and increased opportunities for the organization and participation of women, women's roles in society were not redefined. Instead, their traditional domestic roles were extended into the public realm, as mothers in the human rights organizations and as housewives in the popular economic organizations. Political parties incorporated women's demands in purely formal terms but did not accede to the recomposition of internal political power as women demanded. In this way, party structures continued to be dominated by men, even while politicians proclaimed the equality of the sexes. As the women's movement became stronger, women's branches reappeared within the parties, but they were mere appendages to the central structures that relegated women to segregated spaces and kept them outside the locus of power. This exclusion of women continued after the plebiscite, and in the 1989 legislative elections only 2 of the 38 elected senators and 7 of the 120 deputies were women.

The left was not alone in placing women's principal activity in the family sphere while declaring the equality of the sexes. On the right, the National Renovation (RN) Party, founded in February 1987, proclaimed the equality of women in its declaration of principles, stating that it "values in a special way the virtues and functions belonging to the woman as the bearer of life, center of the family, and principle agent of the transmission of moral values and traditions."[42] This emphasis on the family also motivated the Independent Democratic Union (UDI) to staunchly oppose abortion and the National Party to reject divorce.[43]

The Communist Party gave priority to women's roles within the family, although it also encouraged women to participate in mobilizations to end the dictatorship. The party also proposed social services that would give preferential attention to mothers (maternity subsidies, for example) and legislation that would allow (but not encourage) divorce. In the area of health, the party prioritized mother-infant care and proposed to identify the best way to make paid work compatible with child-rearing.[44]

The Christian Democratic Party drew its views on women's issues from a group of professional women who contributed to the elaboration of the "Alternative Project" in 1984. Putting this moderate program into practice would probably necessitate changes allowing women more power. It is not known, however, to what degree this reform program represented the thoughts of women and leaders of the party.[45]

The PDC took a general Christian-humanist perspective on women's issues, and dealt with conflictive themes by addressing them from the perspective of the Catholic Church.[46] The party would support a divorce law, for example, complementing it with preventive programs, but it would not advocate decriminalizing abortion. The Christian Democratic project proposed legal equality and the end of discrimination in order to democratize social and family relations. To achieve the latter, the project has advocated family guidance centers and training programs for both sexes, which would address family problems and reeducate married couples to share their responsibilities. The platform also proposed programs to facilitate the incorporation of women into paid jobs and to make their work compatible with family life.

The then Núñez Socialist Party founded an organization that defined itself as feminist, the Federation of Socialist Women (FMS), but it was not able to pressure the party leaders for change. The FMS presented a proposal to the party program commission that included provisions for equal rights, divorce law, punishment for domestic and marital violence, elimination of labor discrimination, and reproductive rights. At the same time, the FMS argued for the necessity of opening the party to participation by women. After the plebsicite, both the Socialist Party and the PPD agreed to incorporate a 20 percent quota of women in leadership positions.

The Humanist Party (PH), the newest party in Chile and one that rejected being boxed into the traditional political spectrum, relied on activists whose average age was twenty-five years and more than half of whom were women. This unusual political interest of women was explained by the president of the PH: ". . . we allow them to participate. In our party there is no women's branch, no youth branch, nor any type of discrimination."[47] The party's policies toward women included secular education, freedom of information, sexual education, and participation in mixed organizations. The orientation of the PH reflected a model for the participation and integration of women that was very different from that found in traditional Chilean politics.[48]

Opposition parties wrongly assumed that the alleged conservative attitudes of women and their disinterest in politics would largely benefit the military government.[49] In December 1987, an opposition poll showed a lag in female voter registration. The poll also demonstrated that women perceived politics as something alien and distant, expressed in high rates of "don't know" and "no answer" responses. Rather than showing support for Pinochet, the poll indicated that politics neither motivated women nor addressed their interests. When the opposition focused on women in the plebiscite campaign, it appealed to them as mother-wife-homemakers, ignored their role in political and union activities and in the workplace, and avoided the issue of discrimination against women. When the need to make some reforms for women was recognized, the emphasis was placed on traditional roles. As a PDC propaganda pamphlet during the pre-plebiscite campaign indicated, "all Pinochet has to offer is that women will not have enough money to provide meals [for their families]. Thus they will have to take on work that leaves the family uncared for and destroys the home."

The voting pattern of women in the plebiscite provided an important milestone for the groups that were calling for a more active role for women. The rightist groups thereafter created a new organization to promote women's political participation. In the opposition, pressure increased for greater political spaces for women, which had been ignored during the campaign because of the myth of women's conservative attitudes. Two weeks after the plebiscite, the Women's Department of the Coordinadora Nacional Sindical (CNS) declared that it would demand greater participation for women in decision-making before and during the next democratic government. Similarly, the Women's Department of the PDC called on the party to allow a greater female presence in leadership positions and to include the interests, needs, and aspirations of women in the party's platforms.

Because of the marginal role played by women in the opposition coalition before the plebiscite, the women's organizations of the opposition parties created the Coalition of Women for Democracy (CMD), an entity that was independent from the Coalition of Parties for Democracy. The intent of the CMD to promote the incorporation of women's interests in the government plans of the opposition and to increase women's participation in leadership positions in the entire opposition structure. Even though the number of female candidates for Congress was below 5 percent and no women were appointed to head ministerial posts in the new Aylwin administration, the CMD introduced the women's issue in the national political agenda. The CMD's platform was incorporated in the government's program, which recognized the new role of women in society as well as the need to end all forms of discrimination. The CMD succeeded programmatically, because it developed a single organization that was capable of exerting pressure on issues, but it was less able to penetrate party structures, which explains the low number of women in leadership positions.

Conclusion

The women's issue in Chile is currently a controversial theme that has displaced the class struggle as the only focus of social conflict. It has also been incorporated into the political agendas of various parties and movements. It is a theme that divides the entire political spectrum—including church and government—and prompts a new system of alliances and tensions among political actors. The women's movement has gained political credibility as much for the role it has played in the anti-authoritarian struggle as for the potential for change that the process of redemocratization brings. But the demands of the movement have met strong resistance from inside both the political parties and state institutions.

Since its beginnings in Chile, feminism has been linked to the left; and even though it has claimed its independence, the movement still maintains a strong ideological tie to the left. But other sectors also articulate gender demands, giving the women's movement a high degree of heterogeneity both in composition—cutting across social classes and ideological cleavages—and in its system of alliances. The common gender identity has allowed women to organize across the political spectrum, even during periods of high tension within the opposition. The tendency of the Chilean political system to give greater importance to economic demands could undermine the effectiveness of these groups, however, since they advance their demands from a different perspective.

The democratic transition has benefited from women's proposals to democratize politics, but it has helped restore the role of traditional political organizations more than it has helped the organization of women. Traditional political organizations have shown a relatively open attitude toward incorporating some gender demands, but they have tended to exclude women from the power structure and from political and economic decision-making. This recomposition of the social-political fabric could endanger the new roles played by women during the authoritarian period. The low proportion of women running for popularly elected posts in the first legislative elections, after sixteen years of dictatorship, indicates that electoral participation does not guarantee the participation of women in decision-making.

The political importance of the women's movement during this period did not lie so much in its capacity to mobilize large numbers of people but in its reinforcement of the pro-democracy movement, which brought about greater participation of sectors that would otherwise have remained excluded from the political system. Nevertheless, women's demands have not been fully legitimized by the democratic political forces that took power in 1990.

The Chilean political system has no legitimate form of participation outside the political parties and labor unions, and the parties are not prepared to incorporate women on equal terms. The traditional question of whether autonomously organized groups of women can be more successful in the struggle for power than those who joined preexisting structures has been evident in the democratic transition. While radical feminist groups have insisted on remaining independent of the parties, important numbers of women who define themselves as feminists have joined the parties to fight for a greater space in the power structure. The absence of other effective mechanisms for participation or influence in the political system (such as lobbies) excludes forces that have no representational capacity from the political process. Thus, autonomous feminist groups, as well as other women's organizations, are largely isolated from the political system.

The traditional view of women in politics is that they have no interest in competing with men. This perception has led to the existence of women's departments in the parties and to the emphasis on women in public roles as mere attendants to the wives of political leaders. Even though there is a growing consciousness and a common identity of women with gender problems, large segments of the political spectrum still perceive feminism as an anti-male movement that does not represent the majority of women. In addition, the persistence of traditional values and attitudes concerning the role of women in society has made the work of feminist pressure groups more difficult. At the same time, women's space in the political system remains limited. Under these conditions, the future of the women's movement will depend on its capacity to work in conjunction with other power structures—the state apparatus, political parties, social organizations—without allowing those structures to subordinate or neutralize gender-specific demands.

Notes

1. Josefina Rosetti, "La educación de las mujeres en el Chile contemporáneo," in Centro de Estudios de la Mujer (CEM), *Mundo de mujer: Continuidad y cambio* (Santiago, 1988), pp. 97–181.

2. Ximena Valdés, "Feminización del mercado de trabajo agrícola: Las temporeras," in *Mundo de mujer*, pp. 389–430.

3. Peter Brown, *The Devil and the Flesh* (New York, 1988).

4. Giselle Munizaga, *El discurso público de Pinochet* (Santiago, 1988).

5. Ana María Arteaga, "Politización de lo privado y subversión de lo cotidiano," in *Mundo de mujer*, pp. 565–92.

6. Norbert Lechner and Susana Levy, "Notas sobre la vida cotidiana III: El disciplinamiento de la mujer," *Material de Discusion* FLACSO (Santiago, 1984).

7. Edda Gaviola, Ximena Jiles, Lorella Lopestri, and Claudia Rojas, *Queremos votar en las próximas elecciones* (Santiago, 1986).

8. Julieta Kirkwood, *Ser política en Chile: Las feministas y los partidos* (Santiago, 1986).

9. Patricia Chuchryck, "Protest, Politics and Personal Life: The Emergence of Feminism in a Military Dictatorship, Chile, 1973–1983" (Ph.D. diss., University of York, 1984).

10. Hugo Frühling, "Reproducción y socialización de núcleos de resistencia: La experiencia de la Vicaría de la Solidaridad en Chile" (paper presented at the Seminar on "La cultura del miedo bajo regímenes militares," Buenos Aires, June 1985).

11. Pilar Vergara, *Auge y caída del neoliberalismo en Chile* (Santiago, 1984).

12. Claudia Serrano, "Pobladoras en Santiago: Algo más que la crisis," in ISIS-MUDAR, *Mujeres, crisis y movimiento* (Santiago, 1988).

13. José Pablo Arellano, "La situación social en Chile," *Notas Técnicas CIEPLAN*, no. 94 (Santiago, 1987).

14. Francisco Javier Labbé, "Distribución del ingreso en la teoría económica," *Documento de Trabajo* CED (Santiago, 1986).

15. Osvaldo Rosales, "La mujer chilena en la fuerza de trabajo: Participación, empleo y desempleo, 1957–1977" (M.A. thesis, Universidad de Chile, Escolatina, 1979).

16. Adriana Muñoz, "Fuerza de trabajo femenina: Evolución y tendencias," in *Mundo de mujer*, pp. 185–277.

17. Ibid. Statistical studies consider the head of household to be the person whom the family group recognizes as such. Traditionally, that is the man, even if he is not employed. Thus, the women shown in statistics are usually single women.

18. Eugenia Hola, "Mujer, dominación y crisis," and Ximena Díaz and Eugenia Hola, "La mujer en el trabajo informal urbano," both in *Mundo de mujer*, pp. 13–49, 323–85.

19. Lucía Pardo, "El impacto socioeconómico de la labor de la mujer," *Revista Política*, no. 7 (1985): 81–115.

20. This story illustrates the situation: "When my wife began to work regularly outside the home I felt very small. To see her leave early each winter morning was a sacrifice that I could not conceive of, given that I had married her so that she would be happy in the home, watching the children and waiting for me to come home from work every day." See David Benavente, *A medio morir cantando: 13 testimonios de cesantes* (Santiago, 1985).

21. María de la Luz Silva, "La participación de la mujer en Chile: Las organizaciones de mujeres" (paper presented at the international conference on "La participación política de la mujer en el cono sur," Montevideo, June 1986).

22. Serrano, "Pobladoras en Santiago."

23. This influence came about indirectly because of the ease of communication and directly through the great numbers of Chilean women who had left the country after 1973 for political reasons and who returned to introduce the European and North American strains of feminism in Chile.

24. Following the initial repression of union organizations, changes in the labor code reduced their size considerably. According to Thelma Gálvez and Rosalba Todaro, only 12.4 percent of workers in Gran Santiago were unionized in 1986. This percentage decreases significantly if only female workers are considered. See their "Primera encuesta de opinión política y sindical de los trabajadores. Análisis por sexo," Centro de Estudios de la Mujer (Santiago, 1988).

25. Natacha Molina, *Lo femenino y lo democrático en el Chile de hoy* (Santiago, 1986). The organizations that belonged to MEMCH-83 included the Feminist Movement, MOMUPO, MUDECHI, CODEM, the Women's Department of the CNS, Democratic Women, Chilean Women's Union, and the Commission for the Rights of Women of the Chilean Human Rights Commission.

26. Women's political role has been historically defined as that of elevating the moral level of politics, which is enriched by absorbing women's spiritual values. These values place politics above disputes and conflicts.

27. Muñoz, *Fuerza feminista y democracia* (Santiago, 1987).

28. MUDECHI and CODEM stayed with MEMCH-83. The Feminist Movement, MOMUPO, the Commission of Women's Rights, the Women's Department of the CNS and others withdrew.

29. Kirkwood, *Ser política en Chile.*

30. Molina, "Propuestas políticas y orientaciones de cambio en la situación de la mujer, 1987," *Documentos de Trabajo FLACSO* (Santiago, 1988).

31. Chuchryck, "Protest, Politics and Personal Life."

32. Julieta Kirkwood, "Los nudos de la sabiduría feminista," *Documentos de Trabajo FLACSO* (Santiago, 1984).

33. Molina, *Lo femenino y lo democrático.*

34. The Feminist Movement asked that, once democracy is achieved, the state make the principle of equality between men and women part of the constitution and reform civil, criminal, and labor legislation that discriminates against women. Moreover, it was supposed to create a ministerial office and local organizations to develop public policies that would benefit women, modify educational materials that contribute to the continuance of inequality between the sexes, and establish positive discrimination by hiring women for 30 percent of government positions.

35. The Civil Code establishes the obedience that women owe their husbands and the protection they should receive in return. It also disqualifies women from making fundamental decisions about their lives because of marital authority (the rights that the laws grant to husbands over the person and goods of their wives).

36. *El Mercurio,* July 18, 1986.

37. *El Mercurio,* December 20, 1988.

38. *El Mercurio,* December 11, 1987, December 20, 1988.

39. There is agreement across the political spectrum on this point. Female leaders of right, center, and left parties complain that a masculine conception of politics is dominant. Mariana Aylwin (DC) and Fernanda Otero (RN) agreed when they pointed out that there is a limit to the integration of women in politics because of its function with "masculine styles and schedules." Berta Belmar (PPD) commented that although "we women make up 47 percent of political militants and we had a determining role in the registration campaign and the training of poll watchers for the plebiscite, there are no women on the Board of Directors nor in the Supreme Tribunal, and in the Political Commission we have only María Maluenda and myself." See *La Epoca,* September 5, 1988, January 22, 1989.

40. Elsa Chaney, *Supermadre: Women and Politics in Latin America* (Austin, 1979).

41. Muñoz, *Fuerza feminista y democracia.*

42. Molina, "Propuestas políticas."

43. In the National and the National Renovation parties, calls have been made for changing family rights legislation and also for allowing women greater access to education, so that they can develop professionally, raise their children, and participate in civilian life as informed voters.

44. As Molina wrote in "Propuestas políticas," the Communist Party is an odd case; because it has made no official proposals or declarations concerning women since 1962–63. After the plebiscite, however, PAIS, which includes the PC, created a Women's Committee. This committee took a controversial stand when it publicly called for legal reforms sanctioning the equality of the sexes and the legalization of divorce and abortion.

45. One example of the lack of receptivity of some leaders toward women's demands is given by Claudio Huepe, national advisor for the PDC, who stated: "I do not think that women will be a theme of debate, not even among women themselves, because there are other, more urgent, problems: unemployment, human rights, the soup kitchens." See María Angélica Meza, *La otra mitad de Chile* (Santiago, 1986).

46. Mariana Aylwin, Sofía Correa, and Magdalena Piñera, "Percepción del rol político de la mujer," *Documento de Trabajo*, Instituto Chileno de Estudios Humanísticos (Santiago, 1986).

47. *La Epoca*, January 3, 1988.

48. Molina, "Propuestas políticas."

49. Even though the specific interests of women have been minimally represented, and given that it was assumed that women's demands were the same as their husbands', women had to struggle ha.d to get the right to vote. They showed great interest in participating in politics once they achieved that right in 1949. The study by Aylwin, Correa, and Piñera ("Percepción del rol político de la mujer") showed that the rates of female abstention have been consistently less than those of their male counterparts in the four presidential elections in which they have participated. In 1952, the abstention rate was 13.6 percent for men and 12.4 percent for women; in 1958, it was 17.9 percent for men and 13.9 percent for women; in 1964, it was 16.2 percent for men and 9.6 percent for women; and in 1970, 19 percent of the men abstained and 13.8 percent of the women.

Alan Angell

Unions and Workers in Chile during the 1980s

During the 1960s and until the military coup of 1973, the trade union movement in Chile was an increasingly important economic and political actor. Before 1973, trade unions in Chile enjoyed a relatively high level of internal democracy and participation. Although they relied heavily on the political parties, the negative effects of that reliance were diminished by the variety and pluralism of the possible political allegiances. Trade unions became increasingly involved with the government in matters of economic and social planning and saw themselves as spokespersons for the urban and, to a lesser extent, the rural poor. But the movement had weaknesses as well as strengths. For example, union politics could be sectarian. Union bureaucracies were not well-developed (with certain exceptions, such as the copper miners) and had limited bargaining power with employers and the government. There were large sectors of the urban and rural poor for whom unions were only remote organizations.

After 1973, unions lost most of their power and suffered the effects of severe labor legislation, brutal repression, high levels of unemployment, and widespread economic suffering. The trade union movement was in no condition to resist this onslaught. By the early 1980s, the union movement had weakened; it was poor and politically impotent, recalling the harsh days of the 1930s. Membership dropped to one-third of its highest level, many union leaders were unemployed, sectarian divisions persisted, and the degree of dependence on foreign funding and support became alarming for a movement that had always been proud of its independence.

Nevertheless, unions survived. Although labor organizations were seriously weakened, especially at the national level, memories, loyalties, and political commitment vitalized the rank and file. The major protagonist of the first protest against the regime that broke out in May 1983 was a trade union, the copper confederation (CTC). Unions slowly rebuilt themselves, and in August 1988 they recreated a major confederation, the Central Unitaria de Trabajadores, recalling the old CUT (Central Unica de Trabajadores). Of course, trade unions were only one of the many institutions and movements that combined to oppose the government of General Augusto Pinochet, and it can be debated whether they were among the most important. It will take unions some time before they can recover anything near their former strength. They will have to respond to different challenges and work under a different political context.

The Economic Context

The economic collapse of 1982–83 and the subsequent economic recovery following 1985 were two of the latest cycles in the erratic story of the Chilean economy since 1973. Fairly constant throughout, however, was the process whereby wages were depressed in line with, or even exceeding, any economic recession and recovered less than the economy as a whole during periods of growth. This led to an unequal income distribution, which the unions were unable to change.

According to a survey of earnings in June 1988, the existing legal minimum wage of 10,843 pesos per month was half that necessary to maintain an average family. Moreover, nearly 19 percent of those questioned earned less than the minimum wage. Almost half of the people surveyed earned less than the 20,000 pesos necessary to maintain an average family. At the other end of the scale, 7.3 percent earned at least ten times the minimum wage.[1]

Given the weak power of unions as collective bargainers, the importance of the official minimum wage was much greater under the military than it was prior to 1973. Accepting it as fair and legitimate, employers based their pay offers on the minimum wage or on multiples of it. Therefore, the real value of the minimum wage was of significant concern to the employed labor force. The minimum wage (in 1987 pesos) was much higher in 1981 at 19,169 pesos, or in 1977 at 18,892 pesos, and even in 1979 at 15,839 pesos. The relationship between minimum wage and average earnings is complex. Between

1974 and 1978, the purchasing power of average earnings rose by 17 percent, while the minimum wage rose by 30 percent. Between 1978 and 1982, average earnings rose by 28 percent, but the minimum wage fell by 6 percent. And between 1982 and 1986, average earnings fell by 13 percent, while the minimum wage fell by 35 percent. In 1988, the real average wage was still at the 1980 level.

The government believed that increasing the minimum wage would increase all wages proportionally and, therefore, lead to unemployment. This was by no means certain. For example, the opposite occurred in Chile in the 1960s, when an increase in the minimum wage was linked to an increase in employment. René Cortázar estimated that it was possible to increase the minimum wage by 50 percent without adversely affecting the decisions that entrepreneurs made on the level of employment.[2] But entrepreneurs who were keen to reduce labor costs argued for keeping wages as low as possible, and the government attended to them and not to the workers. In January 1989, the government increased the legal minimum wage to 15,900 pesos. Nevertheless, a leading spokesman of the entrepreneurial associations, Manuel Feliú, stated that the legal minimum could be closer to 18,000 pesos. Industrialist Roberto Fantuzzi agreed that the unions' demand for 25,000 pesos was reasonable.

The unemployment rate is another indicator that demonstrates the lack of union power against a hostile government. The rate of unemployment in the 1960s fluctuated between 5 and 7 percent. Even government figures for Gran Santiago, which underestimate the true rate by excluding those who worked in the government's minimum employment schemes, show that the rate was 11.7 percent in 1980, rising to a peak of 20 percent in 1982 and falling to 11.2 percent in 1988. Unemployment was particularly severe in the industrial and construction sectors, which had been the strongholds of union organization before the coup. These sectors included many of the chronically unemployed who suffered loss of work over several years. Moreover, as a result of the surplus of labor, work became increasingly informal. By 1986, 37 percent of employment fell within the informal sector. It was difficult to envisage how these sectors could be organized in a way that permitted joint action with unions. Work also became less stable and temporary and often was subcontracted to homeworkers.[3]

These conditions of employment were accompanied by greater participation by women in the labor market, though not under favorable conditions. Between 1950 and 1970 the percentage of women in the labor force rose from 20 to 22.4 percent. By 1985, women made up 28.2 percent of Chilean workers. In the 1970s, the annual growth rate of the female labor force was 4.5 percent, whereas for male employment it was 1.8 percent.[4] But even though women in the 1980s were active in a large number of community organizations, from communal kitchens to workshops, they were not active in the trade unions. The great majority of women were not union members, nor could they be, given their occupations. Of the total female urban labor force, 40.2 percent worked in the informal sector (19 percent in domestic service alone), compared with only 22.1 percent of the male labor force. Even those women who worked in the formal sector were rarely in occupations that allowed them to participate in unions. Over half of the women in the formal sector worked for the state, where collective bargaining was prohibited. In the private sector, companies often used tactics that effectively barred women from union participation. For example, many offered short-term contracts of six months, which not only made workers ineligible to join unions but also relieved employers of making social security payments and salary increases based on length of service.[5] These tactics effectively weakened worker unity by dividing the work force into those who enjoyed some degree of employment security and could form unions and those who had no job security and could not join unions. Because of these conditions, unions were unable to adopt a policy to systematically recruit women members. It was a question of attitude as well as opportunity. As Helia Henríquez stated, "Confronting the political parties, the women's movement acts as an alternative structure. Faced with the trade union movement, on the other hand, the basic attitude is one of lack of interest rather than of conflict."[6] According to survey evidence, for many women, paid employment outside the home was a secondary supplementary activity to their main role—as unpaid homemakers. Therefore, it seemed illogical to use the union as the vehicle for collective grievances, since grievances were seen primarily as individual rather than collective.[7]

But it was not only a question of the attitudes of women. In Chile, trade union ideology has traditionally given primary emphasis to class factors, not to gender. Little attention has been paid to the specific problems of women workers, especially to an increasingly important sector of those workers, those who are single parents. Trade union practice—and the Chilean political left as a whole—still only allows women a supporting and secondary role.

Trade unions need to devise not only appropriate strategies to encompass workers whose employment characteristics make them difficult to organize, but also strategies to incorporate women workers. The magnitude of these adjustments should not be underestimated. In other countries, few union movements have been able to deal successfully with problems of incorporating the long-term unemployed or with questions of gender discrimination. To devise novel strategies that reflect these kinds of social change seems a lot to ask of a weak union movement. Yet, the union movement has not yet developed bureaucratic structures that resist change, and the task could be more easily accommodated to the general demand for a participatory role in the construction of a new democratic Chile. If these changes are not made, then the working-class movement could divide into three sectors: (1) traditional unionization based on national confederations that are highly politicized, that speak for a limited part of the union movement as a whole, and that are based primarily on the traditional strongholds of mining and industry; (2) unionization based on individual enterprises, with greater or lesser strength in a specific firm but without overall or national strategies; and (3) a large group of workers with no bargaining power at all that is at the mercy of individual negotiation in the marketplace.[8]

Union Organization, Structure, and Divisions

Figures on the number of unions and unionists must be treated with great caution. They reveal little about the internal life of a union nor about how unions coped with the heavy weight of labor laws. According to Ministry of Labor statistics, Chile had 5,883 unions in 1987, of which 3,834 were enterprise unions. The total number of union members was given as 422,302 (of which 296,914 were members of enterprise unions). In 1981, there were fewer unions, 3,977, with only 395,951 members. There was a sharp decline in the number of unions and union members during the crisis of 1982–1983, followed by a recovery. A more striking indicator of change in the unions is the growth of federations and confederations. In 1982, there were 62 federations and confederations, with some 630 affiliated unions organizing 85,727 members; by 1987, there were 180 federations and confederations with 2,308 affiliated unions and 221,642 members. But even official government statistics classified 25 percent of all unions as "unions in recess."

The highest density of union membership remained, as it had been historically, in the mining sector, where 65.2 percent of the work force was unionized, with mining representing only 2 percent of the total labor force. Of the 606,900 manufacturing workers, 15.2 percent of the total labor force, only 20.1 percent were organized. The single largest occupational category, 28.2 percent of the labor force, was classified as *servicios comunales, sociales, y personales*, and the level of unionization was only 3.9 percent (which is the same figure as that of the second largest category of workers, those in agriculture).[9]

Most unions struggled to perform a minimum of functions. A recent survey of union presidents concluded that virtually all union concerns revolved around the affairs of the enterprise and questions relating to the organization of local unions. Given the generally precarious state of local union finances and the multiple pressures on local union officials, there seemed to be little possibility of developing other activities on a wider scale. Although the union presidents surveyed had close communication with their corresponding federation, contact with national organizations was passive and distant.[10]

This last point indicates one weakness of the major confederations—the fragile contact that existed between the politicized world of the leaders, the major national organizations, and the daily concerns of rank-and-file union members. A 1988 survey of workers in Gran Santiago (of whom 26.5 percent were union members) asked: "Which of the following individuals is the best national union leader?" The respondents replied: Manuel Bustos, 34.5 percent, "don't know any of them," 24.9 percent, "none of them," 24 percent, and Guillermo Medina, a pro-government leader, 6 percent. The only Communist on the list was chosen by 0.5 percent of the workers surveyed; the moderate socialist Arturo Martínez received 0.7 percent, and Nicanor Araya, a socialist of the *histórico* section, received 0.5 percent. This does not mean that rank-and-file members were unsympathetic to the general political concerns of the national leaders. Asked if they favored the formation of a national union confederation (the CUT) 63.3 percent were in favor and only 3.5 percent were against (the others remained indifferent).[11]

The gap between union leadership and the rank-and-file members weakened the influence of the union movement. One of the major goals of the Pinochet government was to decapitate popular movements and to isolate leaders from their followers. A major target of this policy was the trade union movement, weakening the solidarity of the union movement.

The Copper Unions

The copper unions, in spite of their relatively small number of members, have traditionally been in the forefront of union struggles in Chile, and one of the military regime's major objectives was to reduce their power. Overall employment in Gran Minería fell from 32,800 in 1974 to 24,886 in 1986, but union membership fell even more sharply, as mechanisms such as subcontracting and short-term contracts diminished the number of permanent workers who were able to join unions.[12] Total figures were difficult to obtain, but approximately half of the eight thousand workers in El Teniente fell into the categories of temporary or subcontracted labor. The Copper Workers Federation (CTC) estimated that this was the proportion throughout the industry and, moreover, that those workers received wages about 50 percent lower than the permanent CODELCO workers.

Many union leaders were dismissed after the coup, and the government appointed its own partisans to positions of leadership in the CTC. But those leaders gained little support among the copper miners. In 1980, during the first CTC congress held under the military government, the official leaders were defeated in Chuquicamata and El Salvador. And in 1977, the first major demonstration against the government took place in the El Teniente copper mine. The government responded with massive dismissals of strike leaders and workers. Similar action in other mines led to a similar response by the government. In Chuquicamata in 1978, the government declared a state of siege, but even that was not enough to break the strike until some concessions were made. The government obviously wanted to sever the link between the copper unions and the political parties, but weakening the union's power to carry out its normal functions only reinforced its need to seek external support from the parties and to politicize rather than to depoliticize union action.

In May 1983, the leadership role that the copper union took during the first days of the national protests demonstrated the great risks the miners were willing to take to fight for their union and their political rights. The immediate motive for calling the demonstration against the government was the Decree Law No. 18,134, which removed the link between inflation and wage increases. After the initial decision to strike, union leaders decided that broader action would be more appropriate, since unemployment levels of approximately 30 percent made a strike an uncertain venture. The strike call was transformed into a broadly based social protest to demand the restoration of democracy. To ensure its success, the protest was to be called by a leading union, one whose political pluralism aligned all sectors of the middle class and assured them that this was a responsible and representative action that had some chance of influencing events, not merely a wildcat action of the far left.[13]

The successful first day of protest led to a new broad labor confederation; the Comando Nacional de Trabajadores, in which the CTC was prominent. Attempts to repeat the demonstration in June were less successful. Government repression was quicker and more brutal, the strike was less solidly supported, and Chuquicamata did not follow the instruction to strike. Many striking workers and leaders were dismissed, and the union was forced to concentrate on demanding, to little avail, the members' re-employment. The initiative for future protests passed to the political parties.

The copper workers' protest was extremely important in that it opened the way for future demonstrations. The government had created an image of impregnability and had become increasingly confident that it had broken Chileans' dependence on their past political allegiances. The actions of the copper miners showed that the government could be shaken and that a tradition of working class struggle had been repressed but not superseded by a new ideology of materialism and consumerism.

Trade Unions in the Countryside

The real growth of rural unions dates from the mid-1960s. Even though their numerical growth was spectacular thereafter, these unions were not able to resist the repression of a government determined to dominate social relations in the countryside. Left-wing union federations were closed after the coup, and the Christian Democratic unions soon fell victim to the battery of labor legislation that made effective union action next to impossible. Decree Law No. 208 of December 1973, for example, stated that all former beneficiaries of land reform who were involved in land seizures before 1973 would not be eligible for the grant of family farms (*par-celas*). This effectively expelled left-wing peasant activists from the countryside. Later, in 1979, the government's Labor Plan repealed the Christian Democratic Rural Unionization Law of 1967, which had for the first time permitted the formation of effective rural unions. Between 1968 and 1973, rural unions had received an estimated US$8 million from the Fondo de Educación y Extensión Sindical (FEES). Without that soruce of support, Patricio Silva writes, "the peasant movement was reduced to local unions, each acting in isolation."[14] The number of rural workers who belonged to unions in 1985 represented only 20 percent of those affiliated with unions in 1972. A substantial proportion of members claimed by the six union confederations was very nominal, and it is possible that the real figure of active union members was even lower. Moreover, landowners, unlike some urban entrepreneurs, did not discriminate between moderate unions led by Christian Democrats and more radical unions led by Marxists. Rural employers opposed all unions.

But the story is not only one of the repression of union activity. The social and economic change that took place in the countryside was similar to that in cities, producing a much more differentiated occupational structure that was difficult to unite in a common organization. Privatization of the reformed sector of agriculture intended to create an agrarian middle class that would be immune to the Christian Democratic, or the Marxist, ideas on the virtues of communal or collective ownership. There were fewer permanent rural workers (*inquilinos*) and many more temporary workers (*temporeros*), especially in the prosperous fruit industry of the central valley, where more than half the workers were temporary migrants from the towns, many of them women. Only 10 percent of the local rural population enjoyed the benefits and status of permanent workers. Both the power balance and the change in economic organization moved decisively against rural workers. Even though the major confederations did unite in 1982, in the Comisión Nacional Campesina, rural unions remained a pale shadow of what they had been before the coup.

The National Confederations

Union federations formed and reformed after 1975, when the Group of Ten expressed the opposition of the moderate Christian Democratic trade union leaders to the government's labor policy. Nevertheless, a number of groups can be identified. The Group of Ten evolved into the CDT, which continued to voice opposition to both communism and the idea of recreating anything resembling the old CUT. Moreover, the CDT expressed support for at least part of the government's free-market policies. Leftist unions and their Christian Democratic allies formed the biggest group in the union movement. Their organizational efforts culminated in the formation of the new CUT in August 1988.

The pro-government force in the union movement maintained strength in certain sectors, such as banking and the steel industry. Although it is difficult to see why many workers would voluntarily vote for pro-government labor leaders, many believed that opposition union leaders would not be able to accomplish anything, while pro-government leaders could. No doubt fear, intimidation, and associated factors also explain the workers' support for such leaders, though the force of anti-communist sentiment in some sectors of the working population should not be discounted.

Apart from these groups and long-standing white-collar unions like the CEPCH, a new movement took hold. The Movimiento Sindical Unitario (MSU) was founded in 1984 as a reaction of some rank-and-file leaders to the overt partisan commitment of the great majority of national union leaders. Although far from being a majority faction, the MSU did capture the mood of those who wished to move away from the old pattern of union-party relations in order to give more expression to rank-and-file members and create a more democratic internal union structure.

Many of these confederations joined together in the Comando Nacional de Trabajadores (CNT) that formed in June 1983, following the lead of the copper workers. The CNT was an important step in the process of regrouping; it assured the union movement a voice in the development of the opposition to the government.[15] But the CNT was merely a loose coordinating body, and disputes between constituent members weakened its authority. Furthermore, it could not escape the perpetual problem that any opposition movement faced in Pinochet's Chile—knowing just how representative any organization and its leaders were. In addition, the CNT was unable to reconcile the different ideologies of its member unions.

Crucial issues for understanding national union structures include representativeness, the relations between the leadership of the national confederations and the union, and the links with political parties and international organizations. The CNT—and the CUT in 1988—were the product of political accord rather than union matters. They formed because the political moment was propitious, the parties with power in the union movement were in agreement, and such agreement was functional to the strategy of the political opposition. Perhaps there was little alternative to this kind of strategy. As Manuel Antonio Garretón writes:

One of the problems of this type of integration where base organizations are weak, and social movements are dependent upon political ones, is that social sectors not directly linked to the party political structures are reduced to marginal importance. On the other hand, the advantage for that sector that manages to organize itself and to develop a close relationship with the party structure, is that it achieves at least some degree of satisfaction of its claims, even if it remains a subordinate force.[16]

Another aspect of the problem was that the union movement came to rely on both national and international allies. It is no exaggeration to say that without the support of the Catholic Church, especially during the early days, the survival of many unionists, and certainly of many union leaders, would have been almost impossible. But not all help has been so disinterested. The danger of relying on heavy external support was one of reinforcing cold war attitudes or of dividing the opposition, not always accurately, into democratic and nondemocratic groups, rewarding one rather than the other. For example, the American National Endowment for Democracy gave US$856,000 to the CDT from 1984 to 1988 and $185,000 to a joint project of the CDT and the CNT. The CDT was obviously more acceptable to the National Endowment than other trade union confederations, because of its strong anti-communist line. In the world of Chilean unions, where a million dollars is considered a lot of money, it seems reasonable to assume that the existence of the CDT was partly due to the favorable financial treatment it received from such sources.

How much have the traditional divisions in the Chilean union movement been overcome by the formation of the new CUT? Will this new body provide a strong, more representative leadership and be able to participate in the complicated politics that inevitably accompany any period of political transition? The formation of the CUT in 1988 was much different than the formation of the first CUT in 1953.[17] The first CUT was created at a time of political and social turmoil, widespread union militancy, and cooperation between the forces of the left. By contrast, the formation of the new CUT in 1988 was a subdued affair, emanating largely from party agreements, at a time when political attention was concentrated on the plebiscite and when the most popular trade union leader, Manuel Bustos, was sentenced to internal exile.

At the CUT executive election, all four lists presented to members closely identified with a political party. List A consisted of the Almeyda socialists, Izquierda Cristiana, one of the Radical parties, and some independent leftists. This list secured 57,198 votes and elected nine members to the executive. List B, representing the PDC, obtained 106,192 votes and elected sixteen members. List C, representing the Communist Party, the MIR, and some left socialists, got 74,180 votes and elected eleven members. And List D, representing the Núñez socialists, the MAPU, and the MAPUOC, received 52,288 votes and elected eight members. It is interesting that the largest bloc of votes for the PDC list came from the union with the most delegates at the congress, the Colegio de Profesores. This can be seen as an indication of the declining power of the old industrial unions and a rising union militancy of white-collar public employees, who suffered from the government's hostility toward the public sector. The CUT executive board consisted of forty-two men and two women, with six representatives from the Colegio de Profesores, six from peasant unions, five from the CTC, two from the Banking Federation, and only seven from industrial unions. The remainder were from a variety of unions, ranging from university employees to self-employed workers.

There were undeniable differences within the CUT over tactics and objectives. The PC delegates to the inaugural congress attempted to include a reference to the class struggle in the Declaration of Principles, but were defeated. Similarly, some of the PDC delegates tried in vain to include a paragraph rejecting violence and terrorism. There were some hopes that a single list could be presented for election to the executive, but the reality of partisan differences made this impossible. There were also internal disagreements. The PDC list covered the spectrum of opinion inside the party on union matters, and there were no guarantees that internal disagreements would not break out among this group.[18]

The Declaration of Principles and the Plataforma de Lucha agreed to at the congress were notably more moderate than the declarations of the old CUT, with its attack on private property and hopes for a classless society. The Plataforma de Lucha emphasized respect for human rights and the defense of national economic sovereignty, apart from the expected calls for the abolition of labor laws and reform of the social security system. There was also extensive reference to women's rights. The CUT realized that it had to encompass broader issues than it had in the past and included, for example, a declaration of Los 21 Pedidos Urgentes de los Pobres. These statements and the Declaration of Principles showed a greater concern with formal democracy than in the past, but the ritual declaration of the autonomy of the trade union movement from political parties was as accurate for the new CUT as it was for the old.

It is extremely difficult to evaluate properly an organization founded in August 1988, with its two principal organizers (Arturo Martínez and Bustos) exiled to distant parts of Chile for 541 days, a time of momentous political events. The new organization did formally represent the great majority of Chilean unionists, guaranteeing the working class greater influence in the process of political transition, but it could only be as strong as its constituents. Moreover, Chile's unions and federations had been greatly weakened by fifteen years of repression and control. Given the history of Chilean trade unionism, even since 1973, it is unrealistic to assume that the unions' close relationship with the political parties could ever be severed. The idea of an autonomous movement is too divorced from Chilean reality to be feasible, but there are various degrees of dependence. Beyond a certain point, dependence becomes obedience to party dictates, and there is little doubt that such a relationship would damage the possibilities for the union movement to exercise influence over the social and economic agenda of a democratic Chile. But it is possible to retain party attachments and still speak and act with a degree of independence, stressing working-class unity rather than party sectarianism. Such a position—or critical loyalty—to the parties is not easy to attain and will require forbearance by the parties, as well as a strong desire by the unionists for some degree of independence.

Do Unions Represent the Poor?

The CUT indicated that its primary focus was not on issues exclusive to the world of enterprise by including in its initial declarations a document identifying the basic needs of the poor. But in Pinochet's

Chile, what was the relation between organized and unorganized labor? What role did the union movement play in wider social conflict? Did the union have the power to rally the masses? It is difficult to anticipate how much political influence the unions will be able to exercise during the transitional period and once a democratic system is consolidated. The more they can advance and represent the overall interests of the labor force, whether unionized, employed, or not, the more influential they will be.

It can be argued that the union movement should concentrate on the reconstruction of civil society, for one of the legacies of the Pinochet era was a degree of social disorganization and a general weakness of social movements that contrasted markedly with the vigorous social movements of the PDC and Popular Unity administrations. Survey evidence indicates that even in the shantytowns, especially among the unemployed youth of those communities, the trade union movement was viewed as a central actor in the struggle of popular movements. The inhabitants of the shantytowns expected the unions to lead their social struggle. They tended to see violence, the most notable feature of mobilization in the shantytowns, as a defense against government oppression rather than as a demonstration of social power. Active defense of their interests rested more on the possibility of combined action with the unions than on the expectation of a violent political rebellion. In practice, the expectation of practical action and union support was an ideological nostalgia. There is little evidence of real cooperation between the shantytown organizations and the unions, yet the belief that it existed is an indication of the importance of unionism as a political force in the ideological perceptions of the urban poor in Chile.[19]

Trade unions suffered not only from repression but also from legal regulation, and yet they still had some organizational advantages over other movements. On the one hand, there was no large social gap between organized and unorganized labor. But on the other hand, employment was unstable and precarious during the years of military rule. Many workers experienced periods of both employment and unemployment; many families had members who were employed and others who were not; and many trade union leaders were unemployed, especially those who were known to be political militants. Trade unions did not provide a sheltered haven within which political activity could freely take place. On the contrary, fear of reprisals and dismissals made unionists desist from participating in activities of local unions that went beyond those that were acceptable to the authorities. One of the great challenges to social organizations in Chile, including unions, will be to increase participation to such a degree that popular organizations have genuine authority. The weakness of existing popular organizations, including unions, explains the persistence of political party allegiance. It is not that the parties are especially strong or that they can supply massive benefits to their supporters. It is that no other form of social and political articulation exists, either nationally or internationally (and international links can bring all-important financial aid to hard-pressed organizations).

Social organizations in the shantytowns and trade unions suffered from similar problems as they tried to survive under a powerful dictatorship. But shantytown organizers had neither the economic leverage nor the political traditions of the union movement. Most organizations in the shantytowns were concerned with daily survival, not national and political concerns. An estimated 1.3 million inhabitants of Santiago, a third of the total population, live in these settlements, and nearly 70 percent of them are under thirty years of age. There are an estimated 1,383 community organizations in Santiago, encompassing some 200,000 people, mostly families.[20] During the years of military rule, the perspectives of these organizations were very limited. Most attempts to create organizations with a broader perspective were unsuccessful, because of apathy, because the organizations that did exist lacked the time and resources for such activities, and because the new organizations were more visible and invited repression.

The social position of the *poblador* gave rise to a tension between the desire for autonomy and dependence on the state. For *pobladores*, who were excluded from the market and repressed by the government, the *población* was the only community. But social problems can only be solved by state action. One attitude induced apathy and the other the use of violent social protest, the only instrument available to many shantytown inhabitants.

According to Guillermo Campero, *poblador* organizations were torn between an impulse to integrate into society and a feeling of exclusion.[21] Given this tension, it is unlikely that a powerful autonomous *poblador* movement will develop. The groups that did exist during the authoritarian period operated more because of the institutional support of the Catholic Church than because of any intrinsic strength. Politically, *pobladores* were likely to be indifferent to formal democracy and to favor populist measures directed by the state. Their aspirations were based on increased support from the state, not autonomy from it, and they stressed the desire for access to industrial jobs rather than self-sufficient workshops.

It would be a serious error to equate communal organizations in the shantytowns with political organizations. It is undeniable that the Communist Party had some following in these areas, but it is equally undeniable that there were many other organizations whose affiliation was to the church (whether Catholic or Protestant), to some other external agent, or to no one at all. Additionally, not all activists in the shantytowns were political activists, not all shantytowns participated in the days of protest, and not all shantytown dwellers opposed the government. The prevailing attitude of the majority seemed to be a mixture of apathy and indifference. In this context, the recourse to violence should be seen as a measure of desperation rather than as an act of political calculation.

Nonetheless, the creation of wider *poblador* organizations with broader concerns was tempting to the political parties, not only because such organizations could be used for party ends but also because it would alienate rival parties in the struggle to establish party identity and generate support. Moreover, the existence of widespread social organizations that escaped party control was threatening to political parties that were accustomed to monopolizing such institutions.

There were four major poblador organizations: the Movimiento Poblacional Solidaridad, linked to the PDC; the Movimiento Poblacional Dignidad, linked to the Izquierda Cristiana; the Coordinadora Metropolitana de Pobladores, linked to the Communist Party; and the Coordinadora de Agrupaciones Poblacionales, linked to the MIR. The attempt by the three left-wing groups to set up a Comando Unitario de Pobladores was a lesson in party manipulation. Organizations that were not linked to the party were deliberately excluded, and nearly 90 percent of the delegates were party militants. The whole process of electing the executive was marked by bitter struggles between the different parties. In the words of Philip Oxhorn, "the congress was transformed into a political convention, along with pacts and secret agreements in order to control the distribution of power in the developing *poblador* movement."[22] It would be a mistake, however, to assume that the partisan decisions taken reflected some national strategy laid down by party headquarters. Parties had enormous difficulties in communicating with, let alone controlling, the activities of their rank-and-file members, who did not always adhere to the policies of their national leaders. It is not only the popular movements that have to think about their role in a future democratic Chile. It is also the responsibility of political parties to devise methods of incorporating the demands of these groups and of expressing their interests without manipulating them for narrowly partisan considerations. The leadership of political parties in Chile, even those on the left, comes from a relatively small political class, and union and *poblador* representatives are noted by their absence. As one leader of the Comando Unitario de Pobladores observed, "the sad truth is that in the central committees of the parties of the left, there is no poblador."[23]

The link between unions and the organizations of *pobladores* existed at the level of declarations of mutual support by national organizations. At the local level, there seemed to be little sustained contact, with each group isolated in its own community or factory. Examining a number of cases of proposed union-*poblacional* cooperation, Rodrigo Baño concluded that "there exist no significant experiences of cooperation between the union movement and the *poblador* movement." He pointed to two basic factors: the weakness of the *poblador* organizations and the difficulty of the union in moving outside its limited horizons to forge links with the other popular movements.[24] This lack of wider articulation was also a result of government policy. One of the aims of the government was to depoliticize the masses. Although this process was not totally successful (as demonstrated by the outcome of the plebiscite), it undoubtedly led to a widespread lack of trust of parties at the local level, or at least to a fear of becoming involved in parties because of the possible consequences.

The government had somewhat more success in depoliticizing these movements than in creating alternative movements, but there were exceptions. The government used employment in the minimum employment programs (PEM and the POJH) to manipulate the behavior of the urban poor. The latest attempt to divide the union movement, and to win support for the government's economic model, was to sell shares in privatized companies at preferential rates to employees. Of course, this could only benefit those relatively few workers who were employed in the advanced sector of the economy. For example, in the steel plant at Huachipato, the government claimed that one-third of the shares of the company was in the hands of the workers and that of the 7,300 employees of the company, 6,000 owned shares.[25] Such groups may constitute a small percentage of the total work force, but they are groups that exercise considerable economic power. Moreover, widespread employee ownership in their companies (assuming that they are not quickly sold for profit) creates considerable social distance inside the labor movement and makes joint action for wider objectives even more difficult.

Unions and Politics: Has Anything Changed?

Trade unions are very conservative bodies, and they change slowly. Unions will not be able to redefine their role by themselves. Only in a democratic system can the challenges to the union movement be met openly. The role that unions play in the new democratic order will depend on their relationship with the political parties and the entrepreneurial sectors. As J. Samuel Valenzuela has written:

The more various elements of the labor movement see their narrow objectives unfulfilled by the democratic transition, the more the labor sector will be a source of potential semi-loyalty or disloyalty to the new regime. For instance, if state and employer pressures force workers' wages to continue below their collectively organized market power and no other compensations are given to them in exchange, if labor leaders still cannot effectively represent worker interests both at the plant level and nationally given the absence of significant changes in the industrial relations system due to untowards military pressures and so on, then not much has changed for labor and its loyalty to the new regime . . . will be low indeed.[26]

Is the relationship of unions with political parties likely to be different in the future? Do the political parties want a different relationship? The answer to the second question is "probably not." The answer to the first is more complicated. Leaders of the national confederations may continue to define themselves primarily in terms of their militancy in a political party, but can they carry the rank and file with them? The survey conducted by Mario Albuquerque in the mid-1980s indicated that there is considerable distrust of the parties at the local level. Asked who they considered to be the principal allies of the union movement, of the 170 local union presidents surveyed, 18 percent replied that it was the Catholic Church (and the Church-sponsored *Vicaría*), 18 percent identified other workers, 16 percent students, 7 percent international trade union bodies, 12 percent *poblador* organizations, and only 12 percent political parties.[27]

These results reflect the workers' view of a division of functions. The base union defends the specific interests of its members, and the national confederations operate in the sphere of politics. When national trade union leaders called for participation during the days of protest, they did not expect strikes at the factory level. Their appeal was to the unemployed, to the transportation sector, to the small shopkeepers. They were looking for community rather than factory action. Even the first strike called after the plebiscite, in April 1989, was not widely supported, though the ensuing violence led to two deaths and numerous arrests which should have aroused working-class ire.

All sectors of the union movement agree on the need for certain basic reforms, including the abrogation of the labor laws, income redistribution, changes in the social security system, and the defense of national interests against excessive foreign ownership. Trade unions face a double challenge. They will have to lead the movement to reclaim the rights lost by their members and to recover the deterioration in living standards. At the same time, they will face pressure to play the role of conflict manager and restrainer of sectoral demands in order to secure democratic stability and a successful transition from authoritarianism. Some unions will emphasize the politics of compromise and conciliation and accept the need for broad social pacts. Others will stress the logic of confrontation and reject the call for restraint, especially when it comes from entrepreneurial groups that received considerable benefits during the years of military rule. Somehow, the union movement must both represent the interests of the workers and cooperate with other social and political forces and the government to secure the political economy of the transition.[28]

Apart from specific demands for better labor legislation, higher wages, and reintegration of sacked workers, it is possible that rank-and-file unionists will reject attempts to impose broader political tactics on them. The struggle against Pinochet was a struggle against authoritarianism. In the process, the parties and groups that had once downplayed the value of formal democracy in favor of a more utopian goal (whether it be a socialist or a communitarian society) were forced to reconsider the value of democracy. Democratization in the factory or firm is as relevant to workers today as democratization in the larger society. Many workers will continue to focus on that specific aspiration on the grounds that a democratic society can only be constructed on the basis of democratic institutions in civil society. The trade union movement may have to de-emphasize images drawn from the language of class struggle and class identity in favor of themes that emphasize participation, citizenship rights, and social integration. A search for common themes will have to take place in order to unite a union movement that is more fragile and dispersed than in the past. The search for these themes implies more attention by the leadership to the interests and wishes of rank-and-file members. That, in turn, implies the development of better methods of consultation with the rank and file and with the base unions.

Emphasis on processes of internal democratization is likely to concentrate attention on the tasks of reconstructing a union movement that was savagely treated during the dictatorship. Rebuilding is a pre-condition for obtaining a more prominent political role. For example, the union movement was not a critical actor in the mobilization of the opposition that led to Pinochet's defeat in the plebiscite. This is not surprising in that union attention was concentrated on creating the CUT, two of the leading union figures were in internal exile, union activists campaigning for the "no" vote faced the threat of sanctions from their employers, and there were cases of dismissals after the vote. Of course, there was union activity that supported the "no" vote, and at least some of those activities, like the march of El Salvador copper miners and the statements issued by the Chuquicamata copper unions, received considerable publicity. But the major burden of campaigning and organization was undertaken by the parties and ad hoc organizations like the Cruzada Cívica.

In the near future, the focus of political attention is bound to be concentrated on the political parties, whose task will be to construct the framework of the new society. The way in which the new system will work will depend on agreement with its basic premises from sectors that have long been excluded from political influence. The union movement will be called upon first to play a role in the new social order, and that role is likely to include an appeal to its members for moderation. A second responsibility will be to a constituency that has suffered social injustice long enough and that not only demands redress of material improvements but also participation in the shaping of policy. A union leadership that is subordinate to the political parties may accomplish the first but not the second objective. A union leadership that is hostile to the parties may achieve the second objective but will fail to play a general role in society and the political system. The unions cannot define their constituency too narrowly. Those engaged in stable employment, even though they experienced harsh working conditions and low wages, still enjoyed privileges that were denied to the majority of the urban and rural poor. It seems unfair to saddle the weak and divided union movement with such historic responsibility. Nevertheless, one of the consequences of those years of dictatorship is the persistence of problems and difficulties that tax the ingenuity of the most skillful and disinterested democrats, whether their responsibility lies in congress, the executive, the parties, or the institutions of civil society.

Notes

1. Programa de Empleo y Trabajo (PET), "Encuesta de empleo: Santiago" (Santiago, 1988). Cited in *La Epoca,* October 22, 1988.

2. René Cortázar, "¿Qué hacer con los salarios mínimos?" *Notas Técnicas CIEPLAN,* no. 107 (December 1987). In 1982, the government, with Decree Law No. 18,134, substantially worsened wage legislation by eliminating the provision for an automatic increase after a 10 percent increase in the cost of living and by eliminating the guarantee that each collective bargaining process took as a minimum the base established by the expiring contract. Opposition to this law was one of the main factors in the copper workers' call that led to the first mass protest in May 1983.

3. Manuel Barrera, "Consideraciones acerca de la relación entre política y movimiento sindical: El caso de Chile," *Material de Discusión,* Centro de Estudios Sociales, Santiago, no. 6 (October 1988), p. 6.

4. Inter-American Development Bank, *Economic and Social Progress in Latin America, 1987* (Washington, D.C., 1987), p. 90.

5. Thelma Gálvez and Rosalba Todaro, "Chile: Mujer y sindicato," in *Ciudadanía e identidad,* ed. Elizabeth Jelín (Geneva, 1987), p. 203.

6. Helia Henríquez, "Mujeres y trabajo: Un tema político que reclama mayor atención," *Materiales de Discusión,* no. 3 (1987), p. 12.

7. In the words of Gálvez and Todaro, "There is no sense of belonging, nor of a shared oppression, but rather one of competition." In *Ciudadanía,* p. 208.

8. Guillermo Campero, "El sindicalismo ante la democratización," *Mensaje*, no. 378 (May 1989): 144–45.

9. The level of unionization in 1987 was 10.5 percent, with 422,000 workers unionized out of a labor force of just over four million. I am grateful to Manuel Barrera for providing me with copies of these official Ministry of Labor figures and for his constant help and advice.

10. Mario Albuquerque and Victor Zúñiga, *Democracia, participación, unidad: Una mirada a la estrategia sindical desde el sindicato de base* (Santiago, 1987).

11. Quoted in Manuel Barrera, "La coyuntura política preplebiscito en Chile y los actores sociales más significativos," *Material de Discusión*, no. 8 (November 1988).

12. Alberto Bastías, "Factores que inciden en la precarización del empleo: El caso de la gran minería del cobre," *Material de Discusión*, no. 5 (1988).

13. The broad context of the action is discussed in Manuel Barrera and J. Samuel Valenzuela in *Military Rule in Chile*, ed. J. Samuel Valenzuela and Arturo Valenzuela (Baltimore, 1986). A fascinating discussion of the protests is in Manuel Antonio Garretón, *Reconstruir la política* (Santiago, 1987).

14. Patricio Silva, "The State, Politics and Peasant Unions in Chile," *Journal of Latin American Studies* 20: 2 (1988): 441.

15. The CNT was formed by the CTC. The Coordinadora Nacional Sindical grouped progressive Christian Democrats with the left and drew from a wide variety of industrial, mining, and professional unions. The Central Democrática de Trabajadores was a rightist Christian Democratic group based in some peasant enterprises, attracting skilled workers in the manufacturing sector, state employees, and some peasant groups. There was also the CEPCH, one or two smaller confederations, and later on the Petroleum Workers Federation and the Bank Workers. See Garretón, *Reconstruir la política*, p. 187; and Jaime Ruiz Tagle, *El sindicalismo chileno más allá de la crisis* (Santiago, 1984).

16. Garretón, *Reconstruir la política*, p. 161.

17. Manuel Barrera makes this comparison in *Consideraciones*, p. 11.

18. This broad representation may have something to do with foreign funding. According to one journalist, over a year before the congress, a delegation of ten workers from the CDT, twelve from the CNT, and various others went to Washington to seek funding for the CUT from the ICFTU and the American AFL-CIO. Funding was offered if the Chilean delegation could ensure a centrist majority (PDC and PS Núñez). Gonzalo Becerra, in *Qué Pasa*, May 1988.

19. The survey evidence is from a study by Eduardo Valenzuela, cited in Guillermo Campero, *Entre la sobrevivencia y la acción política* (Santiago, 1987), pp. 93–94.

20. Clarisa Hardy, *Organizarse para vivir: Pobreza urbana y organización popular* (Santiago, 1987).

21. Campero, *Entre la sobrevivencia,* p. 134.

22. Philip Oxhorn, "Organizaciones poblacionales: La reconstrucción de la sociedad civil y la interacción elite-base" (mimeograph, Santiago, April 1987). The following account relies on this excellent article.

23. Quoted in *Qué Pasa,* May 14, 1988, p. 34.

24. Rodrigo Baño, *Lo social y lo político* (Santiago, 1985), p. 93.

25. Report in *El Mercurio,* September 26, 1988.

26. J. Samuel Valenzuela, "Labor Movements in Transitions to Democracy: A Framework for Analysis," Working Paper no. 104 (The Kellogg Institute for International Studies, University of Notre Dame, June 1988), p. 10.

27. Albuquerque and Zúñiga, *Democracia,* p. 67.

28. This question is discussed in Guillermo Campero and René Cortázar, "Lógicas de acción sindical en Chile," *Estudios CIEPLAN,* no. 108 (1985); and Rodrigo Baño, "Notas sobre organizaciones de desocupados," *Documento de Trabajo,* FLACSO, no. 297 (Santiago, 1986).

Manuel Antonio Garretón

The Political Opposition and the Party System under the Military Regime

The evolution of the Chilean opposition to the military regime was a process of learning about the type of struggle necessary to put an end to the Chilean dictatorship.[1] This learning process can be described in terms of the phases that the opposition has experienced, culminating in the 1988 plebiscite and its projections for the transition to democracy. The changes from authoritarian, dictatorial, or military regimes to democratic regimes are not necessarily global social transformations.[2] These transitions are far from revolutionary or insurrectional models, insofar as those in power have not been militarily defeated but have decided to withdraw under pressure. The internal decomposition of the regime or the mobilization of the opposition against the government are accompanied by transitions that involve implicit or explicit negotiations between the power-holders (in this case, the armed forces) and the opposition. Transitions also require a regulated area of confrontation between the regime and the opposition using, for example, a plebiscite to solve the conflict.

From this perspective, the opposition's task is to create the best possible space for institutional confrontation with the regime. If this is not achieved, that space will be imposed by the regime in a way that either avoids a transition or limits that space to terms that guarantee an advantageous position for the power-holders when the regime changes. Therefore, it is appropriate to speak of a learning process for a group of political actors facing a historically unique transitional process. This necessarily involves both successes and failures, wherein the opposition redefines its role as it comes to understand what the transition means.

The Original Characteristics of the Chilean Opposition

The Military Regime

The coup of September 11, 1973, put an end to the government of President Salvador Allende and inaugurated a military regime that was characterized by three main features. First, official political power combined a political-military leadership increasingly personalized in General Augusto Pinochet with the authority of the armed forces as an institution. The diverse branches of the military subordinated themselves to the army, which was under Pinochet's command.

Second, the regime, after dismantling the previous sociopolitical system, attempted to implement a new form of relations between state and society, which involved a privatized model of capitalist organization and reinsertion. This arrangement also provided a ready-made individualized model for social organization. These changes characterized a regime that intended to form a totally new order, which was expressed politically through the constitution imposed by the 1980 plebiscite. The constitution institutionalized a military regime of fifteen years' duration (1973–88) and an authoritarian regime of indefinite duration after 1989. According to the constitution, the authoritarian regime would be predominantly civilian but it would give tutelary power to the armed forces, contain a restricted political arena that excluded certain social and political sectors, and guarantee inviolability for certain institutions that determine the character of the state's free-market model of economic and social relations.

Third, the regime's repressive character did not prevent the creation of spaces for social, cultural, and political expression by opposition sectors. The state did not absorb society, but rather repressed, excluded, and controlled it. The expressions of civil society and its organizations were not obliterated, but the regime did restrict those expressions and, more important, eliminated systems of representation before the state.

The Political Opposition

The opposition to the Chilean military regime was made up of a group of political and social actors who were heirs to the previous democratic regime. The opposition retained this inherited character even though new actors appeared and inevitable generational changes took place. Because of this inherited character, certain features that were typical of the relation between politics and society under the democratic regime were reproduced. First, the preponderant role of the state and the party system in constituting social actors meant that social actors had representation but little autonomy with respect to the political system. Second, the preponderance of a political class that tended to be relatively autonomous from its bases of representation exacerbated the problem of party identities in a competitive system. The parties emerged as subcultures, which made them highly ideological and, in certain circumstances, created strong polarizations of the political system and hindered the establishment of alliances.

The military regime profoundly dislocated the relation between politics and society by banning the representative sphere of sociopolitical actors (although the regime could not eliminate them altogether). This dislocation was produced both by the institutional nature of the regime and the type of structural transformations that the regime's project of capitalist recomposition introduced in the society. There were general consequences of this dislocation. Over a long period of time, the Catholic Church emerged as a substitute for the political arena and as an actor that performed additional oppositional functions, without ever being able to replace the party opposition. The party structure remained relatively unaltered, except that its relations with social bases became more difficult and its main purpose became the search for spaces for political expression. Ties were maintained between the leaders of social organizations and political parties. The function of the social organizations, however, went beyond searching for political spaces; social leaders wanted to express and obtain satisfaction for the specific demands of their social bases. The instrumental and expressive-symbolic dimensions that made up political action during the democratic period were disarticulated. These dimensions became identified with different social and political actors. Finally, a responsive state as a basis for the organization and representation of demands disappeared.

Three additional features were added to the characteristics of political actors: (1) the situation of extreme polarization and political division that existed when the democratic regime broke down in 1973; (2) the structural and institutional transformations that took place under the military dictatorship; and (3) the unprecedented character of the dictatorial experience and the struggle against it. As a result, the political opposition confronted three challenges. The first was to reestablish relations between partisan political actors and the organizations and bases of civil society, and at the same time to reconstitute parties themselves. The second challenge was to produce an agreement among the leaders and followers of the parties to unify the political opposition. The final challenge was to confront the dictatorship by opposing government policies and trying to end the regime.

The opposition met this triple challenge in various ways. Some groups extrapolated the experience of the democratic period to the antidictatorial struggle, while others appealed for ideological reasons to models that emerged from other historical contexts (even though they did not apply to the type of transition defined here). Again, the actions and evolution of the Chilean political opposition should be interpreted as a learning process by a political class whose previous formation, practice, and historical memory equipped it to preside over or oppose democratic governments, but not to confront dictatorships.

The Learning Process

The Initial Phases

During the first years of the military regime, there was no opposition, strictly speaking, but rather a resistance by the parties and social sectors that had supported the Popular Unity government.[3] These groups sought to assure the survival of their members and leaders (many of whom were killed, imprisoned, or exiled) and to maintain what they could of their organizational apparatus.

The Catholic Church occupied a semi-oppositional position under military rule.[4] The official function of the Church was the defense of people who were persecuted by security forces, as well as the accumulation and diffusion of information pertaining to these situations. The Church also provided a space where opposition political and social actors could reconstitute themselves. During Pinochet's first years in power, the Church was the only actor to confront the state-military power. But because of its very nature, the Catholic Church could not assume the role of opposition.

The Christian Democratic Party (PDC), which, with some exceptions, had tacitly or explicitly approved the coup, eventually became critical of the military regime through a typical process of dissidence. At the same time, the Revolutionary Left Movement (MIR) undertook armed struggle against the regime.[5] The MIR was fiercely repressed and did not become a significant opposition force, nor did it greatly threaten the stability of the regime.

During this initial period, opposition forces both inside and outside the country discussed the nature, events, and causes of the downfall of the Popular Unity government. They were also concerned with the nature of the dictatorship. This debate had a markedly self-justifying character, with elements of self-criticism emanating mainly from intellectual groups. This led the opposition to misinterpret the military regime as "fascist" or "neo-fascist" and brought about proposals for creating a "democratic anti-fascist front" to oppose the regime. But those views and proposals lacked any basis in reality.

Two important developments introduced changes in the opposition forces. First, the PDC moved to the opposition. Second, beginning in 1976–77, the military regime initiated a process of profound structural and institutional transformations that were intended to reconstitute national capital and reinsertion in the world economy. These developments led to various changes in the opposition.[6]

Although it was officially declared "in recess," the PDC emerged as the most important political actor to oppose the regime.[7] The parties of the left acted clandestinely and were subjected to a harsh, repressive strategy that eliminated various tiers of leadership. Some of those parties developed important opposition activity while they were in exile by bringing Chile to the attention of international organizations and community. Discussions within the parties became critical of their role in the past, although this debate evolved differently inside the country than it did among those in exile. The parties began to interpret and understand the true character of the military regime, and this knowledge was principally expressed in a growing concern for renewing links with social movements. At that point, there was no properly strategic debate, and calls for "broad fronts"—particularly those issued by the Communist Party (PC)—were rejected by the PDC and mistrusted by the Socialist Party (PS). In 1979, the Socialist Party underwent a profound division, and this political debate intermixed with disputes among members of the old leadership.[8]

In addition, the majority of opposition activity, which complemented and was linked to the work of the Church, concentrated on social and cultural issues rather than politics. This was best demonstrated by the emergence and expansion of a fringe of militants within organizations (political, cultural, social, intellectual or academic, parties, churches, popular education, human rights, and so on) who maintained a certain amount of autonomy with respect to their organizations and gave continuity to oppositional activities in different social arenas. Moreover, new forms of organization emerged in the areas of union and student activity, some in relation to the new institutionality generated by the regime and others at the margins of it. Student activities concentrated on institutional demands and especially on cultural events. Union activists tried to rebuild unionism by working through the new labor legislation. They also tried to reestablish coordination among the major labor organizations, which were characterized by partisan political identities and by the structural divisions of the working class.[9] Finally, although these activities called for "the struggle against the dictatorship" as well as the end of the dictatorship and the "quick reestablishment of democracy," their real significance was primarily that of resistance to the changes imposed by the regime, defense of old gains, and maintenance and recreation of threatened collective identities.

The Regime's Institutionalization

The 1980 constitution represented the culmination of the process of the regime's institutionalization.[10] The constitution enshrined the maintenance of a military regime until 1989 and its subsequent transformation into an authoritarian regime that would have a civilian character, a restricted political arena, and tutelary power for the armed forces. The regime then attempted to keep General Pinochet in power through the 1988 plebiscite. In the plebiscite—as dictated by the constitution—the commanders-in-chief of the armed forces would propose a candidate for a presidential term of eight years, during which period the constitution would come into effect. The power scheme installed by the 1973 coup would stay basically the same until 1989: personal dictatorship and military regime, with Pinochet as the chief of state and the junta of commanders-in-chief as the "legislative power."

At the start of the 1980s, a repoliticization of the leadership of the

parties took place around the issue of the political institutionalization of the regime in the 1980 constitution. This repoliticization occurred at an extremely favorable moment for the regime, when it
was having an apparent economic success, which would vanish during the 1982–83 crisis. The PDC assumed public leadership of the opposition to the constitutional plebiscite, but without a coherent or
consensual strategy with the left on how to deal with the plebiscite.
The government won the 1980 plebiscite through widespread fraud
that was denounced by both the opposition and the Church. The
subsequent perception of the regime's indefinite duration had consequences for the opposition.

A period of confusion ensued in the PDC that was compounded by
the death of former president Eduardo Frei and the exile of various
leaders. After two years, the party resolved the problem of leadership
by favoring the faction that proposed greater flexibility in alliances
with sectors of the left. In those sectors, the processes that sought to
turn an oppositional space into an oppositional subject had diverse,
if not contradictory, consequences. The PC, for one, underwent a
shift in both its strategic-political line and its process of growth.
From a gradualist and reformist conception that normally placed the
party "to the right" of the Socialist Party, the PC moved on to a theory
of mass insurrection that brought it closer to revolutionary forms of
political change. This included the party's acceptance of the armed
struggle and the development of a branch of the party linked to an
armed force. Without giving up its character as a workers' party, the
PC grew significantly in the youth, student, and especially shantytown sectors.[11]

The Socialist Party, which had been very fragmented, underwent a
double process of change. On one hand, the party underwent an ideological renovation that led one group away from orthodox positions
linked to the Marxist-Leninism of the 1960s and closer to those
groups that separated from the PDC and the political center during
the Popular Unity period (MAPU, independents). On the other hand, a
partial reunification occurred that later culminated in the emergence of two large socialist parties, one with a renovated socialism
and the other with a classical socialism (though they came together
for strategic reasons by 1988). Smaller groups revolved around these
two parties: the MAPU came ever closer to the socialist parties, and
the Christian Left struggled internally over whether to integrate
into the socialist camp or retain its own identity and destiny.

In any case, these processes at the beginning of the 1980s were marked by certain characteristics that made them different from the period that followed. Politics still lacked a recognized public space and operated in a semi-open and semi-clandestine sphere. Party activities acquired an elitist character that made relations with social movements difficult. Social actors had to confront the regime's transformations and its conception of a new social order that impeded and redefined their struggles for specific demands. Moreover, an incipient strategic debate emerged, hindered by the perception that the regime could not be removed. The debate was highly ideological, lacked the necessary reference points and experiences to participate in this type of struggle, and gave too much importance to abstract questions about legitimizing and delegitimizing the regime through the actions of the opposition. One example of this was the debate over the legitimacy or illegitimacy of a constitution that, whatever its character, was firmly in place and in effect. This situation called for a new way of looking at and confronting the constitution if advances in the process of democratization were desired.

The Opposition in Public Space

In 1981–82, the transformational thrust of the military regime entered a crisis stage, primarily as a result of the failure of the economic model. This failure was manifested in, among other things, the breakdown of the financial system, the changes in the economic team, the large foreign debt, and the generalized indebtedness of vast sectors of the middle class.[12] The most important sociopolitical expression of this crisis within the regime—which many opposition sectors misread as a terminal crisis—was the unleashing of a protest movement that started in May 1983. With this, mass movements were reborn in Chile, forcing the regime to make an initial *apertura*, or opening.[13]

This "opening" represented an attempt by the government to recapture the support of civilian sectors that had distanced themselves from the regime as well as an attempt to involve the opposition in the institutional framework of the 1980 constitution. Toward the middle of 1986, with the discovery of weapons arsenals and the attempt (claimed by the Communist-linked Manuel Rodríguez Patriotic Front) on General Pinochet's life, the cycle of protests and massive mobilizations seemed to come to an end. The regime, for its part, managed to recompose at least part of its economic scheme and proceeded to concentrate on meeting the timetable laid out in the constitution.

This period—from the eruption of politics in public space with the May 1983 protests to the moment in February 1988 when the opposition agreed to reject the armed forces' candidate in the 1988 plebiscite—was the culmination of the learning process of the opposition. This process cannot be understood without reference to other transition experiences, such as those that occurred in Uruguay, Argentina, Brazil, Spain, the Philippines, and Korea. One must also take into account the views of various intellectuals—those both inside and outside Chile and those linked to the political opposition—concerning these experiences, as well as the direct contact that some political leaders had with the other transitions.

The cycle of mobilizations that began in 1983 was directly related to the collapse of the economic model, which affected the middle-class and popular sectors (the latter was already oppressed and impoverished by years of dictatorship). But this crisis would not have had the political effect that it did without certain additional factors, including the level of organization recovered by some unions, the survival of political parties and their underground activity, and the presence of a sociopolitical fringe of militants or activists in many areas of social life. The regime confronted not only a vast source of social discontent, but also organizations capable of turning that discontent into collective forms of expression.

This explains why the process of mobilization lasted three years and led to the mass protests and street demonstations that almost paralyzed the nation. In addition, the electoral triumphs of the opposition in all social organizations led to the isolation of the regime's supporters. Popular protests, which often took place behind barricades, were violently repressed by the police and military. The favored form of protest was the monthly demonstration, in which social and political groups expressed their opposition to the regime under the unified banner of "Democracy Now." The calls for these protests alternated between union and political organizations, which caused some tension.[14]

The surprising and massive size of the first protests gave the opposition three central ideas as it re-emerged in public space. First, members of the opposition believed in the imminent end of the regime if the continuity of pressures and mobilizations could be maintained. Second, they thought that the unity of political organizations was necessary so they could take charge in case the regime collapsed. Finally, the opposition concluded that the traditional connection between politics and social movements had survived relatively intact from the military period.

The Debate Over the End of the Regime

In time, the perception that the regime's fall was imminent led to a relatively incomplete and unrealistic debate over strategy. Instead of a realistic transition strategy or formula, there was the widespread notion that the process of mobilization would create a situation of "ungovernability" that could destabilize the regime. According to some analysts, such a chaotic situation would make the armed forces break away from Pinochet in order to negotiate their withdrawal from power with the civilians. According to other strategists, the mobilizations would provoke the collapse of the regime and the automatic withdrawal of the armed forces, which would leave a power vacuum to be filled by civilian forces. The concept "Democracy Now" accounted for both the perception of the regime's imminent fall and the absence of a proper formula or strategy for the end of the regime. When Cardinal Francisco Fresno called on the opposition to "negotiate" with the regime in August and September 1983, some groups in the center declared that Pinochet's resignation was a precondition for any negotiation and that made the negotiation unviable. The left refused to negotiate at all.

All opposition forces assumed the triple slogan "exit of Pinochet, provisional government and constituent assembly" as a formula and declared the illegitimacy of the 1980 constitution and any of its provisions. Evidently, this idea was influenced by the classical insurrectionary model, which no transition from a military regime to democracy has followed in modern times. For its part, the PC was confronted with the fact that its shift toward more insurrectional forms caused the PDC to exclude the Communists from any alliances. In contrast, this shift was welcomed by a large contingent of young radical shantytown-dwellers, who mistrusted the institutions and formulas of political compromise. These factors reinforced the Communist platform of assuming "all forms of struggle" and prioritizing the most violent and heroic forms of that struggle.

This explains the consolidation of the Manuel Rodríguez Patriotic Front and the Rodríguez Militias with the PC, though the party would later distance itself from these groups.

None of these actions—negotiation aimed at unconditional surrender, mobilization seeking the collapse of the regime, and mass rebellion directed at military defeat—was part of a strategic plan. A real plan would have taken into account the nature of the regime, its level of institutionalization, its resistance to negotiations, and its dual character as a personalized dictatorship and as a military regime providing a constitutional and hierarchical adherence to that personalized government. The price of these deficiencies was that the mobilizations—lacking a transition strategy and institutional formulas that would have made the withdrawal of the armed forces viable in a moment of weakness—made the regime more entrenched and exhausted the protests. Also, Chile's middle-class sectors became discouraged and frightened by the radical forms of mobilization. This led to the isolation of the most militant groups, which promoted the most disruptive forms of struggle in order to create a situation of collapse. During this period, the regime was transformed, spaces for spontaneous collective action were created, and civil society was strengthened. Yet, all of this fell short of the goal of ending the dictatorship and reestablishing democracy.[15]

The Question of Opposition Unity

The theme of opposition unity characterizes another feature of the Chilean opposition: its inherited character and the persistence of organizational ideological identities. Thus, although the opposition re-entered public space and it became clear that many political parties had survived and had gained a significant presence, it did not agree on a transition formula, on the issues the group should face, or on the steps needed to form a multiparty coalition. Instead, there was a cluster of ideological blocs that were more concerned with the identity of those included or excluded than with the terms of a proposal for confronting the regime.

Nevertheless, the configuration of these blocs represented progress from two points of view. First, it was an attempt to overcome fragmentation in the face of a seemingly monolithic adversary. Second, the PDC broke away from the traditional tendency to act alone and accepted alliances, principally with sectors of the left (while always excluding the Communists). There were also changes in some socialist groups, who no longer made the unity of the left a precondition for their participation in alliances. Despite progress in these areas, the first opposition blocs formed in 1983 approached the question of unity in a way that favored preserving ideological identities and affinities over ending the regime and bringing about a transition to democracy. For instance, emphasis was given to the inclusion or exclusion of certain groups on ideological grounds. This occurred even though broader opposition unity was widely desired and considered a prerequisite for the fall of the regime. This situation would not improve until 1988.

The first attempt to unify opposition around ideological-political blocs took place between August and December of 1983, and it set the tone for those that followed. The blocs formed during this period included the Democratic Alliance (small groups of the right, the PDC, other small parties in the center, and some socialist parties and groups); the Democratic Popular Movement (other socialist parties and groups, the PC and the MIR); and the Socialist Bloc (an attempt to unify the socialist camp by grouping socialist sectors that had joined the Democratic Alliance with the Christian Left and MAPU). All of these blocs agreed on the abstract platform of "exit of Pinochet, provisional government and constituent assembly" and on "a social mobilization strategy." But hidden behind this slogan were different perceptions of the nature of the transition, which became evident in the difficulty of establishing a common platform. The partial attempts at unification such as Democratic Intransigence (involving a group of public personalities) or the Civilian Front (inspired by the Alliance's Socialist Party) either never overcame their marginal importance or simply fell apart quickly.

After some years, which allowed the political class to re-emerge through these blocs, the various groups reformed: the Alliance lost its members on the left; the Socialist Bloc dissolved because of the persistence of centrifugal tendencies caused by those who sought to assure the partisan identity of some groups above all else; and in June 1987, the MDP (Democratic Popular Movement) gave way to the United Left (IU), which incorporated MAPU and the Christian Left (IC). But this last effort, which recalled the old theme of "unity of the left" and tried to end the isolation of the PC, had to face the fact that those same parties disagreed on confronting the regime in the 1988 plebiscite. When some of the IU parties joined the remainder of the opposition in their willingness to confront the regime institutionally in the plebiscite, the United Left became a project focused on the post-plebiscite future, without programmatic or strategic content for the short or the intermediate term.

In 1985, another attempt was made to unite the opposition when the Catholic Church initiated the "National Accord for a Transition to Full Democracy."[16] The National Accord, which brought important parties that supported the regime on the right together with the opposition, excluding the Communists, was significant because of the wide spectrum of political parties it managed to incorporate. The National Accord was also important because it made reference to certain transitional mechanisms (such as a plebiscite to reform the constitution), which gave the opposition a better understanding of the nature of these transitions. But several factors—the exclusion of the Communists, the precariousness of right-wing participation, and the disagreements over the methods for precipitating a transition process—turned this National Accord into a symbolic reference point instead of an effective political pact. In fact, attempts to deepen or perfect the Accord led supporters of the regime to regroup and distance themselves from it, although the National Accord succeeded in broadening its representation of leftist groups.[17]

In 1986, the opposition made a new attempt to achieve unity. This effort was made because of the perceived need to renew the social mobilizations that had been losing force and impact. Other factors included the lack of a real political agreement among the parties and the need to re-establish links between political and social forces. The arrangement was named the Civic Assembly, and it worked through social organizations, including Communist entities. The assembly had a great capacity for mobilization, which was evident not only when it organized demonstrations that involved the whole country but also when it promoted a national work-stoppage in July 1986.

In spite of the originality involved in seeking to overcome political differences through social organizations (where all members of the opposition were represented), the Civic Assembly could not avoid two fundamental deficiencies. One was the predominance of middle-class organizations that placed the popular sectors and the left in a relatively subordinate position. The second involved the absence of a real political-strategic design for channeling social mobilization. An unsuccessful attempt was made to resolve the second problem by aggregating the social demands of the assembly's constituent sectors ("The Demand of Chile").[18] But this aggregation was not able to use the advantage that politics brings to collective action. Thus, when political differences reemerged with the discovery of arsenals and the attempt against General Pinochet's life in 1986, the Civic Assembly lost its unity and its capacity to call different groups together.

Political and Social Opposition

Political leaders originally thought that the links that connected social organizations and actors with political parties were the same as they had always been. Thus, they assumed that what happened in the strictly political sphere would immediately be mirrored in the social sphere and, therefore, an agreement among political elites could assure mass mobilization and action. The military regime dislocated this traditional relationship in at least three ways. First, the military regime's structural and institutional transformations weakened material and cultural spaces for the constitution of social actors, and especially for constructing their class bases. This resulted in deep fragmentations and atomizations among social actors.[19] Second, the clandestine or semi-clandestine survival of the political parties, along with the emergence of an intermediate political class of sociopolitical activists and militants, made the crisis of representation even more acute. Third, the absence of a state reference point and the need to resolve pressing problems of material survival and threatened collective identities made the mobilization of social sectors heterogeneous and gave it a different role than that assigned by partisan political logic.

All of this became apparent at the beginning of the cycle of protests and large mobilizations, when political actors had to confront the problem of their constitution and organization as parties after years of clandestine or semi-clandestine politics. The formation of political blocs clashed with the mass movement, which was motivated by a different logic—reconstituting its identity and satisfying various demands—even though it continued to be dependent on political party leadership. The subsequent period saw the exhaustion of mass mobilization and the radicalization of a fringe of sociopolitical activists and militants, but overall it represented an attempt to reestablish the articulation between social and political actors. When this articulation failed to produce a strategic political formula for ending the regime, however, the party fragmentations and configurations of political blocs were transferred to the social organizations themselves. Sectoral, organizational, and demand-making struggles were thereby subordinated to political aims for which there were no sound strategies or intermediate steps. This weakened the collective action that the social organizations, which lacked real autonomy, could undertake.

Many efforts were made to strengthen sociopolitical relations. Even before 1980, activists had attempted to organize the working class beyond local levels in order to achieve national coordination. Local union activity was limited by the restricted institutionalization emerging from the labor legislation that the government imposed as part of its "modernizations." Attempts at national reorganization were made through loose federations (*centrales*) that reproduced party fragmentations or were themselves new political blocs resulting from inter-party agreements or divisions.[20] In 1983, the Confederation of Copper Workers (CTC), representing various facets of the Chilean union movement and its political components, called for the first protest. Soon afterward, the Confederation was replaced by the National Workers' Command (CNT), which involved nearly all of the large union organizations and was able to organize several mobilizations and demonstrations. The Command also officially provided the basis for a new central labor federation founded in August 1988, even though the PDC still tried to maintain several ideologically based *centrales*.

Other attempts at strengthening sociopolitical relations involved students and professional associations. The first democratic elections in the student federations revealed a unified opposition movement, which changed when student groups began to reproduce party groupings and divisions that existed at the national level. The professional associations also reestablished an articulation between political and social spheres in a way that reproduced both conflicts and advances that had been achieved at the political level. In any case, even though new social actors were not fully autonomous from the political parties, a greater tension between social and political actors was generated, which made the purely mechanical reproduction of party-level processes in society more difficult.[21]

The Culmination of the Learning Process

A new phase began in August and September 1986, with the discovery of weapons arsenals, the assassination attempt against General Pinochet (both linked to the Manuel Rodríguez Patriotic Front), and the imposition of a state of siege that demobilized the opposition. From the regime's point of view, this phase was characterized by the implementation of the institutional processes that were established in order to secure compliance with the timetable set out in the constitution, particularly for the plebiscite. This institutionalization involved a certain level of economic recovery (especially concerning the external debt), the promulgation of political laws that complemented the constitution (laws for political parties, electoral registers, votes and vote-counting, and so forth), and efforts to ensure the candidacy of Pinochet and his triumph in the plebiscite.

From the opposition's standpoint, this period marked an increasing, though still uneven, understanding of the character of transitions from military to democratic regimes. The experience of opposition groups during the mobilization cycle, the regime's response to the events of 1986, and the examples of other transition experiences in the Southern Cone, Europe, and Asia led the opposition to agree that the military regime would not end through collapse or defeat but through a political process. The opposition also saw that, given the time lost and its inability to formulate an alternative political scenario for the regime's cessation, this political process would inevitably have to adjust to the institutional forms the regime had devised to perpetuate itself. The opposition's objective would be to reform—not reject—that institutional framework, just as oppositions in the other transitions had done. Given the perceived inevitability of the regime's timetable, the debates over the illegitimacy of the constitution gave way to more realistic discussions about how to precipitate and facilitate the transition process in Chile.

In response to the regime's format for the plebiscite, a group of famous political personalities developed a demand (with origins similar to those of the National Agreement) for "Free Elections," which the parties supported through center and left committees.[22] Compared to the first political blocs, these committees represented an advance in that they sought alternative transitional formulas. Their call for free elections, however, was little more than a step forward in the search for new formulas, because there was no immediate possibility of free elections in Chile. Similarly, the debates over an opposition candidate or program were useless, because there was no scenario for competitive elections as there was in the Philippines.[23] But both debates (which were subsequently rejected) did force the opposition to design political and institutional alternatives. In fact, the "free elections" theme induced both the Catholic Church and the political parties (including a reluctant PC) to encourage the public to enroll in the Electoral Registers, thus complying with the very law they had denounced as illegitimate.[24] This action involved both the regime and its opposition, and it brought both closer to the idea of an institutionalized confrontation.

The debate over the legal registration of the parties—a prerequisite for participating in elections or plebiscites—centered on the illegitimacy of the law. The initial proposal of one sector of the Socialist left in January 1987 to register a single opposition party that would challenge the regime in any electoral contest was discarded because party identities prevailed even after the registration law was seen as inevitable. So the center and pro-regime right-wing parties registered under their traditional names. In addition, one Socialist party joined with other leftist groups and a segment of the nonpartisan right as the Party for Democracy (PPD), which defined itself as an instrument designed to confront the regime in any election.[25]

The Political-Institutional Confrontation of 1988

The process of learning about the need for an institutionalized political confrontation in order to precipitate the transition culminated in February 1988. At that time, all opposition parties, with the important exception of the Communists and some smaller groups, agreed to confront the government in the 1988 plebiscite. The opposition accepted the inevitability of the plebiscite and saw in it a unique opportunity to defeat the regime and its supporters on political grounds.[26] Four months later, the opposition parties (including the PC) adhered—for the first time during the military period—to the same strategy for struggle against the regime. This isolated and defeated the groups that favored armed confrontation with the dictatorship (this has also been the case in all other transitions).

The opposition's realization that the plebiscite presented an opportunity for precipitating the transition process, independent of the outcome, was a very important step.[27] It had learned the lesson that transitions emerge from political institutional spaces that are conquered within a military regime. Moreover, it became clear that in the absence of an alternative politico-military power, it is possible to end the regime and move toward a democracy if the opposition deepens its presence in those spaces. This would have occurred even if the conditions imposed by the government had forced the opposition to abstain from the plebiscite and, therefore, to seek another institutional alternative to end the regime and unleash the process of transition.

The opposition faced various challenges as it prepared to confront the regime in the plebiscite. First, it had to convert a social majority—which had already emerged in 1983 and expressed itself in the public opinion polls—into a political majority.[28] A political majority had already been achieved in part through the creation of the Agreement (Concertación) of Parties for the NO in February 1988 and with the subsequent adherence of all the other opposition groups and parties to this coalition. But it was necessary for them to achieve a consensus on the meaning of the plebiscite and to convey this meaning to the nation. At the same time, they had to establish a single organization and leadership for a campaign that would have to consider the very different sensibilities and tendencies that underlay the common strategy.

Public opinion polls indicated that the majority of Chileans yearned for political change under tranquil and orderly conditions. The opposition used the public perception to give the plebiscite two meanings: rejecting Pinochet and replacing his institutional framework without creating an institutional vacuum. That is, the opposition vowed to bring about change through the regime's own institutions. The triumph of the opposition in the plebiscite would mean not only Pinochet's withdrawal from power, but also the beginning of a process of negotiation or agreement with the armed forces to reform the constitution so that democratic elections and institutions would be implemented within a reasonable period of time. This message, which was used in the public campaign, united opposition sectors, even though the rhetoric of each party conveyed different and seemingly contradictory implications. It is likely that the incorporation of these different forms of rhetoric contributed to gathering, rather than to diminishing, support for the opposition in the campaign.

This message or political line had to be turned into a unified opposition leadership and organization, but history conspired against this type of unity. There were extremely complex problems to resolve, such as the unequal political weight of the member parties, the distinctions between legal and actual parties that did not have access to legal prerogatives, the relations between the Agreement parties and the PC, the disputes among campaign leaders, and the relations with the social organizations that joined the campaign for the NO. All of this could have broken the coalition. Unity seemed to be the capital that the coalition could count on, and, according to public opinion polls, it was the most valued aspect of the opposition campaign. Similarly, opposition unity was the principal target of the government campaign.

Problems of unity were usually successfully resolved, insofar as the unity of leadership and a certain ambiguity in the functions of the different groups were maintained. This ambiguity allowed the opposition to solve problems quickly and pragmatically, without engaging in ideological discussions that had nothing to do with the campaign.

Thus, the leaders of the parties who formed the Command for the NO represented the highest decision-making level. But a more restricted directing nucleus involved the really significant parties, both legal and those of the illegal left. This nucleus helped overcome cleavages that were the result of the personalistic leadership of participating parties and assured a single and efficient leadership by means of a secretariat that had the skilled elements and technical capacities for the task. The illegal parties contributed to the training of poll-watchers and other jobs involved in electoral control that only the legal parties could officially carry out. Disputes over a potential candidate who could personify the struggle against Pinochet were resolved by discarding this unrealistic idea and choosing instead the head of the strongest party, the PDC, as opposition spokesperson. The parties or groups of the left that had not joined the PPD formed the Socialist Command for the NO, a subcoalition that represented them within the Command. This form of participation allowed them to remain in the United Left coalition and to maintain an indirect relationship with the PC. In this way, the PC was persuaded to support the Agreement's strategy, but in a way that did not force the Agreement to formally incorporate the PC or keep it isolated. Therefore, the more electorally inclined sectors within the Agreement became stronger and the insurrectionary factions were weakened.

Finally, two significant developments occurred with respect to the social organizations. In 1988, the creation of the Central Unitaria de Trabajadores (CUT) strengthened the autonomy of the union movement and brought a new actor into the process of democratic transition and consolidation. At the same time, the Acuerdo Social por el No (ACUSO) provided an heir to the Civic Assembly for the purposes of campaign preparation. Moreover, representative associations were organized—composed of independents, entrepreneurs, former regime supporters, and so forth—which carried out their own mobilizational activities yet subordinated themselves to the political leadership of the parties. As a result, parties and social organizations were mutually reinforced, reducing the tensions or contradictions of the past.

The opposition also faced the challenge of turning a political majority into an electoral majority. The opposition had to win an electoral campaign and have its results validated and recognized by the dictatorship.[29] The process of generating and assuring an electoral majority required several steps. First, the opposition needed to register a high number of voters in order to legitimize the plebiscite. The main problem was to overcome the resistance and skepticism of social sectors that opposed the dictatorship but that saw election fraud as inevitable and did not believe in ending the regime through a plebiscite. The result of the opposition's voter registration campaign was the highest number of registrations in Chilean electoral history (slightly more than 90 percent of the eligible voters).

Second, the opposition had to overcome fear and resistance felt by the undecided sectors of the population. If those voters were convinced by government propaganda that the opposition represented either a return to the past or uncertainty for the future, then they could tip the balance in favor of the regime. The opposition knew that it had to combine in its campaign the two popular demands for change and security in order to repoliticize society in a positive way. In order to accomplish this, it was necessary to abandon ideological extremes and isolate the most radical and confrontational sectors of the opposition, or else force them to subordinate themselves to the strategy of the moderate opposition. It was also important to link individual and collective aspirations with the act of voting "No" in the election. To achieve this, the mass media was indispensable in keeping the political class in contact with the people. But this could only be accomplished in a climate of more freedom than had existed during the previous fifteen years.

Consequently, as a third element in the struggle for an electoral majority, the opposition had to secure certain minimal conditions for campaigning during the plebiscite period. Among the guarantees sought by the opposition were the lifting of the states of exception; the end of exile; a fair and public registration process; and access to television, which played a significant role in conveying the dual message of change and stability offered by the NO. Even if this struggle for guarantees did not achieve a climate of complete fairness, which would have been impossible in this type of event, at least it neutralized the government's attempts to manipulate the plebiscite and allowed society to be repoliticized, thus lessening people's fear. As a result, and despite the lack of direct negotiations between the government and the opposition, the government was forced to accede to the pressures of the opposition, the Catholic Church, and international opinion. Only in this way could the regime assure a minimum of credibility and legitimacy for the very device that it had created to stay in power.

Finally, the opposition had to make sure that its electoral victory would be recognized and that neither fraud nor a coup attempt would occur. Once again, the opposition's unity on the basic objective of winning the election allowed them to establish an independent system to monitor the elections (the system of poll-watchers designated by the legal parties) and the vote-counting. This system permitted the opposition to claim its triumph immediately and neutralized the government's incoherent efforts to deny it. The credibility of the opposition depended on the support of an enormous contingent of international representatives and observers, whose presence made the government's dismissal of electoral results and its recourse to extra-legal solutions improbable. The government was never given a pretext for this type of solution, because the parties supporting the NO demanded tranquil behavior in celebrating the victory and managed to control those minority groups that viewed the electoral triumph as an opportunity for staging a mass uprising.[30]

The Results of the Plebiscite and Its Future Projections

Although the plebiscite was devised as a mechanism for perpetuating the regime and keeping Pinochet in power, the opposition turned it into an effective vehicle for the partial politicization and democratization of society. It triumphed by unifying historically antagonistic political blocs and tendencies. Furthermore, winning the plebiscite unleashed a full transition process. This turning point reformulated the tasks of an opposition that had struggled against a dictatorial regime, insofar as the opposition became a leading actor instead of a reactive one.

Once the transition to a democratic regime began, the opposition had two tasks: first, to achieve the constitutional changes that would permit the most democratic elections possible and, second, to construct a majority democratic government that would complete the transition and lead Chilean society toward the global democratization that the military regime had interrupted in 1973. The struggle to obtain institutional changes and, above all, a majority democratic government have forced the existing opposition Agreement to stay together until democratic institutions have been achieved. The opposition also realized the need to work in concert to redemocratize society while avoiding destabilization and possible authoritarian regression. Clearly, both the isolationist tendencies of the center, particularly the PDC, and the temptation of some groups on the left to capitalize on the discontent surrounding an incomplete transition that does not resolve Chile's large socioeconomic problems are centrifugal elements that could tear the coalition apart. The current record of the opposition, however, shows that the learning experience under the dictatorship has had an important effect. That experience strengthened the sense of responsibility of a political class whose incapacity to arrange a majority socio-political pact that could advance democracy and social change had been a significant factor in the breakdown of democracy.

The Recomposition of the Party System

The years of military rule have transformed, but not replaced, the Chilean party system. Changes can be observed in the individual parties, many of which have also inherited certain features of the democratic period, including its institutions, party relations and coalitions, and the links between parties and other social actors.

Changes in the Political Parties

At the time when the military regime seized power in Chile, the party system was made up of three poles: the right, the Christian Democrats, and the left. The right had been unified in the 1960s as the National Party (PN), and it had become increasingly authoritarian and anti-democratic. The PN disbanded voluntarily on the day the coup took place and merged with the military regime. Some PN leaders, as individuals, went on to occupy official posts, and a nucleus of civilians linked to the formulation of the regime's socioeconomic and political model filled positions as ministers, mayors, council members, and so on. The confluence of those who advocated a Chicago Boys economic model with those who were more concerned with a long-term political project (the *gremialistas*) was expressed early through informal relations in government tasks and later through study and action groups, such as New Democracy. The *gremialista* intellectuals and young politicians close to them dominated this last group, which became the Independent Democratic Union (UDI) after 1983. The UDI was closely linked to the government and fought for influence with National Advance (AN), a nationalist sector of the right that descended from "Fatherland and Liberty." The more traditional right, which had become dispersed and had lost a small but significant sector to the opposition in the 1983 Democratic Alliance, tried to regroup. They first worked through the former president of the old PN, Sergio Onofre Jarpa, who was appointed minister of the interior at the height of the protests in order to initiate a very limited "opening." Later, the traditional right tried to regroup through two groups that represented important currents of the old National Party: the National Union (UN) and the National Party.

All groups on the right (principally the UDI, the National Union, and Jarpa's Working Front) except for the National Party and the nationalist sectors tried to reunite as National Renovation (RN), which registered as a legal party in 1987. UDI was expelled from RN when differences arose between the sector that is seen as an heir to the regime and is thus linked to the government apparatus (UDI) and the sector that wanted to become the party of the democratic right. This last group, the former National Union sector, distanced itself from General Pinochet during the plebiscite but continued to support the YES option. UDI then began its own process of legalization. During the 1988 plebiscite campaign, the legalized National Party suffered an important division between those who chose to vote against the regime and those who belatedly announced their support for the YES. The political future of these two sectors remains uncertain, perhaps foreshadowing their eventual relocation in some other collectivity.

The Chilean right, then, divided between those who wanted to preserve the regime's socioeconomic and political model (representing both fascist and more *aperturista* perspectives) and those who saw a democratic regime as inevitable and wanted to occupy the traditional space of the political right in the new arrangement. This second group played the role of "softliners" in the transition period and attempted to win over the center sectors of the electorate by modernizing their style and platform.[31] In all probability, the most a united rightist party could manage in the near future would be to divide the political center and join a center-right coalition as a subordinate.

The second pole of the Chilean political spectrum before the coup was occupied by the Christian Democrats. The PDC played a special role in the center because the party was an alternative pole in itself, highly ideological and unwilling to form alliances and coalitions with other parties. This made Chilean politics enormously rigid and risked the permanent polarization of the system through radicalizations of both the right and the left.

Once the PDC became legal under the law of parties and the entire opposition agreed on pursuing an institutional approach to defeat the regime politically, the most centrist sector reassumed leadership within the Christian Democratic Party. The PDC also participated in the broadest coalition yet, the Concertación (Agreement) for the NO. The predominance of the centrist sectors and their right wing was demonstrated by the party's search for a stronger alliance with other centrist sectors (in the so-called Center Coalition that included the PDC, the Radical Party, and smaller groups) and in the attempt to exercise hegemony within the Concertación. After the plebiscite, the sectors inclined toward Christian Democratic dominance were again in control, despite assurances that the Concertación would be maintained. The internal debate over the presidential candidate for the 1989 elections clearly showed that two distinct projects existed inside the party. One faction wanted to repeat and update the idea of its "own path," this time in cooperation with some minor centrist sectors and in the hope of consolidating a center-right or exclusively center alliance, in which the PDC would have undisputed leadership. The other faction, drawing on the experience of recent decades, wanted to consolidate an alliance with the left, defining its party as one leaning more toward the left than the center. In the short run, the last faction won, although not without producing deep internal tensions.

The PDC emerged as the most organized and structured national party, with a natural tendency toward leading the opposition. But within the party there coexisted a greater receptivity to the idea of alliances, a lesser emphasis on ideology and rigid party machines, and the unwillingness to forge stable agreements with the left, which was exacerbated with regard to the Communist Party. The divisions between the sectors at the center have deepened within the PDC, while a doctrinaire or ideological streak persists. The party also faces competition from a modernizing right and a renovated socialist party that appeals to the electorate both at the center and the left. These are all challenges to the PDC in its role as the principal party of the political spectrum, a position that, according to opinion polls, it still holds. The other parties of the center or center-left, some of which emerged from the old Radical Party, are significant only to the extent that they join alliances with the PDC.

The third pole of the party system before the coup was the left, whose greatest ideological-political expression in the last decades was the Popular Unity coalition. The left has always pivoted on the Socialist-Communist party axis, and sectors of the Radical Party and groups that broke away from the PDC also gathered around this axis. The left was the principal loser and victim of the 1973 coup, and it suffered an especially intense process of repression, fragmentation, dispersion, and clandestinity during the first years of the regime. Because of that, in many cases, the political dynamics of the left developed in exile.

In 1979, the Socialist Party divided into two large sectors, which later gave birth to other factions. A process of ideological-political renovation began among many socialist intellectuals, cadres, and militants, which affected the various factions to different degrees. This renovation recovered and critically examined some traditions of the Chilean socialist camp. The renovators sought to modernize Chilean socialist traditions and re-evaluate political democracy, as well as to critique existing socialist models and depart from the Leninist tradition. This socialist sector stopped making the socialist-communist axis the foundation of leftist politics and sought to develop a "coalition for change" with the center in order to bring about lasting socioeconomic transformations with a sociopolitical majority.[32]

Toward the end of this period, some factions were reunified and rebuilt, and they produced two large socialist parties (the so-called Socialist parties of Ricardo Núñez and Clodomiro Almeyda, after the names of their general secretaries). The Núñez Socialists were more inclined to ally with the center and were more supportive of the socialist renovation than the Almeyda Socialists, who were dominated by orthodox sectors and relied on the old theme of alliance with the PC. The historical differences of the two parties were diluted somewhat during the plebiscite and post-plebiscite periods, because they adopted a single political line and there were internal pressures for reunification. The idea of reunifying the socialists in one large party, which was facilitated by their convergence in the same political line, emerged as one of the crucial points in the recomposition of the post-dictatorial party system. The consequences of this recomposition—such as the isolation of the more traditional and insurrectional sectors of the left, the relaxation of the system of alliances in order to generate a majority coalition with the "progressive" center, and the autonomy of socialism from the center and traditional/orthodox left poles—could be of historic importance.

Another development in the socialist camp occurred when smaller socialist groups either disappeared or were absorbed by the large parties. A similar dynamic can be observed in those groups that, emerging from the PDC (MAPU, Christian Left) or the Radical Party (some of which have already been reabsorbed), vacillated between joining with the reunified socialists or maintaining their "identity" and their "own paths."

Finally, the two main Socialist parties have pursued distinct strategies for legalization, which caused problems for socialist reunification. The Socialist Party (Núñez), which had been part of the Democratic Alliance, created the Party for Democracy (PPD), which was made up of smaller groups of the left, center, right, and independents that had acquired an enormous popularity and following during the plebiscite campaign. The PPD exceeded the purely "instrumental" character that its founders had given it. Moreover, the polls placed the PPD in second place after the PDC. The Socialist Party clearly dominates the PPD, but the electoral potential of the PPD is much greater than that of socialism. The party involves a large number of young people and attracts support from sectors of the modernized left as well as center sectors that perceive the PDC as being highly ideological and traditional.

The Socialist Party (Almeyda) was pressured by other parties of the left and by its own needs to become legal in order to participate in the 1989 elections. Thus, the Socialist Party (Almeyda) joined with the PC, the Christian Left, and others to form the Broad Party of the Socialist Left (PAIS). At the end of 1988, the PAIS began the process of legal registration. As a political entity, it was closer to a federation of parties than the PPD was. Even though it resolved the problem of the legal participation of socialist sectors and previously excluded Communists, PAIS presented two problems for the remainder of the party system. First, because the two socialist parties were legalized in different "instrumental parties," their reunification appeared to be politically and technically more difficult. Second, there was a temptation to reproduce the traditional left (Popular Unity), without taking into account that two lefts had emerged during this period. One group advocated renovated socialism involving parties within the "instrumental" and "legal" parties (PPD and PAIS); the other represented the orthodox-traditional socialism of the PC. This made alliances with center groups difficult, because they were still reluctant to establish relations with the Communists. But if the renovated sectors of "Almeydismo" (those willing to participate in dialogue with the PPD and PDC) become the dominant group within PAIS, then these relations and alliances might be facilitated. This could even lead to electoral pacts among the three or—if there is resistance in the PDC—between the PPD and PAIS, with both parties serving as relational axes to their respective socialist parties.

As had been the case with the PDC, the PC maintained its structure and organization at the national level, despite heavier repression and clandestinity. Perhaps paradoxically, in light of this organizational continuity, the PC underwent the deepest changes in its political lines and practices.[33] Until 1980, the PC followed its traditional line of a workers', Marxist-Leninist party with a gradualist slant. The party was an enemy of the "ultra-leftist" or militarist tendencies, for which it blamed the defeat of Popular Unity. Consequently, the PC sought to form agreements with the center (the PDC) in order to establish anti-fascist fronts (uncritically following the experience of other national contexts).

The PC inaugurated its new line in 1980, at the same time that the regime was institutionalized through the new constitution. The change in the party also reflected criticism by Chilean exiles and the Soviet Union over the PC's lack of military strategy, the effect of Central American and African revolutionary struggles, and the blockaded democratic transitions in the Southern Cone. The new line of the Chilean PC consisted of the "use of all forms of struggle," including "popular rebellion" and "acute violence." The PC had adopted the insurrectional-military model in the struggle against the dictatorship. This was demonstrated when the PC grew closer to the MIR and created its own paramilitary organization, the Manuel Rodríguez Patriotic Front, which carried out armed actions. The change posed internal problems for the PC, whose working-class militants were unprepared for and did not understand the switch.

During the cycle of protests, however, the shift in the PC's strategy resonated with the demands of young people, students, and shanty-town residents. These groups lacked an ideological framework, but they supported epic and heroic radicalism as a result of consistent repression by the regime. The PC's radical posture allowed it to grow—especially through the Rodríguez Militias that were positioned halfway between the Front and the party's youth organization—but in a constituency that was alien to its traditional framework. A division appeared within the PC when, along with advancing its new line, the party was trying to avoid isolation by establishing alliances with other left parties, both at the political level and in social organizations. After the discovery of weapons arsenals and the attempt against Pinochet's life in August and September 1986, and as the protest movement petered out, the opposition decided to confront the regime within the dictatorship's own institutional framework. With that, the PC lost its political direction, cut its ties to part of the Manuel Rodríguez Front, and became subordinate to the political line taken by the opposition in the 1988 plebiscite.

The dual nature of the PC was accentuated during the post-plebiscite period. On one hand, the militarized sector of the Manuel Rodríguez Front became autonomous. On the other hand, a small dissident sector that was closer to euro-communist positions or to renovated socialism distanced itself from the party. A strong debate continued inside the PC over the maintenance of the insurrectional line or the integration into institutional politics, which would let the party reassume its traditional character. This debate was not resolved with the integration of the PC in PAIS, nor were the effects of *perestroika* clearly evident in the party.

The future of the PC is uncertain. Either it will become an extra-system or extra-legal party of the revolutionary type, or it will join the democratic institutions that emerge from the transition. In the first case, the party would be condemned to repression and marginalization. In the second case, even though some more traditional socialist groups might gather around the party, the PC could not occupy a space in the renovated left, which is dominated by the Socialists. Thus, the party would tend to be similar to the old PC, but necessarily diminished in its capacity to gather support and grow, as has been the case with orthodox communism in other national contexts. The presence of the PC will be significant because of what it represents symbolically and socially, but it will be a minority party that is subordinate to the socialist pole of the left.

The MIR (Movimiento de Izquierda Revolucionaria), another component of the left, can be called an "anti-system" party because it has always supported a strategy of armed struggle. During the years following the coup, when the MIR sought to make the struggle against the dictatorship effective, it was marginalized and practically wiped out. The party's line came to have some relevance only when, in 1980, the PC adopted the insurrectional strategy. But the MIR suffered several schisms, and one of the factions that favored a more political line eventually joined the United Left. In short, the MIR was not, nor is it likely to be, a relevant actor in the Chilean political party system.

The Humanist Party (PH) is the only new party in Chilean politics that did not arise from a faction of other parties or groups that were politically active before 1973. The origins of the party go back to a spiritual movement of undefined ideological foundations. The PH, which refers to itself as leftist, is basically a youth party that has contributed new themes to the political debate, including ecology, feminism, and pacifism. The party collected signatures in massive street campaigns during the legalization process and sought to redefine the political style of the Concertación of Parties for the NO, which later became the Concertación for Democracy (CPD). But the party leadership's ties to a foreign-born movement and the lack of a national organizational structure made it closer to a movement than a party, and it was very dependent on its alliance with stronger parties. The Humanist Party is unlikely to achieve sufficient growth to change the relations among the large and historical parties.

The scheme of three poles that characterized the Chilean party system seems to have survived, but perhaps it now has four poles. The first pole is the right, which is divided between its role as heir of authoritarianism and its role as a modernized, renovated democratic right. This duality is expressed in the number and type of parties that make up the right and the relations among them. The second pole consists of the PDC and other center parties. The major problem facing these groups concerns a choice between the adoption of center-right positions (which risk serious internal divisions) or the establishment of a solid alliance with some sectors of the left. The third pole, the Socialist left, confronts questions about its ability to constitute a unified political force that is autonomous of the center and Communist left poles. The fourth pole of the Communist-left, which is likely to attract small Socialist groups, faces problems concerning its definition as an "extra-system" actor that may be condemned to disappear or to be integrated into the political system in a subordinate role to the Socialist left.

Clearly, this four-pole scheme could be affected by the legal parties that are not identified with historical parties (such as PPD and PAIS), because those parties could introduce variations in the party system through the electoral process. In addition, the new scheme depends on the formation of coalitions between the various poles. The Concertación of Parties for Democracy can play a crucial role in redefining this four-pole scheme.

The Institutional Insertion of Political Parties

Under the military regime and as part of the process of political institutionalization that led to the plebiscite, political parties faced legislation that dictated severe restrictions, controls, and exclusions. The parties had to go through complex processes to acquire the legal recognition that would allow them to act politically. For the first time, however, they had access to institutional forms that, despite their shortcomings, allowed opposition parties to register, campaign through television, and monitor the plebiscite. Meanwhile, the government imposed an electoral law that sought to establish a majoritarian, binomial system. In response, the opposition criticized both the law of the parties and the law of electoral districts, which could have ensured government control over parliament. But sectors on the right also saw a danger in establishing a rigid electoral system that could, at any moment, give a majority to the opposition, insofar as the right itself fails to achieve unity.

This institutionality had important consequences for the party system. First, the legal registration of political parties provoked a repoliticization of Chilean society. Because a large number of signatures were required in order for a party to register, the parties had to break their relative isolation from society; they achieved a greater degree of visibility and recognition even before electoral processes began. Moreover, the law called for a system of internal elections that caused a certain democratization and expression from the bases of the parties.

Second, the regime's institutionalization of party politics as well as the opposition's counter-proposals tended to favor a system of large and medium-sized parties and the elimination of small ones. From the government's perspective, this was an attempt to establish a bipolar system, which is unrealistic and ahistorical in the Chilean case, where a multiparty system has existed for a century. In the future, without going to the extreme of bipolarity, a system of large and medium-sized parties might prevail. It could be a multiparty system in which the central question would be that of majority coalitions.

Third, party politics has acquired a dual character. On one side are the recently recognized parties that are the legal expression of historical parties (the Christian Democratic Party, the Radical Party, and the National Party) and parties created under the military regime that correspond exactly to their parties of origin (UDI, National Advance, National Renovation, the Humanist Party, and Radical Democratic Socialism). On the other side are the legalized parties and those in the process of legalization that are distinct from the parties and frameworks from which they evolved, such as the instrumental Party for Democracy (PPD) and the Broad Party of the Socialist Left (PAIS). The PPD is based on the Socialist Party (Núñez), other small parties, and, above all, fractions of parties and many independents. The PAIS is a federation of left parties, in which the Socialist Party (Almeyda) and the Communist Party are more important than smaller parties such as the Christian Left.

This situation has allowed the legalization of sectors that would otherwise be proscribed. At the same time, however, the arrangement poses questions about the future of the party system. Under the democratic regime, will it be easy to put an end to the "instrumental" parties that have been so popular because of their novelty and their "programmatic" nature? How will tensions be resolved between the "instrumental" parties and their original parties or frameworks, which continue to assert separate identities but find themselves sustaining the "instrumental" parties for electoral reasons? Does the existence of a party such as the PPD, which has a high recognition level in the polls and is not easily classified as center or left, call into question the traditional polar scheme of the party spectrum? Will the PPD challenge the traditional hegemony of the PDC in the center and in any future center-left coalition? Will the unity of the socialist camp be gravely compromised by the allegiance of the two principal socialist wings to two distinct legal instrumental parties? Finally, does the presence of the Communist party in one of the legal party conglomerates both create insoluble problems of growth for PAIS and reproduce the image of the PC as a hegemonic party of the left over a divided socialism?

Relations and Coalitions among the Parties

The traditional scheme of Chilean parties, known as the "three thirds" (though it might more appropriately be called the "three poles"), was characterized by the rigidity of the system of alliances, except for those formed within each third. This scheme was also characterized by the predominance of centrifugal and polarizing tendencies that led to minority governments that had global projects of tremendous scope. Such projects elicited majority parliamentary opposition and lacked the sociopolitical backing to succeed. This scheme also tended to reproduce exclusionary and highly ideological party subcultures, which, even if they did not affect the representativeness and stability of the parties themselves, threatened the long-run stability of the entire party system.

This tripolar scheme endured under the military regime to the extent that the right is heir to the regime, the Christian Democratic center is similar to what existed before the coup, and the left has a divided socialism and a radicalized Communist party. Let us assume that the right pole will stay the same, independent of its organizational forms, its modernization, and its adaptation to the incoming democratic regime. But there are still factors that should contribute to the modification of the scheme and that could lead to a more flexible system of relations and alliances among Chile's political parties.

First, the simple necessity of reconstructing an institutional system along truly democratic lines could lead to a foundational pact among all parties, including those on the right, that lays out consensual rules of the game and limits the area of conflict. This potential was seen in 1989 when National Renovation and the CPD reached accords that sought the modification of various aspects of the constitution.

Second, the military regime generated a new bipolarity that could have important repercussions. In this sense, the CPD could be the seed of a lasting majority government coalition that alternates party leaderships.[34] If the group of parties that form the CPD—especially key Christian Democratic and Socialist parties—can administer the first democratic government with a platform of democratic institutionalization, attentive to social change and the achievement of popular aspirations, then they will have simultaneously solved three historical problems. They will have resolved the Chilean dilemma of minority governments facing unmanageable tasks. They will have solved the problem of transitions in which some parties administer the transition while others administer social and popular demands. Such a schizophrenic situation can only lead to a regression to populism and instability or, in the case of Chile, to a return to the three-poled scheme, repeating the 1958–73 cycle of rightist, centrist, and leftist governments. Finally, they will have solved the problem of the integration of the PC, which would not be able to follow an "extra-system" line against a center-left alliance but would have to enter either legal opposition or a tacit alliance with the governing coalition.

A lasting agreement between the center and left, with competition regulated by periodic changes in internal leadership, would go far beyond a simple "transition government." It would inaugurate a new period in the political history of the nation and of the party system. One factor that furthers this possibility is the existence of a generational cohort that has been marked by the same historical-political experience of dictatorship and that runs through all of these political forces, promoting their convergence over and above party allegiances. Clearly, the projects for alliances of parties at the center and right—or at the center alone, which some sectors of the PDC promote—are diametrically opposed to the profound significance of the Agreement for Democracy. Moreover, in practice, these alternative alliance projects represent a return to the three-poled scheme and to minority governments, with the consequent threat that democracy will be destabilized and that the cycle of governments running from right to center to left to military coup will be repeated.

A third set of factors that has caused the three-poled scheme to shift are the transformations in the socialist camp and the socialists' reunification in a political force that could break the traditional Socialist-Communist axis of leftist politics. This poses as a central question the autonomous capacity of socialism to seek alliances with the center and to subordinate the other forces of the left to that project. In this sense, the new four-poled scheme not only reinforces but also perhaps makes viable these types of center-left alliances.

Finally, the emergence of a new force such as the PPD, which has the electoral potential to overcome divisions between center and left and challenges the hegemony of both, raises another question about the old "three poles" scheme and opens new possibilities for agreements and alliances. The PPD's capacity to dispute the leadership of both camps can also bring the three poles together, combining modernity with social justice, invoking the symbolic-ideological force along with a programmatic-pragmatic capacity, and thereby bringing generations and diverse social sectors together. The tendency toward the formation of a durable center-left coalition, however, raises new questions about the leadership of such a historic compromise or agreement.

The Parties and Society

Important changes have taken place in the relations between the party system and other social actors. The opinion polls show that society has a generalized mistrust and low recognition of the political parties. Paradoxically, when the party system articulates clear and unified messages that appeal to common sentiments, there are no actors that can better channel collective actions, as the plebiscite demonstrated. Chileans continue to recognize the role that the parties—and only the parties—should play, but they do not grant parties unconditional trust or easily accept the parties' involvement in areas that are not strictly political. Parties have not lost their place in society, but they are no longer the only channels or actors. The people are demanding participation outside party limits and democratization inside the parties.

The relationship of social actors and movements to the parties has become more complex. While social movements are no longer mere vehicles for the parties, they have not become autonomous actors either. Thus, in union, student, and professional associations, the programmatic and electoral choices continue to be made along the lines of party affiliation, the leadership of these movements closely corresponds to party leadership. It is significant, however, that the struggle for the autonomy or independence of social movements is taking place inside the parties. Political parties should give these movements greater autonomy if they want to maintain a presence in them. The autonomy of social movements and actors seems to be much greater in those new areas or spaces that have emerged as part of the struggle against the military dictatorship: in human rights movements, intellectual sectors, women's movements, and cultural groups and movements. Party militants and leaders have also participated in and founded many of these movements, but these individuals tend to dispense with party direction and define themselves more and more as "militants" of their respective movements. In general, the rhetoric of the "autonomy of the social movements" tends to become relatively operational.

More than having observed the founding of a new relationship between parties and civil society in Chile, we have witnessed the transitional steps from a model of "overlapping" party and social leaderships to one of "tension" between parties and social movements. This has occurred with a tendency toward greater—though relative and unequal—autonomy for the social movements. This tendency might be strengthened through the phenomena of decentralization, transfer of power to middle levels, and participation that should accompany the process of democratic construction. This forces a revision of the courses of action taken by a political class that has adapted to the "overlapping" model and that is in conflict with the new generation that has experienced "tension" and greater autonomy. The concept of a "learning process" does not refer only to the transition from dictatorship to democracy; it also takes place within the party system and in its relations with society.

Conclusions

The evolution of the Chilean political opposition to the military regime can be viewed as a learning process that, given the nature of the opposition and the regime, could be called "late" learning. The process was one of passing from resistance or dissidence to true opposition. It also involved passing from a phase of resistance, dissidence, and opposition to become a subject-actor of opposition. This shift required recognizing the difference between struggles against the dictatorship and struggles for the end of it in a transition to a new regime. The true task of politics in these circumstances consists of the capacity to link the two objectives.

In the case of the Chilean opposition, this learning consisted specifically in overcoming three great obstacles, which stemmed from the inherited character of the opposition as well as the type of dictatorship and social transformations carried out under it. These obstacles were (1) the absence of a consensual and coherent political strategy for the termination of the military regime; (2) the consequent fragmentation of the political organizations that addressed the problem of unity in terms of ideological or organic questions and not in terms of the specific forms of struggle needed to end the regime; and (3) the weakening of relations between the political and social realms.

The learning process and the transformations that have occurred under the military regime have also had consequences for the party system. First, the parts of the political spectrum have changed, with a bifurcation between a right that is heir to the military regime and one that wants to play a modern role in the new democratic regime. The PDC maintains its preponderant role and fluctuates between the tendency of the "own path" (which would lead it to a center-right position) and an alliance with the left. The left is divided between a renovated socialism that still has not resolved the problems of unity and a traditional communism that oscillates between an "extra-system" tendency and the workers' party tradition, which is gradualist and integrated into the institutional system.

Second, the parties have become institutionalized through the creation of "legal" parties that do not always coincide with their "original" parties. These legal parties compete for electoral strength with the traditional center and left.

Fourth, putting together the coalition that defeated the regime in the 1988 plebiscite caused the system of alliances to become more flexible. This coalition then became the first majority democratic government of the past decades to be composed of a center-left alliance. This novel situation has been encouraged both by the shift from a party scheme of "three poles" (right, center, left) to one of "four poles" (right, center, socialist left, communist left) and by the existence of "instrumental" or legal parties. This development tends to lower the degree of strict partisan adherence and ideology of previous periods.

Finally, the relations between the parties and society have been transformed. The public mistrust toward the parties is now combined with the search for new channels of expression and participation in Chilean politics, even while respect for the role of the parties as agents of political representation endures. Moreover, there appears to be a change from a traditional "overlapping" of the party and social movement to a "tension" between the two and a possible greater autonomy of the latter. This is particularly true in the case of movements that emerged in the context of the struggle against the military regime.

Clearly, this learning process has been uneven and contradictory, and it has not ended. It is difficult to make projections, especially if we consider that the role of social actors changes significantly during a transition and under democratic regimes. Nevertheless, it can be predicted for a solid nucleus in the opposition that their learning about transitions from military rule will not be reversed. It can also be said that, in the process of constituting an opposition subject-actor, the foundations have been established for a sociopolitical majority that combines democratic adherence and social change under a democratic regime.

Notes

1. A partly modified Spanish version of this paper has appeared in *Muerte y resurrección: Los partidos políticos en el autoritarismo y las transiciones en el Cono Sur*, ed. Marcelo Cavarozzi and Manuel Antonio Garretón, (Santiago, 1989). I am grateful to Paul W. Drake and Iván Jaksić for their comments on the present version.

2. Many of the conceptual aspects of this paper have been developed in Manuel Antonio Garretón, *The Chilean Political Process* (Boston, 1989), *Dictaduras y democratización* (Santiago, 1984), *Reconstruir la política* (Santiago, 1987), and "Problems of Democracy in Latin America: On the Processes of Transition and Consolidation," *International Journal* (Canada) 43: 3 (Summer 1988): 357–77.

3. For the purposes of this work, I understand resistance to mean the level of individual and organizational subsistence of those who oppose the military regime. By dissidence, I mean the oppositional struggle that does not try to transform or eliminate the regime but rather to express its rejection of it. The opposition involves those actors and struggles that seek to transform or change the regime.

4. Juan Linz, "Opposition to and under an Authoritarian Regime: The Case of Spain," in *Regimes and Oppositions*, ed. Robert Dahl (New Haven, N.J., 1973), pp. 171–259.

5. The MIR has defined itself as an insurrectionary group since the 1960s. Many of the MIR's principal leaders, intermediary cadres, and militants were killed, arrested, or expelled from Chile. In any case, their armed resistance was never very significant, and it is only with the appearance of the Manuel Rodríguez Patriotic Front, which was linked initially to the Communist Party, that theories of armed struggle became more significant.

6. See Arturo Valenzuela and J. Samuel Valenzuela, "Party Oppositions under the Chilean Authoritarian Regime," in *Military Rule in Chile. Dictatorship and Oppositions*, ed. J. Samuel Valenzuela and Arturo Valenzuela (Baltimore, 1986); and Alex Fernández Jilberto, *Dictadura militar y oposición política en Chile, 1973–1981* (Amsterdam, 1985).

7. At the beginning of the military regime, the government officially eliminated the parties of the left and imposed a "recess" of the other parties. The parties of the right complied, but the PDC did not. In 1977, a new decree called for the "dissolution" of all parties. This did not stop the activities of either the PDC or the parties of the left.

8. See "La crisis en el socialismo chileno," *Chile-America*, nos. 54–55 (June 1979): 81–137.

9. Javier Martínez and Eugenio Tironi, "La clase obrera en el nuevo estilo de desarrollo: un enfoque estructural," *Chile 1973–198?* (Santiago, 1983); and Guillermo Campero, *El movimiento sindical chileno en el régimen militar* (Santiago, 1982).

10. See CESOC, *Constitución de 1980: Comentarios de juristas internacionales* (Santiago, 1984). See also note 2 for sources on the political significance of the constitution.

11. This change was announced by the party's secretary general in 1980, but it had an important effect only after 1983.

12. Pilar Vergara, *Auge y caída del neoliberalismo en Chile* (Santiago, 1984).

13. Carlos Huneeus, "La política de la apertura y sus implicancias para la inauguración de la democracia en Chile," *Revista de Ciencia Política* 7:1 (1985): 25–84.

14. Gonzalo de la Maza and Mario Garcés, *La explosión de las mayorías: Protesta nacional 1983–1984* (Santiago, 1985).

15. Garretón, *Reconstruir la política*, esp. chapter 4.

16. This took place in August 1985 under the auspices of Cardinal Francisco Fresno.

17. In 1986, both the National Unity Party and the Christian Left withdrew while some socialist groups and MAPU became part of the National Agreement.

18. Asamblea de la Civilidad, *La demanda de Chile* (Santiago, April 1986).

19. Javier Martínez and Eugenio Tironi, *Las clases sociales en Chile: Cambio y estratificación, 1970–1980* (Santiago, 1985).

20. Campero, *El movimiento sindical.*

21. The most important opposition effort to rearticulate the political and social spheres was the Civic Assembly, but with the drawbacks that I have indicated. An overview of the social movements in Chile during this period is in CLACSO-ILET, *Los movimientos sociales y la lucha democrática en Chile* (Santiago, 1986).

22. See the proclamation of the Council for Free Elections, "Convocatoria a una tarea nacional," March 13, 1987. A committee of parties of the Democratic Alliance and the Left for Free Elections was later formed.

23. The Democratic Alliance, which was already operating without Socialist groups, promoted both the idea of a candidate and a government program during 1987. These platforms were rejected by the left.

24. Because of the destruction of electoral registries in 1973, new ones were created by the Law of Electoral Registries in September–October 1986. The process of registration proper began in February 1987.

25. The parties that registered during this period were National Advance, National Renovation, the National Party, and Radical Democracy (at the regional level) on the right; the Christian Democrats, the Radical Party, and the Social Democrats in the center; and the Humanist Party and Party for Democracy, which had leftist tendencies. The Law of Parties was published in March 1987, and only the parties registered under this law could have official representatives at the voting booths and access to television.

26. On February 2, 1988, thirteen opposition parties signed the "Agreement for the NO," in which they were later joined by other small parties; there was a total of seventeen parties by the end of 1988. After the plebiscite, this became the Agreement of Parties for Democracy (CPD). The principal parties that composed the CPD, and that have agreed to become a government coalition with a single presidential candidate, are the PDC, the Radical Party, the Social Democrats, the Socialist Party (Núñez), the Socialist Party (Almeyda), the PH, the Radical Socialist Democratic Party, MAPU, the Christian Left, and other smaller socialist center and right groups. In reality, the key parties of the CPD are the PDC, the Socialist Party (Núñez)-PPD, and the Socialist Party (Almeyda).

27. I have analyzed the significance of the plebiscite for the transition process in "El plebiscito de 1988 y la transición a la democracia," *Cuadernos de Difusión,* FLACSO (Santiago, May 1988).

28. A general synthesis of the opinion polls in the last years and in relation to the plebiscite appears in Manuel Antonio Garretón and Sergio Contreras, "Sociedad, política y plebiscito: Lo que revelan las encuestas," *Revista Mensaje,* no. 373 (October 1988): 431–37.

29. During the campaign, the government used the entire state apparatus, including regional and municipal authorities, direct intervention by the armed forces' high command, control of television (until the last month, in which the opposition had access to a daily space of fifteen minutes), scare tactics, and direct repression. Neither the date nor the candidate was determined until one month before the plebiscite, which made the opposition campaign difficult.

30. The official results were: 43.01 percent for the YES to Pinochet, and 54.71 percent for the NO, with a registration rate of more than 90 percent and abstentions of 2.39 percent. The last two percentages represent record figures in the history of the country.

31. Guillermo O'Donnell, "Notas para el estudio de procesos de democratización política a partir del estado burocrático-autoritario," *Desarrollo Económico* 22:86 (July–September, 1982): 231–48. This article, which O'Donnell wrote in 1976, called attention to this dynamic of "soft- and hard-liners" (*blandos* and *duros*) in authoritarian regimes. O'Donnell took up this theme again with Phillippe Schmitter in "Transitions from Authoritarian Rule and Prospects for Democracy," in *Tentative Conclusions about Uncertain Democracies* (Baltimore, 1986). In my judgment, the authors have given too much weight to this dynamic in the transition process. As the Chilean case shows, this is a consequence of, not a precondition for, the process.

32. See, among others, CEVAL, *La renovación socialista* (Santiago, 1987); Manuel Antonio Garretón, *Reconstruir la política*, chapter 6; and Garretón "The Ideas of Socialist Renovation in Chile," *Rethinking Marxism* 2:2 (Summer 1989): 8–39.

33. See Augusto Varas, ed., *El Partido Comunista en Chile* (Santiago, 1988).

34. See Garretón, *Reconstruir la política*.

Carlos Portales

External Factors and the Authoritarian Regime

The Military Government and Chile's International Relations

The administration that took power in Chile on September 11, 1973, did more than replace a democracy with an authoritarian regime. It also changed the nation's development model from one based on the expansion of the domestic market and the progressive incorporation of diverse social groups to one directed toward the international market. The shift in orientation from the domestic to the international arena implied deep structural transformations. It entailed a political cost, the loss of democracy, and an economic cost, which later translated into a high social cost for underprivileged sectors.

The radicalism of this process resulted in two crucial changes in international relations. First, structural changes made by the military government were linked to either repression or severe limitation in citizens' participation. Political parties, which were vital to Chile's democracy, were either dissolved or outlawed and social organizations were dismantled.[1] The notion of an "internal enemy" obliterated the distinction between external or internal security issues, placing important sectors of Chilean society outside the "national" realm. Segregation of a large part of the political elite was accomplished through exile, which transferred the locus of domestic politics outside the nation's boundaries. As a result, the domestic political process became the basic issue of Chile's international relations. During the early years of the regime, the agenda was dominated by human rights, which forced the military regime to adopt a defensive foreign policy. The transition to democracy as a foreign policy issue was added later.

Second, Chile's model adjusted to international markets by indiscriminately opening foreign trade, restricting government intervention, and leaving initiative in the hands of the private sector. The model was supposed to increase participation in international capital markets as well as attract foreign investment to accelerate domestic development. These policies directly tied Chile's economy to the fluctuations of international markets and dramatically changed foreign economic policy.

The Basis of the Military Government's Foreign Policy

The institutional and structural changes made by the military government redefined the national interest, which in turn changed Chile's foreign policy. Since the end of the nineteenth century, Chile's international security policy had sought to preserve the territorial status quo through a combination of political tactics and a deterrent military force.[2] This objective claimed a high degree of consensus within the political system. Whatever the differences in the domestic arena, international boundaries policy always enjoyed the support of the population. The pillars of the implementation of this policy were the nation's international prestige, its integration in the international system, and its support for the creation and consolidation of international juridical mechanisms to resolve conflicts.

Although the military government did not change the objective of maintaining the territorial status quo, two elements transformed the country's security policy. First, the nation's diminished capacity to formulate foreign policy as a result of the loss of international prestige rendered diplomacy ineffective. It increased the need for a stronger military deterrent to confront increasing external tensions. Second, the concept of national security was overextended to include not only the territorial status quo but also an internal/external enemy, who was vaguely defined as ranging from "communism" or "soviet aggression" to international critics and internal dissidents. This vagueness confused political conflicts with security problems in both the international and domestic arenas.

At the same time, the objective of national autonomy changed. In traditional Chilean foreign policy, autonomy meant that domestic decision-making and the potential to act at the international level would be in the hands of democratically elected authorities. Under the military government, however, autonomy acquired a defensive character. It became necessary to defend a regime whose practices and legitimacy were questioned throughout the international community. In the economy, the meaning of autonomy changed from a national control (with an important state component) of priorities and of the effects from external variables to a strengthening of economic growth. The nation would adjust to world market conditions and accept the domestic consequences of global economic effects. In practice, it was expected that the compensation for this loss in autonomy would be increased participation in the dynamics of the world economy, which would strengthen Chile's attraction for transnational economic forces.

Transnationalization of Chile's Foreign Relations

The policies of the military regime during its installation and consolidation phase led to the transnationalization of Chile's external relations.[3] This phenomenon was both the expected result of applying the free-market economic development model and the unintended consequence of transferring domestic political conflicts to the international arena. The new style of foreign policy involved not only Chilean and other foreign governments but also domestic actors, such as political parties and human rights organizations. Equally important were numerous nongovernmental actors in other countries, such as human rights organizations, political parties, and labor unions, which intervened at the domestic and transnational levels. Important international intergovernmental organizations also included Chile in their agenda, thus becoming regular actors in domestic debates.

These new foreign policy issues were not just discussed in the forums used in traditional interaction between nations, but they were also debated in the public opinion arenas of other countries, in their domestic institutions, and in governmental and nongovernmental international organizations. Elements that contributed to the formation of these links went beyond bilateral diplomacy and included systematic oversight functions by international organizations, as well as attempts to tie economic and military questions to the issues of democratization and human rights.

The Chilean government—driven by the "soft line" sectors since 1978—emphasized substituting previous democratic prestige, as a source of external power, for prestige based on the implementation of an economic model that was compatible with prevailing prescriptions in the developed capitalist countries, especially in international financial and business circles. It was not government relations per se but rather links with those economic groups that took first priority. The responsibility for this international offensive went to the private sector and to the officials in charge of the economy, leaving the defensive tasks to traditional diplomacy.

Although the regime was unmoved by external pressure up to the 1982–83 period, human rights violations were not as prevalent as they had been during 1973–76. The regime was institutionalized through the 1980 constitution.[4] There was no significant opening for political participation, and dictatorial rigidity was maintained. With the application of the transnational model, the economic growth experienced from 1977 to 1981 created the impression of a "Chilean economic miracle." It seemed as though the new "economic prestige" was going to reincorporate Chile into the international community. At the beginning of the new decade, two significant changes in capitalist powers seemed to provide ample space for the strategy of Chile's military government: the ascension of Margaret Thatcher in Great Britain and Ronald Reagan in the United States. Both leaders advocated a free-market economy that was similar to that adopted by Chile and a benevolent reorientation of their countries' policies toward authoritarian regimes.[5]

The 1982–1983 Crisis

The social conditions that resulted in a serious political crisis for the regime in 1983 were created by the collapse of the economic model in 1982, compounded by the foreign debt. The acute international recession—related to the policies of the Reagan administration—devastated Chile's economy. In 1982, GNP decreased by 14.3 percent. The economic crisis damaged not only low income groups and the growing number of unemployed but also the middle and industrial sectors. The resulting protest movement kept growing until August 1983, when the cabinet headed by Sergio Onofre Jarpa began a period of liberalization. The policies of international openness had increased the vulnerability of the domestic economy and intensified the effects of the recession. Thus, indirectly, the transnationalization sought by the government generated its first serious political crisis.

The crisis was the immediate result of domestic social and political movements, not of international pressure. It should be noted, however, that the policies of external actors had contributed significantly to the preservation of some pluralism within domestic organizations during the previous decade. Foreign influences had particularly encouraged the growth of human rights organizations. Transnational links had aided the survival, however precarious, of opposition parties and the development of intellectual centers and a few independent media that were extremely important in the protest movement. The 1983 policy of liberalization also must be understood by taking into account the development of differences within the bloc that supported the regime. In this case, however, more than coming from a reemergence of the "softliners" strongly linked to the strategy of transnational economic ties, the initiative came from the previously dismantled parties of the right, which represented many segments of the middle and upper classes.

The five-year liberalization period, which began in August 1983 and culminated in the October 1988 plebiscite, was a long, slow, and not always continuous process. To understand the interaction between external influences and domestic factors in that transition, I will discuss four points: (1) the content of the policies of the main international actors with respect to Chile's transition to democracy; (2) the policy priorities of the main international actors as well as the means they used; (3) the responses of Chile's government to these external influences; and (4) the effects of those policies on the transition process.

Motivation and Content of Policies for Democracy

Many international actors considered the promotion of democracy to be one of their most important foreign policy objectives. This was certainly the case with United States foreign policy from 1982 on, after Ronald Reagan's administration reevaluated its criticisms of President Jimmy Carter's human rights policy.[6] Reagan's post-1982 policy coincided with the posture taken by Western European countries, though perhaps for different reasons. "The exportation of democracy" had long been a recurring element in the foreign policy of the United States, but the Western European countries—some of which had consolidated their own democracies during the postwar period—had followed a more cautious path, seeking to reinforce the democratic potential in certain countries, especially those in southern Europe.[7]

The type of democracy preferred depended on the breadth of participation desired. For the United States, the definition of a desired democracy was linked to its concept of security, which was dominated by an ideological confrontation with the Soviet Union. The struggle against the "evil empire" was a key reason why the United States engaged in a crusade for democracy in the 1980s. The European position, more in tune with political systems there, was less preoccupied by the breadth of the political spectrum in Latin America.

The United States' hesitation about Chile's transition was strongly influenced by what was perceived to be the potential role of the Communist Party during Chile's post-authoritarian period, as expressed by Assistant Deputy Secretary for Inter-American Affairs James Michel. Addressing an audience at the University of Arkansas and referring to the position of the United States government with respect to Chile, Michel emphasized the considerable influence that the Communists could have in a political system that allegedly lacked the basic consensus necessary to reestablish a stable democracy.[8] Conversely, the specter of Communism was invoked later to argue that a slow transition was raising the danger that the role of the Communist Party would become increasingly important and that it was therefore necessary to accelerate democratization.[9] This kind of thinking influenced the United States' perception of the Chilean left and accounted for the lack of communication with this sector of the political spectrum; it was only overcome after the departure of U.S. Ambassador James Theberge.

With the perspective gained from having diverse political parties, Western Europeans much more easily related to Chile's pluralistic political system. Partly because of the increasing number of Chileans exiled in Europe, a strong relationship developed between members of the Christian Democratic and Socialist parties of the two continents during the period of the military regime. Because Communists were important political actors in Western Europe, the existence of a Communist Party in Chile did not alarm most Western Europeans.

The position of other Latin American countries with respect to the Chilean process evolved as their own political regimes changed. The decline of authoritarian regimes in South America—particularly in Argentina in 1983, Uruguay in 1985, and Brazil in 1986—added support for Chile's transition. These new democracies saw democratization elsewhere in the region as an element that would strengthen their own governments. Consequently, the new democracies coordinated their foreign policies with other democratic countries, such as Colombia, Peru, and Venezuela, to form the Group of Eight. Chile was obviously excluded.

Policy Priorities in Supporting the Transition

Support for a democratic transition in Chile was neither the only nor often the most important foreign policy goal of any other nation. To understand the extent of this policy objective, it must be analyzed in relationship to (1) other foreign policy objectives, (2) the means of external pressure that a country is prepared to use to accomplish that objective, and (3) the assessment of the total situation of the country where the objective is to be accomplished. This grouping of relationships will illuminate the priorities that underlie a policy of support for democratization and the impact of external influences on that process.

After an initial warming of relations with Pinochet, the Reagan administration recast its policy in the context of the United States' crusade for democracy, the inflexibility of the Chilean regime, and the 1983 crisis provoked by popular protests.[10] The shift in U.S. policy was a long process that began in 1983 with the abandonment of "quiet diplomacy" and the issuance of public statements on human rights and democratic institutions. The U.S. policy transformation concluded with the active advocacy of a gradual and negotiated transition aimed at

restoring democracy through dialogue between those elements within the government favoring the transition and those forces within the opposition favoring negotiation. [The idea was] to initiate a process that Chileans on their own could successfully complete.[11]

The United States did not seek to destabilize the regime but to influence the evolution of internal conditions that were conducive to liberalization. The idea was to encourage the moderate opposition as well as those groups within the government that sought openness. This policy was a safeguard for the United States against the risk of creating instability that could jeopardize its security objectives. The assessment of the internal situation was that

the political transition in Chile has to overcome certain obstacles: up to now the government has not kept its promises of a transition; no consensus has been reached among the different groups within the opposition on a clear basis for negotiations with the military, and the Communists are not interested in compromise formulas.[12]

These conditions convinced the Reagan administration to adopt a policy of gradual intervention into the process of democratization without forcing a breakdown of the regime. This approach allowed for the consolidation of the neo-liberal economic model, which had been harshly criticized and had been modified in some aspects by the military regime after the 1982 crisis but which was essentially restored by 1985.

To implement this policy, the United States applied political-diplomatic pressure through open and discrete messages, through declarations in Washington and Santiago, through symbolic acts, and through pronouncements in international organizations. It emphasized respect for human rights, the avoidance of abuses, the prevention of further delays in the liberalization process, help for internal actors who favored the transition preferred by Washington, and the extraction of guarantees for a plebiscitary process that resembled as much as possible a democratic election.

The change began with the statements issued by the U.S. Department of State at the time of the popular protests, statements that were criticized by the Chilean foreign minister. The change became even more obvious with the arrival in Santiago of U.S. Ambassador Harry G. Barnes Jr. in 1985, with his policy of establishing broad contacts with diverse sectors of the political spectrum. The United States reacted strongly against the imposition of a state of siege in 1984, 1985, and 1986 and condemned the most egregious human rights violations, especially when important actors in the transition process were harmed. The United States also changed its strategy toward international organizations that protested human rights violations in Chile. At the start of 1985, the U.S. influenced the designation of Fernando Volio, former foreign minister of Costa Rica, to monitor the Chilean case for the United Nations. Volio directly linked the human rights situation in Chile to progress made in the transition to democracy, though his reports took into account some positions of the Chilean government. From that time on, the United States' voting record with respect to Chile at the United Nations and the Organization of American States was heavily influenced by what was happening with the transition process, sending warning signals or incentives to the Pinochet government. Support for the National Accord in August 1985 formed part of the policy of encouraging dialogue between the regime and the opposition, since one government supporter—the National Union—signed the accord.[13]

In keeping with this policy, economic pressure was used. Because of the foreign debt crisis, the Chilean government was especially vulnerable when it came to obtaining financial resources abroad. After the withdrawal of private banks in 1982, the foreign public sector—especially international financial organizations—were once again crucial to obtain external financing. Foreign loans had become indispensable, not only for a minimum of domestic growth but also to service the external debt. The approval of these resources was tied on a few occasions and with great caution to changes that favored the process of liberalization. This was the case in June 1985 when Chile requested credit from the World Bank, which was crucial in the nation's renegotiation of its external debt. The United States conditioned its support for the loan on Chile lifting the state of siege implanted at the end of 1984. Warnings that the human rights situation must improve and that guarantees for the plebiscite must be established were sent by the United States' abstention in the structural adjustment credits of the World Bank in 1986 and 1987. This was also the message of the limited economic sanctions imposed by the Reagan administration in December 1987. In no case, however, were economic measures used for destabilization.

Military ties between Washington and Santiago had been severely limited in the 1970s by the Kennedy Amendment. After the partial removal of that legislative barrier, relations remained poor because the White House lacked certification of significant progress on human rights in Chile as well as the regime's refusal to cooperate with U.S. authorities who were investigating the roles of Chilean officials in the assassinations of Chilean Foreign Minister Orlando Letelier and American citizen Ronnie Moffit in Washington. Resolving the Letelier-Moffit case was a precondition from Congress to completely lifting the Kennedy restrictions.

The relations between the military establishments of both countries reached its low point when President Carter imposed sanctions in 1980. Relations improved when the Chilean navy participated in the joint UNITAS operations under President Reagan. But this was not enough to overcome the negative reaction that sanctions had created among Chilean armed forces in 1978. On this matter, the capacity of the U.S. executive branch to act was severely limited by congressional opposition. The cost implied in issuing the certification—a step nearly taken at the beginning of the Reagan administration—was increasing and impeding the greater military cooperation the White House desired. Instead of a program of military assistance, an intense program of exchange visits by high military leaders took place that was limited by the legal restrictions on military aid as well as by the rather cool reception by the Chilean armed forces, especially the army. The lack of a means to act in military relations lessened the possibilities of influencing the Chilean regime through a United States policy of military sanctions and rewards. Furthermore, the effect of the sanctions had been undermined by a policy of transference on the part of European actors.

Western European countries also affirmed their preoccupation with human rights issues and their support for the transition to democracy in Chile.[14] The priority of this objective and the intensity with which it was pursued varied among countries, in some cases because of changes in political orientation. The policies of European governments toward Chile were influenced by each country's general situation, by human rights violations against European citizens, and by diplomatic actions or statements that put European governments in direct confrontation with Santiago.

The 1983 protests drew critical statements from some countries, such as France, as did the arrest of opposition leaders Christian Democrat Gabriel Valdés in 1983 and Socialist Ricardo Lagos in 1986. The regime was also criticized when it proclaimed a state of siege in 1984 and 1986 (including criticism from the European Economic Community), when it closed newspapers and censored the press, and when it expelled British journalist Anthony Boadle in May 1984 (an action later revoked). The ban on the return of some exiles also provoked protests by the international community.

Chilean authorities rejected all critical statements issued by high officials of Western European governments throughout the Pinochet period on the grounds that they interfered in domestic affairs. At the same time, there was not always unanimity in the positions taken by the Western European countries. The military regime in Chile gave special attention to its relations with Great Britain, which improved after Margaret Thatcher replaced the more hostile Labor government, and cooperation was achieved in several areas following the Falklands/Malvinas War in 1982. But this did not mean that Great Britain withdrew from the international European initiatives that favored human rights and the transition to democracy, efforts that intensified as the 1988 plebiscite came closer.

The activism of Western European countries with regard to human rights and the transition to democracy seldom extended to military or economic areas. Purchases of arms and spare parts in Western Europe were subjected to attacks by political forces and suffered restrictions, in Great Britain in the 1970s and in France, West Germany, and Spain. Nevertheless, European countries became the major suppliers of the Chilean armed forces, an extremely important development for the regime's foreign policy. According to the U.S. Arms Control and Disarmament Agency, between 1982 and 1986 Chile imported $550 million in arms—$300 million from France (54.5 percent), $130 million from West Germany (23.5 percent), $60 million from Great Britain (11 percent), and $60 million from other countries. That is, close to 90 percent of the weapons imported by Chile during the critical period of the transition came from Western Europe.[15] Likewise, the policies of Western European countries did not link commerce and trade to the democratic transition results. On the contrary, commercial contacts increased, including agreements on the production of war materials, such as the one between the National Aeronautic Company (ENAER) and the Spanish corporation CASA, which produces military airplanes.

In renegotiating Chile's foreign debt, Europeans followed the leadership of the United States banking industry, headed by Manufacturers Hanover Trust. When voting on structural adjustment loans at the World Bank in 1986–87—which would open the door to renegotiating the debt with private banks and apply pressure on the military regime to move toward a democratic transition—the Western European countries were divided. The representatives from Great Britain (1986, 1987), Germany (1986, 1987), and Spain (1987) voted in favor of the loans. France (1986, 1987), Austria (1986, 1987), and Spain (1986) joined the United States in abstaining. Only the delegates from Sweden and Italy voted against the adjustment credits on both occasions.[16]

During the period leading up to the plebiscite, Western European countries increasingly coordinated their support for the transition. This support was expressed not only through intergovernmental and governmental channels but also through inter-party links. The role that Europeans played in raising the concerns of the international community was symbolized in the multinational membership of the observer delegation funded by the U.S. National Endowment for Democracy, a delegation led by Adolfo Suárez, former prime minister of Spain.

The policies of the Latin American countries, especially those of the Southern Cone, changed as a result of the transitions to democracy that were occurring throughout the hemisphere. Expressions of support for democratization in Chile became an integral part of the foreign policy objective of those countries. But they still emphasized certain widely shared principles that regulate relations among Latin American nations, especially the principles of nonintervention and nonpoliticization of international credit organizations. The governments of the region made their positions known mostly by political means, including official statements, votes in international organizations, and symbolic gestures such as invitations to the opposition to attend presidential inaugurations of democratically elected leaders. A new element in regional politics was the good relationship among democratic governments and between them and the Chilean forces that were fighting for the transition.

During the 1980s, nongovernmental actors intensified their participation in foreign relations. One of the by-products of Chilean exile was the diverse and fluid quality of the personal contacts that opposition leaders made with other Latin American and European elites. The contacts facilitated campaigns for human rights during the transition process and kept domestic political forces in those countries focused on the Chilean case.

In contrast, links among the military establishments of Latin America were not influential. Brazil was the only Latin American country to provide arms to Chile, but its sales were not conditioned by political variables. Other Latin American countries used no economic pressure to encourage the Chilean transition. In the economic realm, the countries of the region had limited means at their disposal, and regional policy—which emerged as a reaction to United States policy—sought to prevent the politicization of multilateral credit organizations. This was why Latin American countries did not join the United States in abstaining during votes at the World Bank and the Inter-American Development Bank in the second half of the 1980s.

For Latin American nations, the relationship between supporting Chile's transition to democracy and other foreign policy objectives, particularly those referring to border conflicts, was very different from that of first world powers. Among the countries of the region, good-neighbor relations were particularly important for democratic governments that had recently emerged from authoritarian experiences and that wanted to limit the role of the armed forces. For those governments, the objective of promoting a transition to democracy had to be coordinated with a good-neighbor policy, which provided a paradoxical contrast with the practices of preceding military regimes.

Thus, Alán García's Aprista government in Peru sought closer relations with the Chilean government in order to encourage arms limitation measures. Although nothing concrete was achieved, at least bilateral relations were improved. The main consequence of Argentina's transition to democracy for Argentine-Chile relations was President Raúl Alfonsín's acceptance of the Papal proposal that ended the border conflict in the austral region through a peace treaty between Chile and Argentina ratified on May 2, 1985. Thus, a conflict that had almost resulted in war in 1978, and had stagnated since then due to the Argentine military government's refusal to accept the Papal proposal, was finally settled. Although an immediate effect was the improvement of bilateral relations, the lack of progress toward democracy in Chile became an obstacle to full normalization of relations. The Argentine government continued to express concern for the Chilean domestic situation. Those worries intensified with the escalation of armed activity by the Manuel Rodríguez Patriotic Front, a situation that the Argentine government believed endangered the stability of Latin American democratic regimes.

Other pressures on Chile came from international organizations that favored improvements in human rights and democratization. Some were intergovernmental organizations, such as the United Nations and, to a lesser extent, the Organization of American States. Nongovernmental actors, such as Amnesty International and Americas Watch, also played a role. The activities of the intergovernmental groups resulted from a consensus or a majority among the member nations, which limited the scope of their action. Nevertheless, the continuous attention these organizations gave to Chile's domestic situation and their dissemination of information kept Chile's internal politics as key issues in the country's foreign policy.

The Chilean Government's External and Internal Response

Faced with accumulated external pressures to change its domestic behavior, the Chilean government systematically invoked the principle of nonintervention when the actions of the international community became too direct. But the government often yielded to external pressures, responding either directly or indirectly. In some cases, it allowed exiled citizens to return or lifted restrictions against foreigners. Another instance of responding to demands without admitting it was suspending the state of siege in June 1985, mostly to prevent negative votes on crucial foreign loans. Some other decisions were made within the context of external pressure or at least with that element taken into account. External leverage definitely contributed to getting Chile's cooperation for the United Nations to enter the country to collect data for its annual report on human rights.

Even so, internal decisions were not directly subordinated to international politics. In 1985, a state of siege was imposed in order to prevent the new eruption of popular protests. Although some ground was lost with respect to civil liberties, there was no return to the grim pre-1983 situation. Human rights violations—which were widespread during brief periods—became more directly linked to repressing and preventing mass movements and to more selective confrontations with armed groups. Nevertheless, incredible brutalities occurred, such as the cases of the "slit throats" in March 1985 and the "burned ones" in July 1986. This second incident particularly captured world attention, because one of the victims was a Chilean resident of Washington, D.C., who was burned to death by a military patrol in Santiago. The Chilean judiciary identified those responsible, but imposed few penalties. At the same time, the United States government continued to insist on prosecuting Chilean officials involved in the 1976 Orlando Letelier assassination, which complicated even more its relationship with the military regime.

The Chilean government responded to foreign demands for institutional changes by opening itself to liberalization in August 1983, which alleviated external pressures and dampened domestic protests. Soon, however, the regime cancelled the dialogue with the opposition. When the anti-government initiatives resurfaced, it reimposed a state of siege, which was lifted in mid-1985 in response to international pressure. After the failed attempt on Pinochet's life, a state of siege was reinstated in September 1986, with lessened severity due, once more, to international pressure. The opposition's failure to make 1986 "the decisive year" focused its desires for institutional change on the 1988 plebiscite.

By August 1986, General Pinochet had already announced the projection of his regime into the future. From the government's perspective, the only response to pressures for a transition to democracy was to implement the permanent institutions in the 1980 constitution. To do so, the cabinet was reorganized to appoint Sergio Fernández as minister of the interior, a post he had held during the 1980 plebiscite to approve the constitution. The objective was to gain recognition and acceptance for the 1980 constitution and to establish an electoral system and political laws that were necessary to designate a presidential candidate for the 1988 plebiscite.[17]

Institutionalization meant reaffirming the 1980 constitution, but the need to legitimize it responded to both domestic and international pressures. Although enjoying some international support, the opposition's campaign for free elections as a mechanism for presidential succession failed to alter the system outlined in the 1980 constitution. Consequently, the debate over the plebiscite became the key issue.

Demands for electoral safeguards came from internal actors such as the Catholic Bishops' Conference, the Committee for Free Elections, and the opposition political parties. Their demands were later supported by the European Community and by an official statement of President Reagan and Secretary of State George Schultz issued on December 17, 1987:

For the ideal of popular sovereignty to become reality in Chile, the United States believes that a climate of freedom and fair competition must be established many months before the actual balloting takes place. This atmosphere will be marked by easy and equitable access to the mass media, especially television, by unrestricted discussion of political issues, broad freedom of assembly, early announcement of the rules of any electoral proceeding, facilitation of registration by prospective voters, and freedom for citizens and political groups to campaign peacefully in favor of their ideas. States of exception which limit freedom of assembly, association, and expression are not compatible with a legitimate electoral procedure.[18]

The opposition parties implicitly accepted the existing institutional framework—if only for the plebiscite—when they united in the Coalition of Parties for the NO, on February 2, 1988. Thereafter the conditions for the plebiscite became the key to the process. Establishing norms for the process was debated even within the regime, where the need to satisfy foreign observers deterred the most extreme hard-line elements. International pressure and the regime's need to seek external legitimation of the plebiscite helped produce an electoral process that permitted a valid expression of preferences.

A series of events provided safeguards for the 1988 electoral showdown. First, the September 24, 1985, decision of the Constitutional Tribunal to establish a Qualifying Elections Tribunal exceeded the constitution's literal requirements and opened an avenue for some civilian control of the plebiscite.[19] Second, the suppression of a series of rules in the Law of Political Parties that the Tribunal declared unconstitutional in February 1987 made it possible for the opposition to finally—and reluctantly—organize itself within the regime's institutional framework. Third, the Project of Law on Voting and Counting approved by the junta did not announce how much time would elapse between the call for the plebiscite and the actual vote; it only established a specific period of time between the election of the candidate by the commanders-in-chief and the date of the national balloting. The ability to shorten the time for campaigning by withholding information on whom the commanders had elected still remained in the president's hands. The Constitutional Tribunal declared that provision invalid in January 1988, and it established a minimum period of thirty days between the time the proposed voting was announced and the plebiscite date. Fourth, in early 1988 it was rumored that the plebiscite date would be set very quickly to limit the number of registered voters. Statements by some members of the junta, however, dissipated fears that the plebiscite would be held before the opposition had had an opportunity to register sufficient voters. A fifth issue concerned freedom of expression as a precondition for the wide acceptance of the plebiscite. Limited time on state-controlled television stations had been made available for debate since the beginning of 1988. Finally, a law was passed at the beginning of August decreeing that fifteen minutes of free television time would be granted to both sides each night of the campaign, a decision that would be crucial to the opposition's victory. Also in August, all states of exception—including the state of siege—were lifted for the first time since 1973.

In this long process of establishing the rules for the plebiscite, international pressure helped those in the regime who favored openness and hindered those who were trying to manipulate the electoral game. Governments and other external actors followed the plebiscitary process closely and repeatedly intervened to protect it. The last such intervention was the unusual call the Chilean ambassador in Washington received from Acting Undersecretary of State John Whitehead warning against any alteration of the process on the eve of the plebiscite. An important contribution during the plebiscite itself was the presence of hundreds of foreign observers.

The military government underwent a fifteen-year process of learning how to deal with foreign influences. During the period 1983–88, the regime developed a growing capacity to evaluate the significance of external pressures. When those pressures occurred on a broad basis and on issues on which the regime was particularly sensitive—such as the question of external credits in 1985—the government gave in, although it retained certain safeguards such as strengthening the state of exception before lifting the state of siege in 1985. But the junta realized that its degree of vulnerability varied with economic issues and external actors.

The Chilean government learned to forge links with developed countries by establishing active contacts with right-wing spokespeople in the United States, West Germany, and England. It countered visits by politicians who were critical of the regime with tours by sympathetic leaders. This strategy changed neither the external image of the regime nor the thrust of foreign influence, but it did blunt some of the pressures.

Since the mid-1970s, the application of a free-market economic model that was widely admired in developed countries, international financial institutions, and the international business community had generated some prestige for the Chilean government until the collapse in 1981–83. When those policies became successful again in the mid-1980s, the government used the economic factor once again to improve foreign relations. Chile's healthy economy provided leverage for foreign debt negotiations and made it easier to

Table 8.1
Chile: Imports and Exports of Arms, 1977–1986
(in millions of 1984 constant dollars)

	Imports	Exports
1977	60	0
1978	60	0
1979	180	0
1980	250	0
1981	310	6
1982	280	0
1983	90	0
1984	160	20
1985	20	19
1986	0	9

Source: ACDA, *World Military Expenditures and Arms Transfers, 1987*, Publication 129 (Washington, D.C., March 1988).

obtain other international resources that were necessary for macro-economic development. The economic "card" also helped diversify external connections and neutralize political pressures from international institutions. Active campaigning by the regime's economic spokespeople helped prevent negative votes in international institutions.

The adoption of measures such as "swaps" to conserve foreign exchange also acquired prestige in foreign financial circles and linked international business interests to the Chilean economy. This new form of transnationalization reinforced the moderate tendencies in foreign governmental policies toward Chile. Chile was cited as a role model among debtor countries, even by those governments that were pressuring the regime to accelerate democratization.

Finally, the Chilean regime responded to international pressure by finding solutions to border problems. The decline in Chile's international prestige had led to increased defense spending as a deterrent against conflict with its neighbors. This situation became particularly difficult when Chile dealt with the conflict with Argentina. Chile responded with an increase in arms imports during the last years of the 1970s and the beginning of the 1980s and with the development of a national arms industry that began exporting in the second half of the 1980s, (see Table 8.1). Because there was an embargo by the United States and the situation with some European countries was difficult at times, the junta diversified foreign relations to purchase arms from Israel and to reach arms co-production agreements with Spain and South Africa.[20]

Chile also used diplomatic means to deal with Bolivia's demand for access to the Pacific Ocean. Beginning in the 1960s, there were no diplomatic relations between Chile and Bolivia. Chile's military regime tried to solve the problem in 1975 by granting access to the ocean through territories that had previously belonged to Peru, in exchange for territorial compensation on the part of Bolivia. This failed attempt led to a new breakdown in relations and to an active Bolivian campaign that sought support for its cause in international organizations. For the first time, Bolivia found sustained international support. Chile's government entered into negotiations in 1983–84 and again in 1986–87, but finally the lack of internal consensus led to the rejection of Bolivia's proposals in June 1987.

Effects of External-Internal Interaction

By observing foreign policies concerning the Chilean transition, we can conclude that a primary objective was to affect an internal process through influence rather than destabilization. The effect of the policies of exerting influence was to limit arbitrary actions by the Chilean regime, which had to calculate the costs of sanctions—mainly political—by the international community. As a result, many elements of liberalization in the post-1983 regime were either maintained or reinstated (such as protection for opposition parties and their leaders and some freedom of the press), thus contributing to the conditions necessary for holding an honest plebiscite.

With respect to internal actors, the policies of the United States, Western Europe, and Latin America encouraged moderate elements in both the opposition and the government in Chile. The broad international support for the National Accord of 1985 combined with the foreign pressures to lift the states of siege and exception and to establish guarantees for the plebiscite made it possible, within the institutional limits of the regime, for groups to promote a reasonably democratic plebiscite. External influences also created space for autonomous political forces to develop among government supporters. In particular, the rightist National Renovation Party played an important role in the recognition of the plebiscite results on October 5 and implemented a political line that favored the transition and that was increasingly independent from the government.

With respect to the opposition, external influences contributed to its survival by supporting human rights organizations such as the Committee for Peace at the beginning of the regime, the Vicariate of Solidarity after the dissolution of the Committee, and the Chilean Commission for Human Rights. Foreigners also facilitated the precarious presence of the opposition in social and labor organizations and after 1983 aided the development of political parties. And last but not least, external influences encouraged citizens' campaigns for the October plebiscite, including promotion of registration, dissemination of information, and development of modern campaign techniques.

The formulation of opposition strategies that ultimately resulted in a transformation in the political system stemmed from the realization that external forces could not destabilize the regime. The foreign and domestic protests changed the regime's policies but not the regime itself. At the same time, the increasing isolation of the Communist Party, which was implementing its "acute violence" policy, reached its peak after the discovery of its arsenals and the assassination attempt against General Pinochet in 1986.[21] Nevertheless, external influences—especially in relations among political parties—still promoted moderation and a common strategy within the opposition. When this approach was consolidated in the Command for the No, external support increased.

In sum, international factors were important but not decisive in the evolution of the Chilean regime. External influences played a role, first in the conservation and consolidation of internal opposition forces, then in limiting the authoritarian attempts to reverse the liberalization process provoked by the protests, and finally in the creation of the proper conditions for the 1988 plebiscite. Above all, foreign actors helped create space for the moderate and liberalizing elements within the regime and for those members of the opposition who were committed to peaceful change; they encouraged "softliners" in both camps to reach a consensus on redemocratization.

International economic factors, by contrast, played a different role. At the beginning of the military regime, United States governmental support was crucial in stimulating the precarious Chilean economy. The regime's plan for transnational economic participation emphasized direct links with the international private sector.

During the final years of the 1970s, these private links compensated for decreased public financial aid imposed by the Carter administration.

When the 1982 crisis closed off access to private financing, the Chilean economy became dependent again on public external financing. But this vulnerability was not used to foment political change. Because Chilean economic policy followed the tenets of the international financial organizations by implementing severe internal adjustments, it received financial support from these organizations with the backing of the United States and Western Europe during the critical period of 1983–84, without being subjected to any political conditions. Only after the Reagan administration switched its policies to promote democracy was U.S. economic pressure used modestly to warn the regime to sustain liberalization and progress toward a gradual, negotiated democratic opening.

With respect to the other central element in Chile's foreign policy, the country paid a high price to maintain the territorial status quo during the prolonged crisis with Argentina. The policies of democratic leaders Raúl Alfonsín in Argentina and Alán García in Peru allowed for an adequate negotiation with the Chilean government. By contrast, Bolivia's demand for an outlet to the Pacific Ocean ceased to be a bilateral issue and became, for the first time, a multilateral question that is constantly being debated. The responses of the military regime, which lacked consensus on this issue, aggravated the problem.

Post-plebiscite, Transition, and International Relations

When Chile's domestic conflicts were transformed into a key element in its external relations, governments, international organizations, and other transnational actors closely followed the nation's internal politics. To the degree that the institutional process leading to congressional and presidential elections in December 1989 produces a complete transition to constitutional democracy, Chile's international relations will no longer be centered on human rights and the system of government. While the process of consolidation continues, external actors will still be attentive to domestic politics. In this regard, there are four elements that Chile holds in common with other nations' experiences with democratic transitions.[22] First, transitions that do not endanger existing international alliances are easier, which was the case with all the leading contenders to succeed

Pinochet. Second, internal forces have the primary role, and external forces play a secondary one. This has been corroborated in the Chilean case where international actors pursued a policy of influencing but not of destabilizing the regime. Third, in countries that operate in the sphere of influence of a superpower, a relative equilibrium between democratic and anti-democratic forces can be influenced decisively by external action. Because Chile is not geographically close to any superpower, external influences did not become too important there. Fourth, transnational forces will continue to influence domestic actors in Chile. In general, the influence of the transition experiences of other Latin American countries on the Chilean armed forces will probably be relevant when decisions are taken to reorient themselves within the democratic system and to establish a new pattern of civil-military relations.

These years of military rule in Chile left a legacy for the nation's international relations. The international community will continue to be concerned with the human rights situation during the post-transitional regime. In addition, greater transnational linkages will persist for domestic actors in Chile, including political parties, labor organizations, and other nongovernmental actors. And finally, the presence of transnational economic actors with strong interests in Chile, including bankers and other investors, will endure.

The transnationalization of internal politics has opened the door for foreigners to manipulate domestic actors, just as Chileans manipulated international support for democratization. Transnationalization could also lead to the development of a far greater capacity for international collaboration and the establishment of more reasonable limits on internal political competition. In any case, external influences on the democratic process seem likely to continue, although with reduced intensity.

The transnationalization of the economy and its enhanced standing with the international business community will also have long-term consequences. Positive evaluation of the economic model places limits on the actions of the next government, which will have to make essential social adjustments during the post-authoritarian period. But the lack of a definitive solution to the problem of the foreign debt, the instability of markets, and the limits of export possibilities in a world economy with protectionist tendencies might reveal the vulnerability of the Chilean economy. Should these factors result in a crisis, the Chilean government might call for solutions that could drastically alter recent economic policies.

In the field of international security, a democratic regime could substantially improve Chile's political-diplomatic resources and avoid the necessity of incurring the dramatic costs of armaments as the only answer to border problems.[23] Furthermore, a democratic regime should be able to launch new international initiatives. These efforts should be based on a realistic appreciation of the national interests of a society undergoing tremendous changes as it enters the twenty-first century. Chile's external capacity for action will be directly related to its internal capacity to achieve an adequate synthesis between a democratic regime and an economic system that has the ability to grow and distribute benefits to diverse social groups.

Notes

1. During the liberalization period that began in 1983, the activity of political organizations was severely restricted and had no possibility of influencing government policies; social organizations enjoyed some degree of freedom but were also subject to limitations. Manuel Antonio Garretón, *The Chilean Political Process* (Boston, 1989).

2. Emilio Meneses, "Los límites del equilibrio de poder: La política exterior chilena a fines del siglo pasado, 1891–1902," *Opciones*, no. 9 (May–September, 1986): 52–66.

3. The most complete information on this period can be found in Heraldo Muñoz, *Las relaciones exteriores del gobierno militar chileno* (Santiago, 1986), and "Chile's External Relations under the Military Government," in *Military Rule in Chile: Dictatorship and Oppositions*, ed. J. Samuel Valenzuela and Arturo Valenzuela (Baltimore, 1986), pp. 304–22. Several of these ideas were originally developed in Carlos Portales, "Transnacionalización y política exterior chilena," *Documento de Trabajo* FLACSO, no. 126, (October 1981).

4. Carlos Portales, "Militarization and Political Institutions in Chile" in *Global Militarization*, ed. Peter Wallensteen, Johan Galtung and Carlos Portales (Boulder, Colo., 1985), pp. 123–44.

5. Joaquín Fermandois, "Chile y las grandes potencias," in *Great Power Relations in Argentina, Chile, and the Antarctic*, ed. Michael A. Morris (London, 1989).

6. See Carlos Portales, "Democracia y derechos humanos en la política ex-

terior del Presidente Reagan," *Estudios Internacionales*, 20:79, (July–September 1987): 352–78.

7. Laurence Whitehead, "International Aspects of Democratization," in *Transitions from Authoritarian Rule. Comparative Perspectives*, ed. Guillermo O'Donnell, Philippe C. Schmitter, and Laurence Whitehead (Baltimore, 1986), pp. 3–46.

8. *La Segunda*, April 18, April 19, 1984.

9. Mark Falcoff, "Chile: The Dilemma for U.S. Policy," *Foreign Affairs* (Spring 1986): 833–48.

10. Heraldo Muñoz and Carlos Portales, *Una amistad esquiva: Las relaciones de Estados Unidos y Chile* (Santiago, 1987); and Carlos Portales, "Estados Unidos y la política chilena en 1988," *Cono Sur* 7:2, (March–April 1988).

11. "Declaración del Secretario de Estado Asistente para Asuntos Interamericanos Langhorne Motley ante el Subcomité del Hemisferio Occidental del Comité de Relaciones Exteriores de la Cámara de Representantes el 29 de enero de 1985," *Texto Oficial*, Servicio de Cultura y Prensa de la Embajada de Estados Unidos en Santiago (February 6, 1985).

12. Ibid.

13. The evolution of U.S. policy can be followed in detail in the journal *Cono Sur* (1985–88), esp. articles by Carlos Portales.

14. One of the most complete sources of annual information on Chile's foreign relations can be found in "Anuarios de Políticas Exteriores Latinoamericanas de PROSPEL," published in Buenos Aires by the Grupo Editor Latinoamericano. See especially Heraldo Muñoz, "La política exterior de Chile: La crisis continua" (1984), "La política exterior de Chile durante 1985" (1985), "Chile: Autoritarismo y política exterior en 1986" (1986); and Manfred Wilhelmy, "Chile: Problemas externos y proyección del régimen" (1987).

15. Daniel Gallik, *World Military Expenditures and Arms Transfers 1987* (March 1988), p. 129.

16. Heraldo Muñoz, *Las políticas exteriores de América Latina y el Caribe: Un balance de esperanzas*, Anuario de Políticas Exteriores Latinoamericanas 1987, Grupo Editor Latinoamericano PROSPEL (Buenos Aires, 1988), pp. 313–25.

17. Ascanio Cavallo, Manuel Salazar, and Oscar Sepúlveda, *La historia oculta del régimen militar* (Santiago, 1988), pp. 428–29.

18. Servicio Cultural y de Prensa de la Embajada de los E.E.U.U. de América, *Declaración del Presidente de los Estados Unidos y del Secretario de Estado en Apoyo a la Democracia en Chile* (December 17, 1987).

19. Cavallo, Salazar, and Sepúlveda, *La historia oculta*, pp. 431 ff.

20. See the talks held when the South African Defense Minister visited Chile to review projects of joint production of arms, *La Epoca*, March 1989, several issues.

21. Due to space limitations, this article does not include an analysis of other international factors that significantly affected some political actors, such as the impact of socialist countries on the Communist Party and other leftist organizations. See Augusto Varas, ed., *El Partido Comunista en Chile* (Santiago, 1988).

22. Whitehead, "International Aspects of Democratization."

23. See Augusto Varas, "La cooperación regional para la paz: relaciones exteriores y defensa nacional," *Cono Sur* 8:2 (March–April 1989), and *Hacia el siglo XXI: La proyección estratégica de Chile* (Santiago, 1989).

Felipe Larraín B.

The Economic Challenges
of Democratic Development

Chile has reached the end of an authoritarian era. The triumph of the "No" option in the October 1988 plebiscite cleared the way for competitive presidential and congressional elections in December 1989. The return of democracy after sixteen years of military rule brings great hopes as well as important challenges. On the political front, the goal is to restore democratic life and institutions and to attain full respect for human rights. On the economic front, the challenge is to achieve sustained and equitable development, an objective shared by the overwhelming majority of Chile's population. The main differences of opinion lie in the policies that are necessary to achieve such a goal.

The achievement of equitable growth in Chile requires striking a delicate balance between growth and redistribution. In the long run, sustained economic growth is the only way to overcome the serious problem of poverty. But a substantial number of Chileans are living under extremely precarious conditions, and decisive action is needed in the short run. Growth alone is not sufficient to solve this problem in the near future. Specific redistributive policies are necessary, and they must be designed in a way that does not jeopardize the creation of wealth. Excessive emphasis on redistribution or the use of inappropriate policies for this end could take a heavy toll on economic growth. In this case, any gains achieved in improving the standard of living of the poor will only be transitory.

Chile faces four main economic problems: (1) a high proportion of the population living in poverty, (2) an insufficient level of investment, (3) a low amount of savings, and (4) a heavy burden of external debt. On the positive side, the fiscal deficit and inflation are under control, and the macroeconomic situation is stable. The economy has started to grow again after a prolonged recovery from the 1982 depression. This growth has been assisted importantly by dynamic entrepreneurial activity, especially in the area of nontraditional exports. The current economic environment is open to world markets, with a coherent trade regime and a competitive exchange rate, and it should be preserved.

The main economic challenges are to eliminate poverty and thus achieve a more equitable distribution of income; to increase investment in order to attain a sustained growth of output; to raise national savings in order to finance a higher level of investment; and to achieve a permanent solution to the external debt problem. Long-term success in attaining these goals can only occur if the basic macroeconomic equilibria are preserved, setting an appropriate environment for the development of private initiative.

The Economic Background, 1974–1988

The Chilean economy has experienced major reforms since the outset of the military regime, and macroeconomic performance, in turn, has exhibited substantial fluctuations.[1] Two deep depressions, in 1974–75 and 1982–83, were followed by recoveries and a resumption of growth. In what follows, I attempt to draw a brief sketch of economic developments during this period.

The Dramatic Changes of the 1970s

Chile's military government undertook major economic reforms during the 1970s, which involved dramatic changes in the roles of the private and public sectors. These reforms can be broadly classified in terms of three different objectives: stabilization, privatization, and liberalization. Stabilization involved a drastic attack on the budget deficit in order to reduce inflation. By the end of 1974 and during 1975, the regime concentrated on correcting the balance-of-payments deficit that had been provoked by the collapse in the price of copper—Chile's main export—and the trebling of oil prices. A first round of privatization (1974–78) was centered on the divestiture of most of the real assets that had been transferred to the state during the Unidad Popular administration as part of a comprehensive attempt to restructure the public sector. Liberalization involved many reforms aimed at increasing the role of market forces in the economy. The starting point was the freeing of most controlled prices in late 1973, followed by a sweeping deregulation of the domestic financial market and the beginning of extensive trade liberalization. This trend was extended to international financial transactions by the end of the decade and, especially, during the early 1980s.

Economic performance experienced wide fluctuations during the period 1974–81. A large contraction took place during 1974–75, with GDP declining by about 13 percent and unemployment surging to 15 percent of the labor force. This could be attributed not only to the terms of trade loss resulting from the rise of oil prices and the fall of copper prices but also to a dramatic decline in domestic demand, brought on by restrictive fiscal and monetary policies and exchange rate devaluation, which sharply reduced real wages.

In 1976 and 1977, the economy recovered from the 1975 depression and experienced four years of growth at an average rate of 7.5 percent. The recovery gave way to a boom in 1980–81, spurred by a major shift in expectations, from a realistic assessment of Chile's prospects to an illusion of sustained, high growth. But unemployment remained high, at well over 10 percent during the entire period.

The opening of the capital account and the abundance of foreign credit in the late 1970s and early 1980s provided the financing necessary for an unsustainable expansion in private expenditures at the time of the boom. By late 1981, Chile had accumulated a stock of foreign debt approaching $16 billion. The economy was particularly vulnerable to an increase in interest rates, because almost 60 percent of the debt was contracted at variable rates, mostly tied to LIBOR (London Interbank Offered Rate). In 1981, LIBOR shot up to 16.5 percent, and the terms of trade declined by 6 percent. The worst would come in the following year.

Crisis, Adjustment, and Recovery, 1982–1988

In 1982–83, Chile experienced its worst economic crisis since the 1930s, with real output collapsing by 15 percent. This major depression was partly a result of external shocks: voluntary external financing had dried up; the terms of trade had deteriorated by 23 percent since 1980; and foreign interest rates had increased significantly.

The effect of external developments was exacerbated by several domestic policy mishandlings: the fixed exchange rate policy cou-

pled with mandatory indexation of wages at 100 percent of past inflation; the sweeping opening of the capital account at the time of the
boom; the radical liberalization of domestic financial markets without the provision of proper regulations and controls; and the belief in
the now-infamous "automatic adjustment" mechanism, by which
policy-makers expected the market to produce a quick adjustment
to the new recessionary conditions without interference by the authorities.

Initial efforts to cope with the 1982 crisis were primarily directed
at Chile's external payments problem. But the nation experienced
significant uncertainty from the middle of 1982 to the first quarter of
1983. During this period, regulators assumed control of several trou-
bled financial institutions, including the two largest private banks.
In addition, exchange rate policy was erratic, as shown by the implementation of five different exchange rate regimes. The external dis-
equilibrium was reduced in 1983, but the economy continued to be
depressed. This is not surprising, since most of the adjustment to the
balance-of-payments crisis occurred through import contraction,
while exports showed little response. In 1983, imports were at less
than 50 percent of their 1981 level.

The expansionary policies pursued during most of 1984 helped to
achieve a recovery in output, but proved to be unsustainable. The
current account deficit almost doubled, surpassing $2 billion. In
September 1984, the exchange rate was devalued and tariffs were
raised, sending conflicting signals to economic actors.

A new macroeconomic policy was implemented at the beginning
of 1985 in an effort to produce a recovery of output and employment
through the structural adjustment of the economy. Policy actions
centered on three fronts: the promotion of non-copper exports, the
enhancement of domestic savings and investment, and the strengthening of the corporate and financial sectors.

The heavy burden of a foreign debt in excess of GDP required a vigorous effort to promote exports. At the same time, the regime had
recognized the need to diversify exports beyond copper, and a process of export diversification had been underway since the
mid-1970s. To strengthen this effort, the government relied on several policies: a series of devaluations followed by the stabilization of
the real exchange rate at a competitive level;[2] a reduction of import
tariffs from 35 to 15 percent in three steps; and various fiscal and administrative measures, including a 10 percent tax rebate on minor

exports and an acceleration of existing tax refunds for exporters. Although these measures were primarily oriented toward exports, they also provided an incentive for import substitution stemming from the high level of the exchange rate.

By 1982, national savings had reached a remarkable low of 2 percent of GDP. As foreign savings (that is, external borrowing and direct foreign investment) became severely limited, it was imperative to improve the domestic effort in order to finance higher levels of investment. At a broad level, the restoration of macroeconomic stability was essential to increase savings. Specific policies were also pursued, such as the tax reform of December 1984, which attempted to promote corporate savings through a radical reduction in the tax rate that affected retained earnings. Household savings were also encouraged by allowing a reduction from the tax base of 20 percent of qualified investments.

Public revenues were hurt by several factors: the depressed levels of economic activity; the social security reform of mid-1981, which required the government to make a greater contribution to the state social security system; and the 1984 tax reform, which significantly reduced direct taxation. In view of the bleak picture of public finances, the government implemented a series of measures to improve its financial position. Wage adjustments in the public sector were set systematically below inflation, and social security disbursements ceased to be adjusted automatically to lagged inflation. Several other categories of current and capital expenditures were also curtailed.

Nonfinancial corporations became very weak—and some were outright insolvent—as a consequence of three major factors: extremely high real interest rates, the effects of currency devaluation on dollar-denominated debt, and the economic depression. These factors, coupled with faulty banking practices in a permissive regulatory environment, set the stage for a major crisis in the financial sector.

Clearly, the future of most banks and nonfinancial companies would depend on the general course of the Chilean economy. In the short run, the government reacted to the crisis with a substantial aid package for the banking system and local debtors. The package included a preferential exchange rate for dollar debts, which at times was 40 percent below the official rate; credit lines at below-market rates for the financial sector; and the Central Bank's purchase of bad loans from the banking system with a repurchase agreement, which also involved a subsidy.[3]

The programs were phased out by the end of 1986, but the public sector had paid a substantial cost. The total value of subsidies for financial rehabilitation is estimated at $6 billion, or about 35 percent of 1986 GDP.[4] In an attempt to avoid the mistakes of the earlier financial liberalization, bank regulation was strengthened and the regulatory powers of the Superintendency of Banks and Financial Institutions were enhanced. By mid-1985, government authorities started a major recapitalization program for private banks.

Macroeconomic performance has significantly improved over recent years. In 1986, Chile started a sustained recovery that by its fourth year was accompanied by a steady improvement in the external accounts. These results are due to a combination of internal and external factors. Internally, the structural adjustment program has been accompanied by macroeconomic stability, which has enabled the economy to respond to the new policies. The fiscal deficit has declined from 4.3 percent of GDP in 1984 to less than 0.5 percent in 1988. On the external front, the decline of world interest rates during a good part of the program and the improvement of the terms of trade in 1986–89 have certainly helped Chile's current account status and economic growth.

The structural adjustment program has been quite successful in promoting non-copper exports and efficiently substituting imports. The combination of a competitive exchange rate, low and flat tariffs, and specific fiscal incentives has produced a strong response from nontraditional exports. At the same time, the generalized economic recovery has strengthened substantially both the financial and nonfinancial sectors. Despite these accomplishments, the economy still has important problems. Savings and investment have improved, but their levels are still significantly short of the country's needs. The external accounts look better, but the foreign debt problem is far from over and poses substantial challenges for the future. And the widespread problem of poverty demands immediate attention.

The Pressing Social Agenda

Poverty and income distribution are different concepts. Poverty refers to insufficient means to meet a specific level of basic needs; income distribution refers to the relative share of different groups in the national income. It is not necessarily true that high levels of poverty must be accompanied by extremely unequal income distribu-

Table 9.1

Income Distribution and Poverty: An International Comparison

| | Percentage Share of Income | | | Per capita US$ |
| | Lowest 20% | Highest 20% | Ratio | Income |
	(1)	(2)	(²/₁)	(3)
Asia				
Bangladesh	6.6	45.3	6.9	160
India	7.0	49.4	7.1	300
Sri Lanka	5.8	49.8	8.6	400
Latin America				
Argentina	4.4	50.3	11.4	2,390
Brazil	2.0	66.6	33.3	2,020
Chile	4.2	60.4	14.3	1,310
Mexico	2.9	57.7	19.9	1,830
Peru	1.9	61.0	32.1	1,470
Venezuela	3.0	54.0	18.0	3,230
Industrialized Countries				
France	5.5	42.2	7.7	12,790
Italy	6.2	43.9	7.1	10,350
Spain	6.9	40.0	5.8	6,010

Source: Columns 1 and 2: World Bank, *World Development Report 1989* (Washington, D.C., 1989), whose figures apply to different years; Instituto Nacional de Estadísticas, "Resultados Encuesta Suplementaria de Ingresos" (September 1989), Figures for 1988. Column 3: World Bank, *World Development Report*, whose figures correspond to 1987.

tions. In some third world countries, income inequalities are not excessively pronounced even though poverty is widespread, as is the case in some Asian nations. In Latin America, however, poverty tends to coexist with highly skewed distributions of income.

Bangladesh, India, and Sri Lanka are all classified as low-income economies, yet the poorest 20 percent of the population in those countries receives a share of national income that is similar to the pattern in industrial economies (see Table 9.1). In contrast, Latin American middle-income countries with significantly higher levels of per-capita income have extremely skewed distributions of income. Although Chile lies at the lower end of the inequality scale in Latin America, its income distribution is much more unequal than in the very poor countries of Asia and in industrialized economies. The economic record in terms of income distribution during the authoritarian period in Chile points toward a deterioration. This is not

Table 9.2
Chile's Income Distribution in Time

Year	Real Wage Index (1)	Per Capita GDP Index (2)	Unemployment Rate (3)	Unemployment Rate (4)	Gini Coefficient (5)
1970	100.0	100.0	5.7	5.7	50
1974	68.1	95.9	9.2	9.2	45
1975	65.9	82.1	13.5	15.5	47
1976	67.8	83.6	15.9	20.6	54
1977	74.8	90.2	14.2	19.2	53
1978	79.6	96.0	14.2	18.0	52
1979	86.1	102.2	13.8	17.2	52
1980	93.5	108.3	11.8	16.5	53
1981	101.9	112.4	10.9	15.1	52
1982	102.0	94.9	20.4	25.7	54
1983	91.0	92.7	18.6	30.1	54
1984	91.2	96.9	19.1	22.9	55
1985	87.1	97.7	16.0	20.9	
1986	90.5	101.5	13.9	18.0	
1987	88.7	105.6	12.6	15.2	
1988	94.5	111.6	12.2	14.0	

Note: Column 3 is the open unemployment rate; Column 4 is the unemployment rate, including emergency programs.

Sources: Column 1: Andrés Solimano, "Política de remuneraciones en Chile: Experiencia pasada, instrumentos y opciones a futuro," *Colección Estudios CIE-PLAN*, no. 25 (December 1988), for 1970–87; and Banco Central de Chile, *Informe Mensual*, various issues, for 1988. Column 2: Banco Central de Chile, *Indicadores Económicos y Sociales* and *Informe Mensual*. Columns 3 and 4: Luis Riveros, "Macroeconomic Adjustment and Labor Market Response in Chile," mimeo, The World Bank (Washington, D.C., January 1989). Column 5: Arístides Torche, "Distribuir el ingreso para satisfacer las necesidades básicas," in *Desarrollo económico en democracia. Proposiciones para una sociedad libre y solidaria*, ed. Felipe Larraín (Santiago, 1987).

surprising, given the two sharp depressions that Chile experienced under military rule and the painful adjustments that followed. In each case, real wages declined significantly and unemployment increased to unprecedented levels (see Table 9.2).

The income of the poor can be accurately explained by the unemployment rate and the wage index.[5] On the whole, wages in Chile declined more than per-capita output, and unemployment was quite high on average.[6] It is likely, then, that income distribution worsened under military rule.[7] As shown in Table 9.2, the Gini coefficient deteriorated from 50 in 1970 (used as a base year) to 55 in 1984 (no information was available beyond 1984).[8] After 1983, unemployment declined substantially. Real wages, following a long depression, recovered strongly in 1988 but were still below the 1970 level.

There is no clear way to determine the optimum income distribution, but the level of poverty is a specific criterion to guide distributive policy. In fact, one might argue that distribution would not be such a pressing issue if poverty did not exist. This is clearly not the case in Chile. In a recent and widely publicized study, Arístides Torche has determined that about 45 percent of the country lives in poverty.[9]

The problem of poverty should become the primary social concern in Chile and should be the guiding principle for distributive policy. Chilean society must make a commitment to provide all of its members with their basic needs, including nutrition, health, housing, and education. As much as we value freedom, there needs to be a minimum base of equality that enables all people to make effective use of their liberty.[10] Otherwise, freedom becomes an empty concept for a vast portion of the population. On more practical grounds, poverty has become a significant concern in public opinion. According to a September 1988 poll conducted by the Centro de Estudios Públicos, poverty and low income levels were the principal reasons behind the vote for the "No" option in the October 1988 plebiscite.[11] Economists would say that there is "demand" for decisive action on this front. Thus, the redistribution of income should be oriented toward the elimination of poverty.

Given the significance of this issue, it is important to review how Torche determined that 45 percent of Chileans were living in poverty and to revise the results of other studies. Torche used two criteria in his study: current income and permanent income.[12] A household was considered *indigent* if it devoted all of its income to food and still did not have enough money to purchase a consumption basket that filled the minimum acceptable level of nutrition.[13] A household was classified as *poor* if, dividing its income according to normal spending patterns, the portion assigned to food was not enough to acquire the minimum consumption basket. The concept of permanent income combined specific indicators of housing, health, education, and current income to assess a family's ability to satisfy its basic needs. The results according to both criteria were remarkably similar. About 45 percent of Chileans lived below the poverty level and 25 percent were indigent as of November 1985 (the date to which the basic information applies). Furthermore, the 10 percent lowest-income group of the population appeared to live under particularly bad conditions, and their situation received the *critical poverty* label. People in this group do not have the abilities to obtain a productive job. The economic recovery and the resumption of growth in 1986–88 have probably improved this situation, but it is unlikely that the effect has been significant. It takes decades of economic expansion to break the circle of poverty.

Other studies show similar results. Jorge Rodríguez calculated that 30 percent of Chilean households lived in indigence as of 1982, but he did not provide a magnitude for the number of poor.[14] Moly Pollack and Andras Uthoff studied poverty in Santiago and its surroundings in 1984 and found indigence to affect 23 percent of households and poverty to cover 49 percent of them.[15] Only the "Map of Extreme Poverty" produces different results. This method was first worked out by Sergio Molina and others, who estimated that 20 percent of Chilean households suffered from extreme poverty in 1970.[16] Rodrigo Mujica and Alejandro Rojas concluded that the figure had declined to 15 percent in 1982.[17] These two sets of results differ so dramatically because they measure different things. The "Map" considers three indicators related to housing conditions: overcrowding, equipment, and sewerage. These are basic needs, but not the only ones. The "Map" is valid for what it measures, but it gives only a partial view of the extent of poverty in Chile.

Poverty is not a new problem in Chile. But the extremely high proportion of Chileans living in poverty at the end of 1985 was largely the result of the 1982–83 depression and the adjustment pattern followed by the economy. The open rate of unemployment increased to over 20 percent. If we include the emergency employment programs (PEM and POJH), unemployment surpassed 30 percent and was still at

19 percent as late as 1986. Average real wages declined by almost 20 percent, and the minimum wage was reduced by 40 percent in the 1981–85 period.

In addition, the adjustment severely affected some social expenditures, especially in education and health. Low levels of investment and depressed wages have taken a heavy toll on the physical and human capital of these sectors. The revenues of the public health system have also been damaged with the privatization of middle- and high-income health care. When the option to switch to the private health institutions was given, 8 percent of the affiliates did so, carrying with them 40 percent of the revenues of the public entity. Although the reform certainly increased the quality of service for those who switched, the lower income groups suffered significantly from the decline in resources. Chile must make an aggressive effort to improve health services for the poor and the lower middle-income sectors.

Investment, Savings, and Sustainable Growth

In the long run, the only way to reduce poverty is with sustainable growth. It is also the way to avoid destabilizing social conflict. Chile presently has highly valuable macroeconomic stability, dynamic entrepreneurial activity, and a sound openness to trade with the rest of the world. But the nation must overcome three major obstacles to sustained growth: insufficient investment, a low level of savings, and a heavy burden of external debt.

A high and productive level of investment is essential to support a sustained and significant rate of output growth in the intermediate to long run. This is not necessarily true in the short run. The country can rely on available unutilized capacity to expand production even with relatively low levels of investment. But there is a limit. When the utilization rate approaches capacity, investment becomes a constraint on growth. This appeared to be the situation in Chile in 1989.

For decades, Chile has had a chronically low rate of capital formation (see Table 9.3). Considering five-year averages to smooth out short-term fluctuations, the investment-to-GDP rate has not surpassed the 15 percent range since the early 1960s. Taking these annual averages into account, output growth has not exceeded 4.5 percent during the period. In 1980–81, the economy experienced an investment surge (parallel to a consumption boom) financed with

Table 9.3
Investment, Savings, and GDP Growth

Annual Averages	Investment (% GDP)	Savings (% GDP)	GDP Growth (%)
1960–64	15.2	10.3	
1965–69	14.4	14.4	4.4
1970–74	14.5	12.4	0.9
1975–79	14.8	11.6	3.0
1980–84	14.8	6.3	0.6
Year			
1980	16.6	13.9	7.8
1981	18.6	8.2	5.5
1982	14.6	2.1	−14.1
1983	12.0	4.4	−0.7
1984	12.3	3.0	6.3
1985	14.2	5.4	2.4
1986	14.6	8.1	5.7
1987	16.0	12.6	5.7
1988	16.3	16.2	7.4

Note: Investment figures refer to gross fixed capital formation.
Source: Central Bank of Chile, *Indicadores Económicos y Sociales* and *Informe Mensual*, various issues.

foreign credit. The depression of 1982–83 provoked a sharp drop in the rate of capital formation to such an extent that investment in 1983 was barely enough to cover the depreciation of the existing capital; there was little room left for an increase in productive capacity. The recovery that began in 1984 was then based principally on the existing stock of capital. Even if investment has recovered since then, by 1987 there were clear signs that capacity utilization was reaching its limits in several industrial sectors.

If Chile wants to increase its output at a rate of 5 percent per year, it will be necessary to invest efficiently between 20 and 25 percent of GDP.[18] A brief examination of countries that experienced high growth in the 1980s shows that their investment efforts are substantially higher than Chile's.

Korea, Malaysia, and Singapore had average GDP growth rates of 4.9 to 8.2 percent between 1980 and 1986 (see Table 9.4). During the same period, they invested, on average, between 30 and 44 percent of GDP. In comparison, the investment goal set to support 5 percent

Table 9.4
Investment and GDP Growth: Selected Countries
(average rates, 1980–86)

	Investment (% GDP)	GDP Growth (%)
Korea	29.8	8.2
Malaysia	32.2	4.9
Singapore	43.9	5.3

Source: International Monetary Fund, *International Financial Statistics*; The World Bank, *World Development Report* (Washington, D.C., 1989).

GDP growth in Chile looks quite moderate. This rate of economic expansion, although significantly higher than the historic average, is not overly ambitious. Chile needs to develop economically and also to solve the problem of poverty in a reasonable period of time. It should not settle for less.

The recovery pace of capital formation has continued, but it decelerated in 1988 when investment reached 16.3 percent of GDP. This magnitude must be increased by about 5 points of output, an increase that cannot be accomplished in one year. It requires increased savings from both the public and private sectors and an effective solution to the debt problem, which can only be achieved in an environment of macroeconomic stability. In Chile's current situation, investment is constrained by the availability of savings, and it is unlikely that foreign savings will finance the bulk of this extra effort. The devastating effects of the crisis of the 1980s are too current and still persist in Latin America. And although Chile presents a better economic picture than many third world debtors, the foreign debt problem is far from over. Contrary to some perceptions, it is highly unlikely that the country can return to voluntary international credit markets in the short run. Thus, the additional investment effort will have to be financed principally from domestic sources. A permanent reduction in the foreign debt burden can also increase the resources available for domestic investment.

National savings have been chronically low in Chile, even more so than investment (see Table 9.3). During the 1970s and especially in the early 1980s, savings were clearly insufficient to finance domestic investment. The gap was translated into significant current account deficits. Although the recovery of savings from the lows of the 1982 depression has been impressive, its sharp increase during

1988 has to be viewed with circumspection. To a great extent, the increase was the result of extraordinarily favorable conditions in the copper market, which generated substantial extra revenues for the country, a good part of which were accumulated in the Copper Stabilization Fund. But the booming conditions of the copper market are unlikely to continue. Thus, an additional domestic savings effort is crucial for financing the higher level of investment.

The Foreign Debt Problem

Chile's economy faces a heavy external burden, despite how light that burden may have looked in the favorable external scenario of 1988. Domestic savings of about 8 percent of GDP are used to comply with financial services. Thus, the country is forced to make a major overall savings effort, compressing—among other things—the funds available for social programs. It also limits the resources that are left in the economy to finance productive investment.

It is a very demanding task for the country simultaneously to grow at 5 percent, to eliminate poverty in a reasonable period of time, and to service foreign obligations in the present terms. Moreover, an attempt to achieve the three objectives simultaneously—given the expected external conditions, especially with respect to copper prices—can destabilize the economy and, ultimately, the new democratic government. This would not be good for Chile or for its external creditors. The nation's top priorities should be to grow and build a more equitable society in the new democracy, with the service of the external debt being subordinated to those objectives. In practical terms, this amounts to searching for ways to reduce the external transfer through negotiations with foreign creditors.

The authoritarian government followed a policy of debt negotiation at the limits of the traditional approach. Reschedulings of principal, new money, and retiming of interest payments have been part of the agreements with commercial bank creditors. A renegotiation in mid-1988 allowed for limited amounts of new operations, such as debt buybacks. The country has also pursued two voluntary debt reduction schemes since 1985: debt capitalizations and indirect debt buybacks. The first scheme (known in Chile as Chapter xix) involves the swap of external liabilities for real domestic assets and is generally referred to as debt-equity swaps.[19] The second scheme (known as Chapter xviii) allows private agents (intermediaries) to purchase debt certificates in international markets in order to negotiate their prepayment with the Chilean debtor. The results of the two schemes have been substantial. Through debt capitalization and debt repurchase, Chile has cut $4.2 billion of its foreign debt as of December 1988. This represents some 22 percent of the country's debt at the end of 1985, the year the operations started. A further $1.9 billion has been reduced through direct negotiations between debtors and creditors, including condonations.[20]

In spite of significant debt reduction, Chile's external problem has not been solved. By the end of 1988, total foreign debt was still close to $19 billion, or about 90 percent of GDP. During that year, the country was favored by unexpectedly high copper prices, and it reduced the current account deficit to less than $200 million. But these conditions are bound to change. The future prospects in the copper market point to a deterioration in prices (from its peak of $1.65 a pound in December 1988, it was down to a dollar by July 1989); projections for the early 1990s are currently based on $0.85–0.90 per pound.

In addition, the $2.1 billion in debt-equity swaps have implied a change of one liability for another, but not necessarily a reduction in Chile's foreign obligations. The country will pay less interest on debt but more repatriation of investment profits. Through debt-equity swaps, Chile has captured less than one-third of the secondary market discount, with the rest going principally to subsidize foreign investors and intermediaries. In addition, the rate of profit repatriation is bound to be substantially higher than the real interest rate on debt. It is not clear whether these operations will result in reduced pressure in the payment of financial services to the rest of the world. Thus, debt capitalizations have provided only temporary relief from the external constraint, since profit repatriation starts at the fifth year of the swap operation. The pressure will be felt in the early 1990s.

Indirect debt buybacks appear to have been a better arrangement for the country. Through them, Chile has captured approximately three-quarters of the secondary market discount. The direct repurchase of $300 million of debt last October allowed the country to obtain the whole discount. But the wisdom of using international reserves to repurchase a small part of the debt is questionable, especially in light of the likely deterioration in external conditions expected to occur in the not-too-distant future.

Some schemes for reducing a country's debt are better than others. On several criteria, indirect debt repurchase appears to be preferable to capitalization. A common feature of all of the mechanisms used thus far, however, is that they represent piecemeal approaches. Rather then providing a permanent solution to the debt issue, they only reduce marginal amounts of the debt. A comprehensive arrangement is needed that will permanently reduce the burden of foreign debt and will let the country pursue its development agenda while it restores and solidifies its democracy.

A Strategy for Equitable Growth in Democracy

The widely shared goal of growth with equity requires the elaboration of specific policies to tackle the challenges I have identified. There are two important aspects of this problem: the formulation of a concrete social agenda and a proposal to ease Chile's debt burden.[21] But the achievement of equitable growth requires more than specific economic measures. Chile must also maintain an adequate macroeconomic environment in the context of a stable development strategy. The challenge is to preserve macroeconomic stability in the face of strong social demands.

Social Demands and Macroeconomic Stability

Chile's new democratic government will face many pressures from different groups of the population, and as always, there will not be enough resources to satisfy everyone. Moreover, an attempt to give in to all demands will only produce short-term benefits at the cost of sacrificing macroeconomic stability and future growth. The consequences of such folly are evident in the problems that Argentina, Brazil, and Peru faced in reconciling the different claims that arose with the restoration of democracy.

The most important domestic pressures in Chile could come from organized labor. After all, real wages were particularly hard hit after the 1982–83 depression and at the end of 1988 were still 5 percent below their 1970 level. A successful recovery probably did not need such stringent wage policy, especially in 1987, when the economy grew at almost 6 percent and real wages fell by 1 percent.[22] Although there is room for wage improvement, however, it is necessary to be cautious in this area. There are several important reasons to refrain

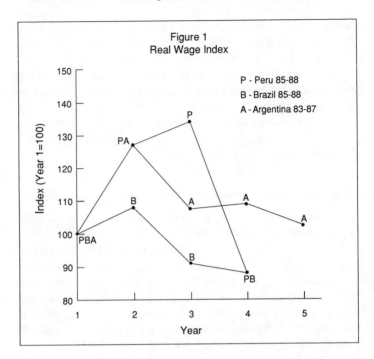

Figure 1
Real Wage Index

Source: CEPAL, *Balance Preliminar de la Economía Latinoamericana* (1988)

from wage increases that go beyond productivity improvements. First, the reduction of unemployment is an important concern, which could be jeopardized by excessive wage pressure. Second, real wages recovered significantly in 1988, increasing by almost 7 percent over 1987. This is a clear indication that the labor market is tightening and that it will further increase wages as long as the economic expansion continues. Third, capacity constraints and the need to increase investment put a strict limit on wage increases that are not based on productivity changes.[23]

Aggressive wage adjustments are likely to be short-lived and to quickly result in wage contractions. Argentina, Brazil, and Peru attempted a policy of major wage expansions at the outset of their recent democratic administrations (see Figure 9.1). The rise lasted for just one year in Argentina and Brazil and then gave way to an enormous contraction that soon left workers with lower real wages than they had before the expansion.[24] In Peru, wages increased for two years and then suffered a major setback, leaving workers making wages substantially below their initial level in 1985. It is in the interest of workers to avoid this pattern.

Cooperation from organized labor will be critical to preserving macroeconomic stability in the near future. Moderation in labor's demands will be an extremely important contribution by workers to the nation's democracy. How can this be achieved? "Concertation" and compromise among workers, entrepreneurs, and the government has produced good results in many countries and is a promising avenue to explore.[25] In Spain, the Socialist government of Prime Minister Felipe González had a favorable experience with the Pactos de La Moncloa. In Israel, the main confederation of workers (Histadrut), the associations of entrepreneurs, and the government agreed to moderate wage and price increases in order to control a high inflation rate.[26] A similar consensual effort was attempted recently in Mexico, also as a way to control triple-digit inflation. Preliminary results there have been satisfactory. Chile should not wait for an economic crisis to pursue this kind of agreement; an attempt should be made at the outset of the democratic government.

Concertation should also help Chileans agree on reforms in the current labor code. Workers have the right to have their opinions adequately considered in this process. Revisions to the current legislation should try to achieve an effective equilibrium of the bargaining power of the parties in labor contracts while also considering the interests of society. But reforms should not attempt to revert to old practices such as the Ley de Inamobilidad (Immobility Law), which introduced unnecessary rigidities in the labor market. Job stability cannot be guaranteed by law; it should be pursued through efficient mechanisms, such as profit-sharing.[27] In addition, the concept of real wage adjustments based on productivity should be maintained. Basically, reforms should produce a moderate piece of labor legislation that avoids radical changes.[28]

In Pursuit of Social Equity

In the long run, only sustained economic growth can provide the basis for a permanent solution to the problem of poverty. But with vast numbers of the population living below the poverty level, immediate action is necessary. According to Torche, with a real GDP growth of 5 percent per year, it will take more than three decades to reduce indigence from 25 to 5 percent.[29] Chile cannot afford to wait. The challenge is to devise policies that can eliminate the problem without compromising the dynamism of sustained economic growth.

An expansionary wage policy is not an appropriate tool to achieve social equity. With respect to wages, the government should concentrate on two main areas. First, it should avoid the deterioration of real wages through inflation. In particular, it should protect the minimum wage from this erosion. Second, the government should improve the nation's institutional and legal framework in such a way that workers can effectively capture increases in productivity. The adequate redistributive tools are primarily the spending and tax decisions of the public sector.

Several general policies can improve the situation of the poor. For example, the poor could be given quick and expeditious access to credit. It is no secret that in most cases the absence of tangible collateral is an unsurmountable obstacle to obtaining loans, especially among the very poor. The efforts of the private sector in providing funds to microenterprises can be an important complement to government assistance in this area. Experience shows, for example, that a loan as small as $30 can double the income of a poor family in six months.[30] In some sectors, such as agriculture, financial resources must be complemented with enhanced technical assistance.

Social policies should generally be based on special programs directed to lower income groups, which encourage the poor to break their circle of marginality. Thus, the programs should not be limited to subsidies and should emphasize the access of poor Chileans to productive jobs. This is one reason why economic growth is so crucial in eliminating poverty.

Specific programs are generally more efficient when they are directly targeted to the lower income groups, and they should be favored over indirect policies like subsidized prices. For example, nutritional programs for infants and pregnant women, implemented by the military government, have been successful. But in cases where the costs of identifying the beneficiaries are too high or when the targeted group will not accept a program, an indirect approach may be tried. In all cases, it is necessary to reduce the leaks of social programs to higher income groups. It has been estimated that only about 40 cents of each peso spent on social programs in Chile reach the lower two quintiles of the population.

Targeting has increased over recent years, but an effort must be made to improve it further.

Investment programs (for example, those affecting health, education, and child nutrition) are highly desirable, as they affect the wealth-generating capacity of the beneficiaries and point toward a long-term solution to poverty. Furthermore, by increasing labor productivity these programs also contribute to economic growth. But consumption programs—which are less efficient—are necessary for those sectors of the poor that live under especially harsh conditions, especially for the group in the lowest decile of the income distribution spectrum.

Improving the efficiency of social programs will help, but it will not be enough. Chile will also have to increase the amount of public resources spent on basic social needs (the so-called *gasto social*) in order to accelerate the reduction of poverty. I have suggested a strategy that would reduce indigence to minimum levels in five years and reduce poverty in one decade.[31] The prospects for an earlier solution are not realistic because of the limited public resources that can be applied to ending poverty and the time needed for programs to produce their intended results.

The strategy suggested requires Chile to spend about 3 percent more of GDP in social spending for education, employment subsidies, health, housing, nutrition, social security, and labor training.[32] Some 70 percent of the extra resources should be spent on the indigent, with the rest targeted on the remaining 20 percent of the poor. About half of the financing for this program could come from a reallocation of public expenditures, primarily from current rather than capital outlays, and from a reduction in defense spending.[33] Some 0.4 percent of GDP could come from economic expansion, since growth has a positive effect on employment and family income, with the remaining 1.1 percent coming from taxes. The extra resources for social spending might be channeled to a special solidarity fund. Adequate knowledge of the beneficial destiny of the contributions would help to reduce the resistance of those sectors that would be negatively affected by the redistributive policies.

The contribution to this program from taxes is not excessive, especially if it is collected in a way that does not discourage the productive activity of the private sector. At the same time, the additional revenues have to be collected in a progressive way. The current Chilean tax system is efficient, but it has signs of regressivity, as direct taxes contribute about one-fifth of total revenues.[34] The solution should not be based on higher personal tax rates, which are currently at 56 percent marginal. This would discourage productive activity and increase tax evasion. There are other avenues to explore, including the reduction of Value Added Tax (VAT) evasion, estimated at about 20 percent; the adjustment of urban and agricultural property valuations to market terms; and the imposition of luxury consumption taxes on a limited number of products. Tax reforms along these lines would increase progressivity while maintaining efficiency.

Reducing the Debt Burden

The maintenance of the current growth rate and the elimination of poverty will require allocating significant additional resources to investment and social programs. The democratic government will also have to cope with major social demands that will be difficult to resist. At the same time, Chile's large external debt and the expected future profit repatriation from debt capitalizations place a heavy burden on domestic savings. In order to comply with the development agenda new solutions are needed for the debt problem.

In spite of massive transactions, the current schemes to reduce Chile's debt have not permanently solved the debt problem. Given the likely levels of international interest rates, copper prices, and the coming amortization payments, Chile will face uncertainty in its external financing as early as 1991. This uncertainty will have adverse effects on domestic expectations and can affect investment decisions. It is in the interests of Chile and its creditors to reduce the debt burden to levels that are compatible with stable democratic development.

Chile should seek a comprehensive solution to its debt problem that allows for a sensible rate of GDP growth. This would entail a negotiated settlement with commercial bank creditors over all or most of their medium- and long-term credits. An agreement could include ways to permanently reduce the nation's interest bill, with the secondary market price of the debt serving as a reference point. The reduction could be achieved in two ways: first, preserving the value of the principal while reducing the interest rate to submarket levels or, second, decreasing the nominal value of the debt while maintaining interest rates on market terms. Both schemes, or a combination of the two, can produce an identical outcome in terms of the economic value—and the burden—of the remaining debt. The option for one or the other depends only on practical considerations, such as bank regulations. For example, commercial banks might prefer to keep the value of the principal stable and reduce interest rates if they can spread the accounting loss over a period of time. It should be kept in mind, however, that the reduction of commercial bank debt can only offer limited relief, because these obligations have declined in relative importance to about one-third of Chile's *total* foreign debt.[35]

For debt reduction to be part of a negotiated settlement, it must be attractive to the banks. This can occur only if the flow of interests, after the agreement is reached, is substantially more secure than the current one is. In addition, Chile can offer an escalating clause on interest rates if, for example, the price of copper increases significantly. Thus, the government might consider providing some form of collateral for the future interest obligations, which amounts to securitizing the debt—that is, converting it into bonds with some guarantee over the flow of payments. The better the guarantee is, the higher the discount will be that the country will capture. Good collateral can be obtained in part through guarantees from multilateral and bilateral institutions. To complement this, Chile could commit a limited portion of its future copper revenues to an escrow account that might be used to pay the interest on the bonds. The guarantee over the principal could come from a long-term zero-coupon bond of the U.S. Treasury, which would not be too burdensome to finance, especially if it implies a permanent and significant reduction in the debt burden.[36]

A democratic government will clearly enhance Chile's standing in the international community. Although the nation's new standing will provoke a more favorable climate for negotiations with industrial governments, commercial banks are unlikely to grant greater concessions based on a change of political regime. They will have to be enticed by economic arguments (for example, collateralization and regulatory and tax amendments) and by whatever pressure their respective governments and the multilateral institutions can put on them to grant debt relief. The Brady proposal from the Bush administration is a welcome step, in that it accepts the principle of debt reduction as a fundamental element of solving the debt problem.[37] At the time of its announcement, however, the plan was short on specifics and uncertain about the source of financial resources to support it.

Conclusion

An objective assessment of the problems and strengths of the Chilean economy is imperative for the success of the economic policies of the democratic government and, therefore, for the consolidation of democracy. A good reason for optimism is the existence of some consensus on the nation's problems and strengths.[38] This does not necessarily mean, however, that the restoration of democracy will be smooth. There are real economic problems to tackle, and the new government will have to cope with a likely increase in the expectations of the people.

The Chilean economy has substantial challenges to confront in eliminating poverty, in enhancing investment and savings, and in achieving a permanent solution to the external debt problem. But it is also important to recognize the strengths of the economy. The macroeconomic situation is solid, with the public budget under control and inflation, at 12 percent in 1988, within reasonable boundaries. The current trade and exchange regimes have fostered a dynamic increase in trade, pushed by the growth of nontraditional exports. These conditions are objectively positive, and especially so when viewed in comparison to other Latin American countries. More generally, the private sector in Chile has taken an active role in the nation's economic development, a role that should be expanded with the cooperation of the state. But this will only be possible in an environment of economic freedom and respect for property rights, which precludes expropriations as a tool of economic policy.

Chile has learned from painful experience about the costs of high policy variability. During the 1970s and 1980s, the economy experienced radically conflicting models and wide policy swings. Such major fluctuations have had a negative effect on the nation's economic performance, and it is extremely important to reduce this variability. Under the present circumstances, the Chilean government must preserve the favorable aspects of the current economic scheme and correct its shortcomings. The time is ripe for the end of ideology and the flourishing of pragmatism.

Notes

I have benefited from discussions with Jeffrey Sachs and from the comments of Paul W. Drake, Sebastián Edwards, Albert Fishlow, Iván Jaksić, Jeffrey Sachs, Arístides Torche, Andrés Velasco, and Rodrigo Vergara.

1. For a more detailed analysis, see *The Public Sector and the Latin American Crisis*, ed. F. Larraín and M. Selowsky, (San Francisco, 1990).

2. This was complemented by the creation of a Copper Stabilization Fund, which was designed to sterilize the domestic effects of sharp fluctuations in copper prices.

3. Private banks exchanged their bad loan portfolios for Central Bank bonds, which gave a real interest rate of 7 percent per year. At the same time, banks incurred in a liability with the monetary authority for a similar amount, whose interest rate was only 5 percent. The net subsidy was then an annual 2 percent of the value of transactions.

4. Felipe Larraín, "Public Sector Behavior in a Highly Indebted Country: The Contrasting Chilean Experience," in Larraín and Selowsky, *The Public Sector*.

5. See Jorge Rodríguez, "La distribución del ingreso en la gestión económica, 1973–84," ILADES (Mimeograph, Santiago, 1987).

6. Ideally, I would use a concept of per capita income rather than GDP, but that figure was not readily available for the whole sample period.

7. For an analysis of unemployment, real wages, and income distribution, see René Cortázar, "Distribución del ingreso, empleo y remuneraciones reales en Chile, 1970–78," *Colección Estudios CIEPLAN* (Santiago, June 1980); and Sebastián Edwards and Alejandra Cox-Edwards, *Monetarism and Liberalization: The Chilean Experiment* (Cambridge, 1987).

8. The Gini coefficient measures the distribution of income with values between 0 and 100. The higher this index, the more concentrated income is.

9. Arístides Torche, "Distribuir el ingreso para satisfacer las necesidades básicas," in *Desarrollo económico en democracia: Proposiciones para una sociedad libre y solidaria*, ed. Felipe Larraín (Santiago, 1987).

10. For an analysis of the relationship between liberty and equality, see Oscar Godoy, "Bases para una estrategia de desarrollo," in Larraín, *Desarrollo económico*.

11. Centro de Estudios Públicos, "Estudio Nacional de Opinión Pública," *Working Paper*, no. 111 (Santiago, January 1989).

12. Torche, "Distribuir el ingreso."

13. According to United Nations standards.

14. Jorge Rodríguez, *La distribución del ingreso y el gasto social en Chile*, ILADES (Santiago, 1985).

15. Moly Pollack and Andras Uthoff, "Pobreza y mercado de trabajo: aspectos conceptuales y metodología," PREALC (Mimeograph, Santiago, 1986).

16. "Mapa de la extrema pobreza en Chile," *Working Paper*, no. 29, Pontificia

Universidad Católica de Chile (Santiago, 1975).

17. "Mapa de la extrema pobreza en Chile," *Working Paper,* Pontificia Universidad Católica de Chile (Santiago, 1986).

18. See Dominique Hachette, "El ahorro y la inversión en Chile: Un gran desafío," in Larraín, *Desarrollo Económico.* This calculation assumes depreciation to absorb about 10 percent of GDP and an incremental capital-output ratio of between two and three.

19. Its characteristics and regulations are specified in Chapter 19 of the Law of International Exchanges.

20. For a detailed analysis of Chile's debt reduction schemes, see Ricardo Ffrench-Davis, "Conversión de pagarés de la deuda externa en Chile," *Colección Estudios CIEPLAN* (Santiago, December 1987); and Felipe Larraín and Andrés Velasco, "Can Swaps Solve the Debt Crisis? Lessons from the Chilean Experience," *Princeton Essays in International Finance,* forthcoming.

21. The analysis of a detailed development strategy for Chile can be found in F. Larraín, "Desarrollo económico para Chile en democracia," in Larraín, *Desarrollo económico.*

22. Real wages are influenced by conditions in the labor market, but the adjustment conditions of public wages also exert an important influence over private wage negotiations.

23. For a detailed analysis, see Andrés Solimano, "Política de remuneraciones en Chile: Experiencia pasada, instrumentos y opciones a futuro," *Colección Estudios CIEPLAN* 25 (December 1988).

24. In Argentina, the 1988 real wages were about 3 percent lower than in 1983.

25. This has been discussed extensively in Chile. See, for example, Alejandro Foxley, *Chile y su futuro: Un país posible* (Santiago, 1987).

26. In spite of some recent problems, the agreements in Spain and Israel have been useful for several years.

27. See Martin Weitzman, *The Share Economy: Conquering Stagflation* (Cambridge, 1987).

28. See Alejandro Foxley, "Chile: After Pinochet Comes Progress," *The International Economy* (January–February 1989). Foxley stated that a compromise before the December elections would likely avoid the more radical reforms that could come out of open discussions in Congress. This is an important strategic point.

29. Torche, "Distribuir el ingreso."

30. A number of private foundations and organizations provide very small loans. One of them, ACCION (Americans for Community Cooperation in Other Nations), has recently started operations in Chile. For an interesting account of their work, see *New York Times,* February 21, 1988.

31. See Larraín, "Desarrollo económico."

32. The 3 percent figure relates to 1988 GDP, but the annual flow of resources spent is fixed in real terms. Thus, the figure will decrease as a percent of GDP with economic growth.

33. See Larraín, "Desarrollo económico."

34. This figure refers to 1986–87.

35. The structure of Chile's debt has changed dramatically since 1982, principally shifting to official creditors. For an analysis of this issue, see Larraín and Velasco, "Can Swaps Solve the Debt Crisis?"

36. For example, a thirty-year zero-coupon bond that pays 10 percent interest will only cost 6 percent of face value.

37. U.S. Secretary of the Treasury Nicholas Brady advanced his proposal in the Conference on Third World Debt, sponsored by the Brookings Institution and the Bretton Woods Committee, Washington D.C., March 10, 1989.

38. This is demonstrated by, among other things, an open letter of the economists of CIEPLAN, "El consenso económico-social democrático es posible," *La Epoca,* August 27, 1988, and by many declarations of leading politicians.

Selected Bibliography

Alexander, Robert J. *The Tragedy of Chile*. Westport, Conn., 1978.

Arellano, José Pablo. *Políticas sociales y de desarrollo: Chile 1924–1984*. Santiago, 1985.

Arellano Iturriaga, Sergio. *Más allá del abismo*. Santiago, 1988.

Arriagada, Genaro. *Pinochet: The Politics of Power*. Winchester Mass., 1988.

———. *El pensamiento político de los militares*. Santiago, 1986.

Aylwin, Patricio. *La alternativa democrática*. Santiago, 1987

Baño, Rodrigo. *Lo social y lo político*. Santiago, 1985.

Bitar, Sergio. *Chile para todos*. Santiago, 1988.

Bouvier, Virginia M. *Alliance or Compliance: Implications of the Chilean Experience for the Catholic Church in Latin America*. Syracuse, 1983.

Brunner, José Joaquín. *Informe sobre la educación superior en Chile*. Santiago, 1986.

Bulnes Aldunate, Luz. *Constitución de la República de Chile*. Santiago, 1981.

Campero, Guillermo. *Entre la sobrevivencia y la acción política*. Santiago, 1987.

———. *Los gremios empresariales en el período 1970–1983: Comportamiento sociopolítico y orientaciones ideológicas*. Santiago, 1984.

Campero, Guillermo and José A. Valenzuela. *El movimiento sindical en el régimen militar chileno, 1973–1981*. Santiago, 1984.

Canovas, Rodrigo. *Literatura chilena y experiencia autoritaria*. Santiago, 1986.

Carrasco Delgado, Sergio. *Génesis y vigencia de los textos constitucionales chilenos*. Santiago, 1980.

Cavallo, Ascanio, Manuel Salazar, and Oscar Sepúlveda. *La historia oculta del régimen militar.* Santiago, 1988.

Cavarozzi, Marcelo, and Manuel Antonio Garretón, eds. *Muerte y resurrección: Los partidos políticos en el autoritarismo y las transiciones del Cono Sur.* Santiago, 1989.

Chavkin, Samuel. *Storm over Chile: The Junta under Siege.* Westport, Conn., 1985.

CIEPLAN. *Modelo económico chileno: trayectoria de una crítica.* Santiago, 1982.

Collados, Modesto. *Formas de vida para Chile.* Santiago, 1988.

Corporación de Promoción Universitaria. *Las ciencias sociales en Chile, 1983.* Santiago, 1984.

Correa, Raquel, Malú Sierra, and Elizabeth Subercaseaux. *Los generales del régimen.* Santiago, 1983.

Correa, Raquel, and Elizabeth Subercaseaux. *Ego sum Pinochet.* Santiago, 1989.

Cortázar, René, Alejandro Foxley, and Víctor E. Tokman. *Legados del monetarismo en Argentina y Chile.* Buenos Aires, 1984.

De la Maza, Gonzalo, and Mario Garcés. *La explosión de las mayorías: Protesta nacional, 1983–1984.* Santiago, 1985.

Domic K., Juraj. *Política militar del Partido Comunista de Chile.* Santiago, 1988.

Dooner, Patricio. *Iglesia, reconciliación y democracia.* Santiago, 1989.

Drake, Paul W. *Socialismo y populismo en Chile, 1932–1988.* Santiago, 1991.

———— and Arturo Valenzuela. "The Chilean Plebiscite: A First Step Toward Redemocratization," *LASA Forum,* 19:4, (Winter 1989): 18–36.

Edwards, Sebastián, and Alejandra Cox-Edwards. *Monetarism and Liberalization: The Chilean Experiment.* Cambridge, Mass., 1987.

Falcoff, Mark. *Modern Chile, 1970–89: A Critical History.* New Brunswick, N.J., 1989.

————, Arturo Valenzuela, and Susan Kaufman Purcell. *Chile: Prospects for Democracy.* New York, 1988.

Feliú, Manuel. *La empresa de la libertad.* Santiago, 1988.

Fischer, Kathleen B. *Political Ideology and Educational Reform in Chile, 1964–1976.* Los Angeles, 1979.

Flaño C., Nicolás, and Gustavo Jiménez F. *Empleo, política económica y concertación*. Santiago, 1987.

Fleet, Michael. *The Rise and Fall of Chilean Christian Democracy.* Princeton, 1985.

Flisfisch, Angel. *La política como compromiso democrático.* Santiago, 1987.

Fontaine Aldunate, Arturo. *La historia no contada de los economistas y el presidente Pinochet.* Santiago, 1988.

Foxley, Alejandro. *Chile y su futuro: Un país posible.* Santiago, 1987.

———. *Latin American Experiments in Neo-Conservative Economics.* Berkeley, 1983.

Foxley, Alejandro, et al. *Reconstrucción económica para la democracia.* Santiago, 1983.

Frühling, Hugo, Carlos Portales, and Augusto Varas. *Estado y fuerzas armadas.* Santiago, 1982.

Garretón, Manuel Antonio. *The Chilean Political Process.* Boston, 1989.

———. *Propuestas políticas y demandas sociales.* 2 vols. Santiago, 1989.

———. *El plebiscito de 1988 y la transición a la democracia.* Santiago, 1988.

———. *Reconstruir la política.* Santiago, 1987.

———. *Dictaduras y democratización.* Santiago, 1984.

González Camus, Ignacio. *El día que murió Allende.* Santiago, 1988.

Hojman, David E. *Chile After 1973: Elements for the Analysis of Military Rule.* Liverpool, 1985.

Huneeus, Carlos. *Los chilenos y la política: Cambio y continuidad bajo el autoritarismo.* Santiago, 1987.

———, ed. *Para vivir la democracia: Dilemas de su consolidación.* Santiago, 1987.

Jaksić, Iván. *Academic Rebels in Chile.* Albany, N.Y., 1989.

Jarvis, Lowell S. *Chilean Agriculture Under Military Rule.* Berkeley, 1985.

Kirkwood, Julieta. *Feminismo y participación política en Chile.* Santiago, 1982.

Lagos, Ricardo. *Hacia la democracia.* Santiago, 1987.

———. *Democracia para Chile, proposiciones de un socialista.* Santiago, 1985.

Larraín, Felipe, ed. *Desarrollo económico en democracia: Proposi-*

ciones para una sociedad libre y solidaria. Santiago, 1987.

Lavín, Joaquín. *Chile: revolución silenciosa.* Santiago, 1987.

Loveman, Brian E. *Chile: The Legacy of Hispanic Capitalism.* 2d ed. New York, 1988.

Marras, Sergio. *Confesiones.* Santiago, 1988.

Munizaga, Giselle. *El discurso público de Pinochet.* Santiago, 1988.

Muñoz, Heraldo. *Las relaciones exteriores del gobierno militar chileno.* Santiago, 1986.

———— and Carlos Portales. *Una amistad esquiva: Las relaciones de Estados Unidos y Chile.* Santiago, 1987.

O'Brien, Phil, and Jackie Roddick. *Chile: The Pinochet Decade.* London, 1983.

O'Donnell, Guillermo, Philippe Schmitter, and Laurence Whitehead, eds. *Transitions from Authoritarian Rule: Comparative Perspectives.* Baltimore, 1986.

Ortega, Eugenio, and Ernesto Tironi. *Pobreza en Chile.* Santiago, 1988.

Pinochet, Augusto. *Pinochet: Patria y democracia.* Santiago, 1985.

Politzer, Patricia. *Altamirano.* Santiago, 1990.

————. *Miedo en Chile.* Santiago, 1987.

Prats González, Carlos. *Memorias. Testimonio de un soldado.* Santiago, 1985.

Programa Interdisciplinario de Investigaciones en Educación. *Las transformaciones educacionales bajo el régimen militar.* 2 vols. Santiago, 1984.

Ramos, Joseph. *Neo-conservative Economics in the Southern Cone of Latin America, 1973–1983.* Baltimore, 1986.

Ruiz-Tagle, Jaime. *El sindicalismo chileno después del plan laboral.* Santiago, 1985.

Sigmund, Paul E. *The Overthrow of Allende and the Politics of Chile: 1964–1976.* Pittsburgh, 1977.

Silva, Patricio. *Estado, neoliberalismo y política agraria en Chile, 1973–1981.* Dordrecht-Holland, 1987.

Smith, Brian H. *The Church and Politics in Chile.* Princeton, 1982.

Stepan, Alfred. *Rethinking Military Politics: Brazil and the Southern Cone.* Princeton, 1988.

Tironi, Eugenio. *Los silencios de la revolución.* Santiago, 1988.

————. *El liberalismo real: La sociedad chilena y el régimen militar.* Santiago, 1986.

Tupper, Patricio. *Opciones políticas en Chile.* Santiago, 1987.

Valdés, Juan Gabriel. *La escuela de Chicago: Operación Chile*. Buenos Aires, 1989.

Valenzuela, Arturo. *The Breakdown of Democratic Regimes: Chile*. Baltimore, 1978.

Valenzuela, J. Samuel, and Arturo Valenzuela, eds. *Military Rule in Chile: Dictatorship and Oppositions*. Baltimore, 1986.

Valenzuela, María Elena. *La mujer en el Chile militar*. Santiago, 1987.

Varas, Augusto, ed. *La autonomía militar en América Latina*. Caracas, 1988.

———, ed. *El Partido Comunista en Chile*. Santiago, 1988.

———, *Los militares en el poder: Régimen y gobierno militar en Chile, 1973–1986*. Santiago, 1987.

———, ed. *Transición a la democracia*. Santiago, 1984.

Verdugo, Patricia. *Los zarpazos del puma*. Santiago, 1989.

Vergara, Pilar. *Auge y caída del neoliberalismo en Chile*. Santiago, 1984.

Vicaría de la Solidaridad. *Chile, la memoria prohibida*. Santiago, 1989.

Vidal, Hernán, Carlos Ochsenius, and María de la Luz Hurtado. *Teatro chileno de la crisis institucional: 1973–1980*. Minneapolis, 1982.

Walton, Gary M., ed. *The National Economic Policies of Chile*. Greenwich, Conn., 1985.

Washington Office on Latin America. *Chile's Transition to Democracy*. Washington, D.C., 1989.

———. *Conditions for Chile's Plebiscite on Pinochet*. Washington, D.C., 1988.

Zaldívar, Andrés L. *Por la democracia ahora y siempre*. Santiago, 1987.

The Contributors

Alan Angell is Director of the Latin American Centre at the University of Oxford and a Fellow of St. Antony's College. He is the author of *Politics and the Labour Movement in Chile* and has recently completed a chapter on Chile since 1958 for the *Cambridge History of Latin America*.

Guillermo Campero is Academic Director of the Instituto Latinoamericano de Estudios Transnacionales in Santiago. A sociologist, he is an expert on labor, shantytown dwellers, and entrepreneurs. His most recent book is *Entre la sobrevivencia y la acción política: Las organizaciones de pobladores en Santiago*.

Paul W. Drake is Professor and Chairman of the Department of Political Science at the University of California, San Diego. A historian, Drake is also past president of the Latin American Studies Association. His books include *Socialism and Populism in Chile, Elections and Democratization in Latin America* and *The Money Doctor in the Andes*.

Manuel Antonio Garretón is a Senior Researcher at the Facultad Latinoamericana de Ciencias Sociales in Santiago and a political sociologist. His most recent books include *The Chilean Political Process* and *Reconstruir la política*. He has held the Tinker Chair at the University of Chicago and has been a Fellow with the Kellogg Institute of International Studies at the University of Notre Dame.

Iván Jaksić is Associate Professor of History and Director of the Center for Latin America at the University of Wisconsin–Milwaukee. An intellectual and social historian, he was previously vice-chair of the Center for Latin American Studies at the University of California at Berkeley. He is the author of *Academic Rebels in Chile*.

Felipe Larraín is Associate Professor of Economics at the Pontificia Universidad Católica in Santiago. He was recently a visiting scholar at the Department of Economics at Harvard University. An adviser to several Latin American governments, he is editor of *Desarrollo económico en democracia* and co-editor, with Sebastián Edwards, of *Debt, Adjustment and Recovery: Latin American Prospects for Growth and Development*.

Carlos Portales is a political scientist at the Facultad Latinoamericana de Ciencias Sociales in Santiago. He is a specialist on the Chilean constitution and on international relations. One of his recent publications is *Una amistad esquiva: Las relaciones de Estados Unidos y Chile*, with Heraldo Muñoz.

Eduardo Silva is a Ph.D. candidate in political science at the University of California, San Diego. He is co-editor of *Elections and Democratization in Latin America* and is currently completing a dissertation titled "Capitalist Coalitions and Economic Policymaking in Authoritarian Chile, 1973–1988."

Arturo Valenzuela is Professor of Political Science and Director of the Latin American Studies Program at Georgetown University. He has been a visiting scholar at Oxford University, the University of Chile, and the Catholic University of Chile. He is the author of several books on Chile, including *Political Brokers in Chile* and *The Breakdown of Democratic Regimes: Chile*, and the co-editor, with J. Samuel Valenzuela, of *Military Rule in Chile*.

María Elena Valenzuela is a sociologist with the Institute of Women and coordinator of the Study Group on Women and Militarization of the International Peace Research Association (IPRA). A specialist on the condition of women in Chile, she is the author of *La mujer en el Chile militar*.

Augusto Varas is a sociologist at the Facultad Latinoamericana de Ciencias Sociales in Santiago and one of Latin America's leading specialists on the armed forces and international relations. His most recent books include *Militarization and the International Arms Race in Latin America* and *Los militares en el poder*.

Index

Other volumes in the Latin American Studies Series include: